Contributions to Management Science

More information about this series at http://www.springer.com/series/1505

Katrin Blankenburg

Intellectual Capital in German Non-profit Organisations

An Empirical Study

Springer

Katrin Blankenburg
Hamburg University of Applied Sciences
Hamburg, Germany

ISSN 1431-1941 ISSN 2197-716X (electronic)
Contributions to Management Science
ISBN 978-3-319-62654-3 ISBN 978-3-319-62655-0 (eBook)
DOI 10.1007/978-3-319-62655-0

Library of Congress Control Number: 2017947909

Printed on acid-free paper

This Springer imprint is published by Springer Nature
The registered company is Springer International Publishing AG
The registered company address is: Gewerbestrasse 11, 6330 Cham, Switzerland

Definitions

Association	A union of people working towards a common social goal on a voluntary basis, for a certain amount of time, which is not dependent on certain individual members, consisting of at least seven people at time of the foundation (§56 BGB), have a charter (§57 BGB) and a board (§64 BGB) (Menges, 2004).
Benevolence	NPOs that support individuals are labelled benevolent according to §53 AO (Bundesministerium der Justiz und für Verbraucherschutz, 1976).
Charitable limited liability companies	NPO consisting of a small and closed group of people. The liability of the members of its board is limited since the organisation is liable for its assets (Menges, 2004).
Churchliness	NPOs that support religious groups are labelled churchly according to §54 AO (Bundesministerium der Justiz und für Verbraucherschutz, 1976).
Demographic change	This development is the consequence of a decrease in the birth rate and an increase in life expectancy, with the result being that the number of young people living and working in Germany decreases, while the number of elderly people living in Germany increases over time (Berthel & Becker, 2010).
Direct	As a characteristic for the public benefit status, direct refers to the work done towards the aim which must be provided by the organisation itself (Anheier & Seibel, 1993).
Donation	A voluntary financial or material spending or provision of time and know-how to support a purpose of a charitable organisation and without the expectation of a return service for the benefit of the donor (Menges, 2004)

Expert	Someone who is not only familiar with every aspect of a specific topic, process or resource but is able to develop improvements for everyone within their area of expertise (Sveiby, 1997).
Expertise	Expertise is building on the usage of knowledge, i.e. experience (Sveiby, 1997).
Firm resources	"strengths that firms can use to conceive of or implement strategies that improve its efficiency and effectiveness." (Barney, 1991, p. 106)
Foundation	A foundation is characterised by three common features: it needs to be purposive, have financial or material assets (§82 BGB) and be neither an association nor an organisation (Menges, 2004).
Gemeinnützigkeit	In order to gain public benefit status (*Gemeinnützigkeit*), an organisation must show that it is selfless, exclusive, and provides its service directly (Anheier & Seibel, 1993).
Goodwill	"the consequence of a firm's above-normal ability to generate future earnings, or as a set of assets controlled by an acquired company but not reported in its financial statements." (Canibano et al., 1999, p. 10)
Grants	Are given by a legal person or entity, often tied to requirements or restrictions and to a specific purpose (Lichtsteiner et al., 2013; Glassman & Spahn, 2012).
Human capital	"what the single employee brings into the value adding processes" (InCaS, 2008, p. 7), including knowledge, experiences and abilities of people.
Image	(a) picture (b) "the general impression that a person or organisation gives to the public" (c) "a mental picture or idea of somebody/something." (Oxford Wordpower Dictionary, 2006, p. 368)
Information	Raw material, data—without further interpretation (Bontis, 1998, p. 67).
Institution	"Institutions comprise regulative, normative, and cultural-cognitive elements that, together with associated activities and resources, provide stability and meaning to social life." (Scott, 2013, p. 56).
Institutionalisation	"social process, obligations, or actualities come to take on a rule-like status in social thought and action." (Meyer & Rowan, 1977, p. 341 cited by Greenwood et al., 2008, p. 5)
Intangible	"intangible things have value but do not exist physically—used in business." (Longman Dictionary of Contemporary English, 2012, p. 916)

Intangible assets	"A claim to future benefits that does not have a physical or financial embodiment." (Andriessen, 2004, p. 407)
Intangible resources	"an identifiable non-monetary asset without physical substance" (IPSASB, 2010, p. 11) that is able to produce future benefits for an organisation (InCaS, 2008; Barney, 1991)
Intellectual capital	No commonly accepted definition exists. For this project, the definition developed by InCaS is utilised, defining IC as "the intangible resources of an organisation". (InCaS, 2008, p. 7)
Isomorphism	Refers to the relationship between an organisation and its institutional context; organisations conform to rule-like expectations of society (Greenwood et al., 2008).
Knowledge	Information put into context. Knowledge can be tacit (implicit) or codified (Sullivan, 1998).
Legitimacy	"a generalized perception or assumption that the actions of an entity are desirable, proper or appropriate within some socially constructed system of norms, values, beliefs, and definitions" (Suchman, 1995, p. 574)
Linguistic message	Words as part of a picture, e.g. a product label, logo, or caption, etc. (Davison & Skerratt, 2007)
Mission	The mission of an organisation is its signpost and shows internal as well as external stakeholders the raison d'être of the organisation and its self-understanding (Keehley & Abercrombie, 2008).
Measurement	A tool for the comparison of things with respect to their usefulness and desirability (based on Andriessen, 2004).
Natural capital	"The world's stock of natural assets." (Kenner, 2014, p. viii)
Non-profit organisation	Organisations that are "formally constituted, nongovernmental in basic structure, self-governing, non-profit-distributing, and voluntary to some meaningful extent" (Salamon & Anheier, 1992, p. 1).
Organisational culture	Giving every member of the workforce of an organisation a common perspective and view on how to handle information, how decisions are made and what values are pursued (Marr & Roos, 2005).
Principles	Principles are a general idea of what good behaviour constitutes "based on what a person believes is right" (Oxford Wordpower Dictionary, 2006, p. 563).
Professional	"1) connected with a job that needs a high level of training and/or education; 2) doing something in a way that shows skill, training or care" (Oxford Wordpower Dictionary, 2006, p. 566)

Professionalisation	Professionalism in the sense of an "occupational value" (Evetts, 2011, p. 33) is linked to the trust of a client that a person or organisation has the appropriate knowledge and experience to manage and finish a task successfully and to a certain quality.
Relational capital	"The relations of the company to external stakeholders" (InCaS, 2008, p. 7), including the perceptions that are held about the company
Resources	see "firm resources".
Selfless	§55 AO: members do not receive any compensation in form of profits or anything similar (Bundesministerium der Justiz und für Verbraucherschutz, 1976)
Spiritual capital	"the essence or positive spirit of the organization" (Hall, 1998, p. 78), providing an emotional connection or return, often connected with religion or the church (Oxford Wordpower Dictionary, 2006)
Stakeholder	Stakeholders are individuals or groups who are affected by an organisation or who have an influence on the survival of an organisation in a positive or negative way (derived from Post et al., 2002; Brugha & Varvasovszky, 2000; Reed et al., 2009).
Structural capital	"what happens between people, how people are connected within the company, and what remains when the employee leaves the company" (InCaS, 2008, p. 7) such as organisational routines, procedures, cultures, databases, etc.
Sustained competitive advantage	A value-creating strategy that no current or potential competitor has implemented already or implements simultaneously and that other organisations are unable to copy the benefits of (Barney, 1991)
Sustainability	A concept that aims for a holistic and lasting development of the economic, environmental and social performance of a company (DRS 20.11) (Deutsches Rechnungslegungs Standards Commitee e.V., 2012).
Tangible resources	Nonmonetary resources with physical substance that in combination are able to produce future benefits for an organisation (derived from IPSASB, 2010)
Trust administration	according to law, is either the investment of funds to earn interest or the renting and letting of material assets—both forms are tax privileged for NPOs (Menges, 2004).
Value	The degree of usefulness or desirability of something, especially in comparison to other things (Andriessen, 2004, p. 18).

Valuation — A comparative assessment or measurement of something with respect to its embodiment of a certain value (Andriessen, 2004, p. 18).

Workplace spirituality — expresses "the effort to find one's ultimate purpose in life, to develop a strong connection to co-workers and other people associated with work" (Milliman et al., 2003, p. 427), as well as consensus of the beliefs and values of the organisation and the individual.

References

Andriessen, D. (2004). *Making sense of intellectual capital: Designing a method for the valuation of intangibles*. Oxford: Elsevier.

Anheier, H. K., & Seibel, W. (1993). *Defining the nonprofit sector: Germany*. Baltimore, MD: Johns Hopkins Institute for Policy Studies.

Barney, J. (1991). Firm resources and sustained competitive advantage. *Journal of Management, 17*(1), 99–120. doi:10.1177/014920639101700108.

Berthel, J., & Becker, F. G. (2010). *Personalmanagement* (9th ed.). Stuttgart: Schäffer-Poeschel Verlag.

Bontis, N. (1998). Intellectual capital: An exploratory study that develops measures and models. *Management Decision, 36*(2), 63–76. doi:10.1108/00251749810204142.

Brugha, R., & Varvasovszky, Z. (2000). Stakeholder analysis: A review. *Health Policy and Planning, 15*(3), 239–246. doi:10.1093/heapol/15.3.239.

Bundesministerium der Justiz und für Verbraucherschutz. (1976). *Abgabenordnung (AO)*. Berlin: Bundesministerium der Justiz und für Verbraucherschutz. http://www.gesetze-im-internet.de/ao_1977/

Canibano, L., Covarsí, M. G.-A., & Sánchez, M. P. (1999). The value relevance and managerial implications of intangibles: A literature review. In *Measuring and reporting intellectual capital, Amsterdam* (pp. 1–74). Paris: Organisation for Economic Co-operation and Development. Accessed August 07, 2012, from http://www.oecd.org/sti/industryandglobalisation/1947974.pdf

Davison, J., & Skerratt, L. (2007). *Words, pictures and intangibles in the corporate report*. Edinburgh: The Institute of Chartered Accountants of Scotland.

Deutsches Rechnungslegungs Standards Commitee e.V. (2012). *Deutscher Rechnungslegungs Standard Nr. 20 (DRS 20)* (pp. 1–56). Accessed November 23, 2015, from www.drsc.de/docs/press_releases/2012/120928_DRS20_nearfinal.pdf

Evetts, J. (2011). Professionalism and management in public sector (Not-for-profit organizations): Challenges and opportunities. In A. Langer & A. Schröer (Eds.), *Professionalisierung in nonprofit management* (pp. 33–44). Wiesbaden: VS Verlag für Sozialwissenschaften.

Glassman, D. M., & Spahn, K. (2012). Performance measurement for nonprofits. *Journal of Applied Corporate Finance, 24*(2), 72–77. doi:10.1111/j.1745-6622.2012.00381.x.

Greenwood, R., Oliver, C., Sahlin, K., & Suddaby, R. (2008). Introduction. In R. Greenwood et al. (Eds.), *The SAGE handbook of organizational institutionalism* (pp. 1–46). London: SAGE.

InCaS. (2008). *Intellectual capital statement – Made in Europe*. Accessed January 31, 2010, from www.incas-europe.org

International Public Sector Accounting Standards Board (IPSASB). (2010). *Intangible assets*. New York: International Federation of Accountants.

Keehley, P., & Abercrombie, N. N. (2008). *Benchmarking in the public and nonprofit sectors* (2nd ed.). San Francisco, CA: Wiley.

Kenner, D. (2014). *Who should value nature?* London. Accessed January 18, 2015, from http://whygreeneconomy.org/wp-content/uploads/2014/12/Who-should-value-nature.-Why-Green-Economy.pdf. ISBN: 978-0-85760-938-0.

Lichtsteiner, H., Gmür, M., Giroud, C., & Schauer, R. (2013). *Das Freiburger Management-Modell für Nonprofit Organisationen* (7th ed.). Bern: Haupt Verlag.

Longman Dictionary of Contemporary English. (2012). *Longman dictionary of contemporary English* (5th ed.). Harlow: Pearson Longman.

Marr, B., & Roos, G. (2005). A strategy perspective on intellectual capital. In B. Marr (Ed.), *Perspectives on intellectual capital* (pp. 28–41). Oxford: Elsevier Butterworth-Heinemann.

Menges, E. (2004). *Gemeinnützige Einrichtungen.* München: Deutscher Taschenbuch Verlag.

Meyer, J. W., & Rowan, B. (1977). Institutionalized organizations: Formal structure as myth and ceremony. In W. W. Powell & P. J. DiMaggio (Eds.), *American Journal of Sociology, 83*(2), 340–363.

Milliman, J., Czaplewski, A. J., & Ferguson, J. (2003). Workplace spirituality and employee work attitudes: An exploratory empirical assessment. *Journal of Organizational Change Management, 16*, 426–447. doi:10.1108/09534810310484172.

Oxford Wordpower Dictionary. (2006). In J. Turnbull (Ed.), *Oxford wordpower dictionary* (3rd ed.). Oxford: Oxford University Press.

Post, J. E., Preston, L. E., & Sachs, S. (2002). Managing the extended enterprise – The new stakeholder view. *California Management Review, 45*(1), 6–28.

Reed, M. S., Graves, A., Dandy, N., Posthumus, H., Hubacek, K., Morris, J., et al. (2009). Who's in and why? A typology of stakeholder analysis methods for natural resource management. *Journal of Environmental Management, 90*(5), 1933–1949. doi:10.1016/j.jenvman.2009.01.001.

Salamon, L. M., & Anheier, H. K. (1992). *In search of the non-profit sector II: The problem of classification.* Baltimore, MD. doi:10.1007/BF01397460. Accessed March 24, 2012, from http://www.springerlink.com/index/K1UQQ84225324356.pdf

Scott, W. R. (2013). *Institutions and organizations* (4th ed.). Thousand Oaks, CA: SAGE.

Suchman, M. C. (1995). Managing legitimacy: Strategic and institutional approaches. *Academy of Management Review, 20*(3), 571–610.

Sullivan, P. H. (1998). Advanced definitions and concepts. In P. H. Sullivan (Ed.), *Profiting from intellectual capital – Extracting value from innovation* (pp. 35–42). New York: Wiley.

Sveiby, K. -E. (1997). *The new organizational wealth* (1st ed.). San Francisco, CA: Berrett-Koehler.

Acknowledgements

There are several people without whom this project would have been impossible:

Essential in the endeavour to conduct this research were the interview respondents. I am very grateful that they took the time and granted me their trust in sharing their knowledge and experiences with me. It is only through the insight they offered that this project is as practice related as I aspired it to be. I hope that these findings will support them and their organisations in their essential and wonderful efforts towards improving the lives of those in need.

For the PhD project this book is based upon, I was blessed with supervisors who guided, challenged and supported me: Prof. Angus Duff of the University of the West of Scotland and Prof. Dr. Thomas Pfahler of the Hochschule für Angewandte Wissenschaften Hamburg. Thank you both for the chance to embark on this adventure and for your faith in me! Additionally, I was in the unique position to have Dr. Doris Merkl-Davies of Bangor University as my "Patendoktormutter". Doris, your support was invaluable, and your feedback and our discussions allowed me a more comprehensive understanding of the theory underlying my topic—thank you so much!

Sincere thanks go to Prof. Dr. Zita Schillmöller and the team of the Promotionszentrum of the HAW Hamburg. Their valuable feedback, advice, critique as well as the discussions we had during as well as outside the workshops they offered were immensely helpful.

Jasmina Crcic and Thea Freese: our regular discussions provided a lot of valuable feedback, helped to overcome doubts and undeniably helped to raise the quality of my research.

Last but definitely not least, I owe a huge thank you to my parents, Axel und Elke Blankenburg, as well as to Alexander Koch, and to the rest of my family and to my friends. I am thankful beyond words for your love, your continuous support and that you always believe in me!

Ein besonderer Dank gilt meiner Tante Trudchen, die mich in ihrer wundervollen Art inspiriert hat und ein großes Vorbild für mich ist und immer bleiben wird.

Contents

List of Abbreviations

AO	Abgabenordnung (German Fiscal Code)
BGB	Bürgerliches Gesetzbuch (German Civil Code)
CGMA	Chartered Global Management Accountant
DMSTI	Danish Ministry of Science, Technology and Innovation
DRS	Deutscher Rechnungslegungs Standard (= German Accounting Standard)
DRSC	Deutschen Rechnungslegungs Standards Committee
DZI	Deutsches Zentralinstitut für soziale Fragen
GG	Grundgesetz (German Basic Law)
HAW	Hochschule für Angewandte Wissenschaften
HC	Human Capital
HGB	Handelsgesetzbuch (German Commercial Code)
IAS	International Accounting Standards
IC	Intellectual Capital
ICS	Intellectual Capital Statement
IFRS	International Financial Reporting Standards
IIRC	International Integrated Reporting Council
InCaS	Intellectual Capital Statement—Made in Europe
IPSASB	International Public Sector Accounting Standard Board
<IR>	Integrated Reporting
k	kilo = thousand
n.d.	no date
n.n.	no name
NPO(s)	Non-profit Organisation(s)
URL	Uniform Resource Locator
UWS	University of the West of Scotland
VHS	Video Home System

List of Figures

List of Tables

Chapter 1
Introduction

The existence of intangibles within a company has been known for a long time, but was not considered important, since the relevant resources for value creation were tangible, like land, location and technology. In the last three decades, however, most economies have shifted towards a knowledge- and service-based focus and intellectual capital (IC) replaced the traditional tangible resources determining competition (Guthrie, 2001; Kong, 2008; Möller & Gamerschlag, 2009). The concept of IC gained momentum in the early 1980s with the recognition that organisational performance could not be expressed via the traditional financial reporting system and thus hidden value exists (Edvinsson, 1997; Petrash, 1996), making predictions as to the future of an organisation challenging. Hence, the concept can be regarded as practice-driven, since the discussion about IC was started by practitioners (Bontis, Dragonetti, Jacobsen, & Roos, 1999). So far there is no commonly agreed upon definition of IC. The definitions of intangible capitals utilised for the current research are provided by the group that developed the "Intellectual Capital Statement—Made in Europe (InCaS)", as their definition is straightforward, practice-oriented, and transnational due to the involvement of 25 companies from five European countries (InCaS, 2008).

InCaS defines IC as "the intangible resources of an organisation" (InCaS, 2008, p. 7) which is comprised of human capital, i.e. "what the single employee brings into the value adding processes" (InCaS, 2008, p. 7), structural capital, which is defined as internal relationships and networks that are independent of individuals, and relational capital, which is the relationships to external stakeholders. An intangible capital that is not defined by the InCaS but considered in the current research is spiritual capital. Spiritual capital is defined by Hall (1998) as "the essence or positive spirit of the organization" (Hall, 1998, p. 78) and, based on this definition, it can be assumed that it is an important resource for NPOs to differentiate themselves from for-profit businesses and other organisations. Furthermore, all capitals are regarded as interrelated; a concept introduced by a group of practitioners around Petrash (1996), one of the pioneers in the field of IC.

K. Blankenburg, *Intellectual Capital in German Non-profit Organisations*,
Contributions to Management Science, DOI 10.1007/978-3-319-62655-0_1

Non-profit organisations (NPOs) are defined as being "formally constituted, nongovernmental in basic structure, self-governing, non-profit-distributing, and voluntary to some meaningful extent" (Salamon & Anheier, 1992, p. 1). NPOs are highly knowledge- and service-based, yet IC and its disclosure are thus far topics mainly researched from a for-profit perspective (Guthrie, Ricceri, & Dumay, 2012). The few papers that explicitly address IC in NPOs, (Kong, 2003, 2007a, 2007b, 2010a, 2010b; Kong & Prior, 2008), focus on Australia and are based on literature reviews. NPOs are generally seen as supporting the stabilisation of a society through the procurement of norms and the support of conflict avoidance, consequently furthering integration of individuals into society (Wex, 2004). Also, NPOs are a voluntary consolidation of people with the same aim. This group chooses the social aim they want to work towards voluntarily (Wex, 2004) based on needs that are not met by the state but which this group of people regard as essential (Lichtsteiner, Gmür, Giroud, & Schauer, 2013). The reason for the focus of the current research on the German non-profit sector is a unique feature: its dichotomy, based upon the principles of both self-administration and subsidiarity (Anheier & Seibel, 1993).

Subsidiarity principle is also evident in social policy in Germany and requires individuals to exhaust their own resources before the state provides any support (Anheier & Seibel, 1993; Priller, Zimmer, Anheier, Toepler, & Salamon, 1999). As a result of the principles, some NPOs, particularly organisations within the health sector and social services, are commissioned, partly supervised, and financially supported by the state (Helmig & Boenigk, 2012; Zimmer & Priller, 2007) to ensure support if necessary. Other NPOs, in contrast, are fully dependent on donations (Zimmer & Priller, 2007). For these organisations, it is imperative to signal proper handling of resources. Not only is the tax shelter status of NPOs dependent on the information on the allocation of resources (KPMG, 2012), but donors and volunteers want to be sure that the money and time they donate is used in a considerate way towards the social aim (van Broekhoven, 2008). Another challenge for NPOs and reason for IC disclosure is that success cannot be signalled via profits or margins. Also, donors do not necessarily benefit from the services that they enable an NPO to provide (Grossekettler, 2006) and are consequently not able to evaluate differences in the service quality of different NPOs. Stakeholder theory and resource dependency theory support this perspective.

Resource dependency theory regards organisations not as isolated, but as interacting and dependent on their environment with their survival reliant on the effective acquisition and maintaining of resources (Pfeffer & Salancik, 2003). Resources are often taken for granted within an organisation (Barney, 1991) but the external communication of unique resources, such as IC, is essential to highlight the ability to successfully face the competitive environment and to distinguish itself from other organisations working in the same field. Marr and Roos (2005) segment resources into monetary capital, physical capital and intellectual capital. Since most of these resources are not produced by the NPOs themselves, but rather need to be obtained, a link to stakeholder theory exists. Stakeholders are individuals or groups who are affected by an organisation or have an influence on the survival of an organisation in a positive or negative way (a derivation of this definition will be presented in Sect. 5.3), thus including suppliers of resources. Stakeholder theory argues that organisations have to take the demands of their stakeholders into account for every decision made and action executed to ensure their continued support (Freeman & McVea, 2001; Post, Preston, & Sachs, 2002; Reed et al., 2009). Information on IC provides stakeholders with the means to evaluate the organisation more realistically than what traditional financial accounting reports allow.

Prior work experience gained within the non-profit sector demonstrated that NPOs are not necessarily aware of the concept of IC. There is no information available in literature on what German NPOs know of IC or on actual reporting practices for IC disclosure. Also, apart from the aforementioned importance of the disclosure of IC, literature on the motives of NPOs to disclose IC is scarce, and no empirical research examining the disclosure of IC of German NPOs has been conducted so far.

The current research examines four questions. First, are German donation-soliciting NPOs aware of the term intellectual capital and its concept? Second, is IC currently disclosed by German NPOs? Third, how is IC currently disclosed by German NPOs? Fourth, what are the reasons for German NPOs to disclose their IC? Based on the answers to these questions researched, a practice related framework for German NPOs will be developed. This framework serves as the final aim of the current research to support German NPOs by pointing out how information on their IC might be disclosed and their competitive advantages communicated, which in turn helps these organisations to save resources and remain competitive.

The current research is expected to offer contributions to knowledge in three areas. First, while stages one and two of IC research are centred upon "developing IC as a research field" (Guthrie et al., 2012, p. 70) through raising awareness of the topic of IC and establishing the topic as a genuine research field, the current research will contribute to the third stage of IC research. This third stage is described by Guthrie et al. (2012) and centres upon linking the use of IC to the performance of a company via empirical research. Second, the research will add a non-profit view on the disclosure of IC to literature. Third, a new perspective shall be added to the literature on NPOs in Germany. Since the research is practice-oriented, it is expected that implications to practice and policy are going to emerge as well. Finally, reasons for the disclosure of IC in practice shall provide a foundation for discussion on a common approach to IC reporting.

Before an outline of the chapters is presented, it must be noted that the differentiation of male and female forms of address is avoided in order to reduce complexity. The use of the male form of address should thus be regarded as symbolising both forms of address and as non-discriminating. Additionally, the terms company, firm and organisation are used interchangeably and utilised as synonyms for the people working therein.

Eight further chapters follow this introduction. The following two chapters present the literature review. A conceptual framework of intellectual capital is developed in the first chapter of the literature review (Chap. 2). To this end, definitions and concepts of IC are presented first, followed by insight into the historical background of IC. Related concepts are defined next to avoid misunderstandings. Since the current research considers IC disclosure, the next section focuses on this topic. IC is a challenging field from the accounting perspective, which is introduced in Sect. 2.4. Existing rules and regulations for financial reporting do not facilitate the inclusion of information on IC. Information on important intangibles is therefore not available for stakeholders via traditional financial reporting, leading to unrealistic evaluation of an organisation. Correcting this unrealistic picture is one of the motivations for organisations to disclose information on their IC (Beattie & Thomson, 2010). Further incentives and disincentives for IC reporting are discussed in Sect. 2.5. When an organisation decides to disclose information on its IC, it faces the challenges of IC reporting introduced in Sect. 2.6. Countable assets and liabilities are easy to report in the form of numbers; intangibles, however, are not countable. The measurement of IC is therefore a topic of ongoing discussion in the field of IC and closely related to its disclosure. Main arguments of this discussion are presented in Sect. 2.7. The consequent topic an NPO is confronted with, after finding an answer for itself on the question of measurement, is the question of how information on IC can be disclosed. An overview on general information on external communication of IC is therefore presented in Sect. 2.8 and, since several frameworks for the disclosure of IC exist already, these are introduced in Sect. 2.9. Chapter 2 closes with an interim summary, outlining the significance of IC and highlighting the key characteristics of IC for the current research.

Chapter 3 constitutes the second part of the literature review, concentrating on the non-profit sector, also called third sector. However, before the non-profit sector is introduced, a distinction of the three sectors is necessary and thus presented in the first section. Non-profit sectors worldwide did not develop equally, but based on the historic development and culture of their particular country. As the current research focuses on organisations in Germany, the non-profit sector of this particular country is introduced in the Sect. 3.2, highlighting its history and characteristics. Furthermore, a variety of organisations are part of a third sector; therefore, possibilities to divide organisations into more homogeneous and more manageable segments are highlighted in the third section, as well as different types of NPOs. Next, the two main topics of the current research, i.e. IC and NPOs, are linked by offering insight into research on IC in NPOs. The final section of this third chapter offers a review of the literature on IC reporting of NPOs, thus building the foundation and starting point for the empirical research.

Before the empirical research is presented, the methodology, theoretical framework, and methods applied are introduced. The methodology chapter contains a description of the aims and expected impacts of the current research, followed by the research philosophy applied. Reflections on the influence of the researcher and of ethical issues are also highlighted. Literature review on reasons for NPOs to engage in reporting of IC revealed theories applied previously and some of the theories used most frequently (Dumay & Cai, 2015) are introduced in Chap. 5: agency theory, stakeholder theory, legitimacy theory, resource-based-view, institutional theory, and resource-dependency theory. Additionally, the applicability for explaining IC disclosure of NPOs of all theories is illustrated as part of their individual introductions. Based on the six theories, a theoretical framework for the motivation of IC disclosure of NPOs is developed and presented in Sect. 5.7.

Chapter 6 starts with an overview of the research approaches chosen to answer the aforementioned research questions posed. In the second section, characteristics of problem-centred semi-structured expert interviews are introduced, including a discussion on what constitutes an expert. Thirdly, content analysis is introduced as the method chosen for analysis. Since the terms or description of IC were not expected to be explicit based on prior work experience, a quantitative content analysis or a questionnaire would have been inapt. Therefore, the focus is on qualitative content analysis. As the available approaches to qualitative content analysis by Mayring (1996), Schreier (2012) and Gläser and Laudel (2010) are either too comprehensive or not comprehensive enough, an overlapping combination of their approaches is used for the current research as described in Sect. 6.3. Furthermore, measures taken to satisfy quality criterion are also highlighted in Sect. 6.3 as well.

Section 6.4 describes the development and composition of the sample utilised for the current research. Since there is no register of all German NPOs, the sample for data collection was based on the information provided by the Deutsches Zentralinstitut für soziale Fragen (DZI), which collects and provides information on German donation-soliciting charities (DZI, n.d.). Donation-soliciting charities are of special interest for the current research since they depend the most on external communication to ensure the availability of resources. Of all NPOs listed by the DZI, the most contrary organisations based on longevity, size and composition of workforce, revenue generated, level of internationality, fundraising performance, and location were identified to establish similarities and differences in the way IC is disclosed.

In accepting recommendations by various researchers (see for instance Brüggen, Vergauwen, & Dao, 2009; Denzin & Lincoln, 2011; Dumay & Cai, 2014) to use more sources than annual reports to allow a validation of data and findings, various publicly available documents are considered. These publications are produced by the NPOs themselves and available via their websites. All documents were analysed via qualitative content analysis. Additionally, face-to-face or telephone interviews with twelve representatives of the nine German NPOs were conducted, transcribed, and analysed via qualitative content analysis as well, but independently from the documents. The approaches to analysis of the documents and interviews and the software utilised are introduced in Sect. 6.6. Next, the development of the coding frame and the frame itself are described and the last section of the chapter and offer insight into the process of coding, including coding rules applied and quality measures taken.

Results of the analysis are presented in Chap. 7: first the documents, followed by the interviews. Both sections are structured the same way. A description of the advancement of the coding frame is offered first, followed by the illustration of changes to the coding frame and the introduction of new codes established. Next, findings regarding the disclosure of each of the capitals are presented, followed by findings on the form of disclosure, and finally, on the aforementioned variables that were used to establish the most contrary NPOs for the sample. A third section offers a comparison of these findings. As the theoretical framework presented in Sect. 5.7 pointed out the importance of stakeholder support and the availability of resources, crucial resources and demands imposed on NPOs were also researched during the analysis. These resources and demands as well as their dependencies and interdependencies are highlighted in Sect. 7.4. Finally, a summary of the main findings is offered.

Chapter 8 brings the literature presented in Chaps. 2 and 3 together with the findings presented in Chap. 7, based on the methodology described in Chap. 4, the theoretical framework introduced in Chap. 5 and the methods highlighted in Chap. 6. The chapter starts with an overview of the current state of disclosure of IC by German NPOs. This section also highlights the awareness of IC by German NPOs and highlights whether and how IC is currently disclosed by German NPOs i.e. answers to the research questions one, two, and three are presented. The fourth research question on the reasons for German NPOs to disclose information on their IC is discussed in Sect. 8.2.

Implications for the disclosure of IC are highlighted in the third section of the eighth chapter, facilitating the foundation for a framework for the disclosure of information on IC by German NPOs. Before the framework is presented, Sect. 8.4 begins by pointing out possible applications and target groups. The framework itself consists of questions clustered into three sections, inspired by the parts through which NPOs connect their purpose to their everyday operation, namely outcomes, outputs, processes and inputs as defined by Keehley and Abercrombie (2008).

Concluding, contributions to knowledge, policy implications, as well as implications for practice, and limitations and opportunities for further research are described in Chap. 9. This book closes with a recapitulation and reflection of the findings and of the current research in general.

References

Anheier, H. K., & Seibel, W. (1993). *Defining the nonprofit sector: Germany*. Baltimore, MD: Johns Hopkins Institute for Policy Studies.

Barney, J. (1991). Firm resources and sustained competitive advantage. *Journal of Management, 17*(1), 99–120. doi:10.1177/014920639101700108.

Beattie, V., & Thomson, S. J. (2010). *Intellectual capital reporting: Academic utopia or corporate reality in a brave new world?* Edinburgh: The Institure of Chartered Accountants of Scotland.

Bontis, N., Dragonetti, N., Jacobsen, K., & Roos, G. (1999). The knowledge toolbox: A review of the tools available to measure and manage intangible resources. *European Management Journal, 17*(4), 391–402. doi:10.1016/S0263-2373(99)00019-5.

Brüggen, A., Vergauwen, P., & Dao, M. (2009). Determinants of intellectual capital disclosure: Evidence from Australia. *Management Decision, 47*(2), 233–245. doi:10.1108/00251740910938894.

Denzin, N. K., & Lincoln, Y. S. (2011). The discipline and practice of qualitative research. In N. K. Denzin & Y. S. Lincoln (Eds.), *The Sage handbook of qualitative research* (pp. 1–17). Thousand Oaks, CA: SAGE.

Dumay, J., & Cai, L. (2014). A review and critique of content analysis as a methodology for inquiring into IC disclosure. *Journal of Intellectual Capital, 15*(2), 264–290. doi:10.1108/JIC-01-2014-0010.

Dumay, J., & Cai, L. (2015). Using content analysis as a research methodology for investigating intellectual capital disclosure: A critique. *Journal of Intellectual Capital, 16*(1), 121–155. doi:10.1108/JIC-04-2014-0043.

Edvinsson, L. (1997). Developing intellectual capital at Skandia. *Long Range Planning, 30*(3), 366–373. doi:10.1016/S0024-6301(97)00016-2.

Freeman, R. E., & McVea, J. A. (2001). *A stakeholder approach to strategic management.* Charlottesville, VA. doi:10.2139/ssrn.263511.

Gläser, J., & Laudel, G. (2010). *Experteninterviews und qualitative inhaltsanalyse* (4th ed.). Wiesbaden: VS Verlag für Sozialwissenschaften.

Grossekettler, H. (2006). Verbände zwischen Markt und Staat aus finanzwirtschaftlicher Sicht. In H.-J. Schmidt-Trenz & R. Stober (Eds.), *Jahrbuch Recht und Ökonomik des Dritten Sektors 2005/2006 (RÖDS)* (pp. 13–35). Baden Baden: Nomos Verlagsgesellschaft.

Guthrie, J. (2001). The management, measurement and the reporting of intellectual capital. *Journal of Intellectual Capital, 2*(1), 27–41. doi:10.1108/14691930110380473.

Guthrie, J., Ricceri, F., & Dumay, J. (2012). Reflections and projections: A decade of intellectual capital accounting research. *The British Accounting Review, 44*(2), 68–82. doi:10.1016/j.bar.2012.03.004.

Hall, M. L. W. (1998). The confusion of the capitals: Surveying the cluttered landscape of intellectual 'capitals' and terminology. In P. H. Sullivan (Ed.), *Profiting from intellectual capital – Extracting value from innovation* (pp. 76–83). New York: Wiley.

Helmig, B., & Boenigk, S. (2012). *Nonprofit mangement.* München: Verlag Franz Vahlen GmbH.

InCaS. (2008). *Intellectual capital statement – Made in Europe.* Accessed January 31, 2010, from www.incas-europe.org

Keehley, P., & Abercrombie, N. N. (2008). *Benchmarking in the public and nonprofit sectors* (2nd ed.). San Francisco, CA: Wiley.

Kong, E. (2003). Using intellectual capital as a strategic tool for non-profit organisations. *The International Journal of Knowledge, Culture and Change Management, 3*(1), 467–474.

Kong, E. (2007a). A review of the strategic management literature: The importance of intellectual capital in the non-profit sector. In *28th McMaster world congress on intellectual capital and innovation* (pp. 1–26). Hamilton, ON: McMaster University. doi:10.1108/14691930710830864.

Kong, E. (2007b). The strategic importance of intellectual capital in the non-profit sector. *Journal of Intellectual Capital, 8*(4), 721–731. doi:10.1108/14691930710830864.

Kong, E. (2008). The development of strategic management in the non-profit context: Intellectual capital in social service non-profit organizations. *International Journal of Management Reviews, 10*(3), 281–299. doi:10.1111/j.1468-2370.2007.00224.x.

Kong, E. (2010a). Analyzing BSC and IC's usefulness in nonprofit organizations. *Journal of Intellectual Capital, 11*(3), 284–304. doi:10.1108/14691931011064554.

Kong, E. (2010b). Intellectual capital and non-profit organizations in the knowledge economy: Editorial and introduction to special issue. *Journal of Intellectual Capital, 11*(2), 97–106. doi:10.1108/14691931011039624.

Kong, E., & Prior, D. (2008). An intellectual capital perspective of competitive advantage in nonprofit organisations. *International Journal of Nonprofit and Voluntary Sector Marketing, 13*, 119–128. doi:10.1002/nvsm.

KPMG. (2012). *Rechnungslegung in der Praxis – Bilanzierungs- und Bewertungsfragen nach deutschem Recht bei Non-Profit-Organisationen*, (Homepage). Accessed January 08, 2014, from http://www.kpmg.com/DE/de/Bibliothek/2012/Seiten/Rechnungslegung-in-der-Praxis.aspx

Lichtsteiner, H., Gmür, M., Giroud, C., & Schauer, R. (2013). *Das Freiburger Management-Modell für Nonprofit Organisationen* (7th ed.). Bern: Haupt Verlag.

Marr, B., & Roos, G. (2005). A strategy perspective on intellectual capital. In B. Marr (Ed.), *Perspectives on intellectual capital* (pp. 28–41). Oxford: Elsevier Butterworth-Heinemann.

Mayring, P. (1996). *Einführung in die qualitative Sozialforschung* (3rd ed.). Weinheim: Psychologie Verlags Union.

Möller, K., & Gamerschlag, R. (2009). Immaterielle Vermögenswerte in der Unternehmenssteuerung - betriebswirtschaftliche Perspektiven und Herausforderungen. In K. Möller, M. Piwinger, & A. Zerfaß (Eds.), *Immaterielle Vermögenswerte – Bewertung, Berichterstattung und Kommunikation* (pp. 3–21). Stuttgart: Schäffer-Poeschel Verlag Stuttgart.

Petrash, G. (1996). Dow' s journey to a knowledge value management culture. *European Management Journal, 73*(4), 365–373.

Pfeffer, J., & Salancik, G. R. (2003). *The external control of organizations.* Stanford: Stanford University Press.

Post, J. E., Preston, L. E., & Sachs, S. (2002). Managing the extended enterprise – The new stakeholder view. *California Management Review, 45*(1), 6–28.

Priller, E., Zimmer, A., Anheier, H. K., Toepler, S. & Salamon, L. M. (1999). Germany: Unification and change. In *Global civil society: Dimensions of the nonprofit sector* (pp. 99–118). Baltimore, MD: The John Hopkins Center for Civil Society Studies. Accessed March 24, 2012, from http://scholar.google.com/scholar?hl= en&btnG=Search&q=intitle:Global+Civil+Society+Dimensions+of+the+Nonprofit+Sector#4

Reed, M. S., Graves, A., Dandy, N., Posthumus, H., Hubacek, K., Morris, J., et al. (2009). Who's in and why? A typology of stakeholder analysis methods for natural resource management. *Journal of Environmental Management, 90*(5), 1933–1949. doi:10.1016/j.jenvman.2009.01.001.

Salamon, L. M., & Anheier, H. K. (1992). *In search of the non-profit sector II: The problem of classification.* Baltimore, MD. doi:10.1007/BF01397460. Accessed March 24, 2012, from http://www.springerlink.com/index/K1UQQ84225324356.pdf

Schreier, M. (2012). *Qualitative content analysis in practice.* London: SAGE.

van Broekhoven, R. A. (2008). *Engaging Donors' Trust.* Accessed February 20, 2014, from http://www.icfo.org/ICFO-Publications

Wex, T. (2004). *Der Nonprofit-Sektor der Organisationsgesellschaft* (1st ed.). Wiesbaden: Deutscher Universitäts-Verlag.

Zimmer, A., & Priller, E. (2007). *Gemeinnützige Organisationen im gesellschaftlichen Wandel* (2nd ed.). Wiesbaden: VS Verlag für Sozialwissenschaften.

Chapter 2
A Conceptual Framework of Intellectual Capital

The existence of intangibles, including intellectual capital, within a company has been known for a long time but has not been considered important, since the relevant resources for value creation were largely tangible (Guthrie, 2001; Möller & Gamerschlag, 2009). However, in the last three decades, most economies shifted towards a knowledge- and service-based focus and IC replaced the traditional tangible resources determining competition, such as land, location and technology (Guthrie, 2001; Kong, 2008; Möller & Gamerschlag, 2009). The aim of this chapter is to ensure a common understanding of the term intellectual capital and its concept and to provide an insight into the current discussion on the measurement and reporting of IC.

To this end, definitions and perceptions of intellectual capital are introduced in the first section. The second section offers insight into the historical background of IC and the research in this field to facilitate the relation of the current research with prior literature. Next, to prevent confusion, concepts associated with IC are defined, namely knowledge, expertise, and goodwill. Section 2.4 highlights the accounting perspective on intellectual capital since IC is a growing area of interest in this field. In light of the current research, an important question is why organisations engage in the reporting of intellectual capital. Answers given in literature to this question are presented in Sect. 2.5, followed by an introduction to the challenges of intellectual capital reporting in Sect. 2.6 and an overview on the discussion on intellectual capital measurement in Sect. 2.7. External communication with a focus on financial reporting is discussed in Sect. 2.8. The ninth section introduces available frameworks for the management and disclosure of IC. These frameworks are the Intangible Asset Monitor, the Skandia Navigator, the Intellectual Capital Statement by the Danish Agency for Trade and Industry, the MERITUM project, the Wissensbilanz—Made in Germany, the Intellectual Capital Statement—Made in Europe, and Integrated Reporting. The chapter closes with a summary putting the topic of intellectual capital into the context of the current research.

K. Blankenburg, *Intellectual Capital in German Non-profit Organisations*,
Contributions to Management Science, DOI 10.1007/978-3-319-62655-0_2

2.1 Intellectual Capital

A vital basis for the current research is a common understanding of the term and concept of IC used. To this end, first, it must be acknowledged that the term 'intellectual capital' is contested in literature. The main criticism is based on the term 'capital'. Originally, 'capital' derives from the Latin word for 'head' (Andriessen, 2004; Edvinsson, 2013; Langenscheidt Verlag, 2010). It implies similarities to physical capital which can be measured and managed (Dumay, 2009b). Additionally, in the traditional accounting sense, the word 'capital' is connected to the liability side of the balance sheet (Alwert, Heisig, & Mertins, 2005; Andriessen, 2004) but IC is also an asset. An ethical argument that should not be overlooked is that the valuation of human beings (e.g. employees) in form of capital is contested (Gowthorpe, 2009). However, there have not been any attempts to suggest a less controversial term. Therefore, the term intellectual capital is used for this book.

Another challenge in the field of IC is that there is no generally agreed-upon definition yet (Abeysekera, 2006; Alwert et al., 2005; Dumay, 2009b). Researchers and practitioners have offered a number of possible definitions, depending on their respective world view and area of expertise. These views can be classified into two broad groups: the accounting view and the management view. The accounting view describes IC as static, implying that it is a measurable position and the term 'intangible asset' is favoured. A comprehensive introduction to the accounting view on IC is offered in Sect. 2.4 of this chapter. From a management perspective, the preferred term is 'intellectual capital', which is often described in context of the competitive advantages of an organisation, i.e. the focus adopted is external; the organisation is regarded in relation to its environment. Also, IC is viewed as dynamic (Beattie & Smith, 2013) and as a process or a resource that can be actively influenced. For example, from a management view, human resource management is regarded as responsible for the development of human capital through hiring new staff, staff development, and knowledge management. Relational capital is affected by every department and individual in contact with external stakeholders, such as clients, journalists, suppliers, or possible future employees. Company culture as part of structural capital is influenced by individuals and strategic decisions. On the whole, the management perspective implies that IC is a complex topic which is relevant in and dependent on every department and individual employee of an organisation, and that it is not available in the same quantity at all times since it is dynamic and elusive. The accounting and management perspectives cannot be strictly separated. A selection of definitions sorted by the view the respective author adopted and the date of publication is presented in Table 2.1.

Despite the various definitions for IC in literature, some common basic characteristics can be identified. In all definitions, IC is viewed as intangible, which is defined by Dictionaries as "difficult do describe, understand or measure" (Oxford Wordpower Dictionary, 2006, p. 388), "an intangible quality or feeling is difficult

Table 2.1 Selection of definitions for intellectual capital

Source	Definition	Underlying concepts
Stewart (1991, p. 44)	"it's the sum of everything everybody in your company knows that gives you a competitive edge in the marketplace"	**Management view External focus**
Petrash (1996, p. 336)	"Intellectual Capital = Human Capital + Organizational Capital + Customer Capital" "Dow must focus on the management of its intellectual assets and intellectual capital not only to survive, but to prosper"	
Edvinsson (1997, p. 368)	"the possession of knowledge, applied experience, organizational technology, customer relationships, and professional skills that provide [. . .] a competitive edge in the market"	
InCaS (2008, p. 7)	IC "describes the intangible resources of an organisation" and "[. . .] Intellectual Capital is linked to corporate goals, business processes and the business success of an organisation [. . .]"	
Sullivan (1998, p. 4)	"Intellectual capital may be thought of simply as knowledge that can be converted into profits."	**Accounting view Internal focus**
Caddy (2000)	IC = intellectual assets—intellectual liabilities	
Lev (2001, p. 7)	IC is a "nonphysical source of value [. . .], generated by innovation (discovery), unique organizational designs, or human resource practice. Intangibles often interact with tangible and financial assets to create corporate value and economic growth."	
Abeysekera (2006, p. 61)	IC is "unaccounted capital", which "can be described as the knowledge-based equity that supports the knowledge-based assets of a firm"	
International Federation of Accountants	"the knowledge-based equity of a company" (Tan, Plowman, & Hancock, 2008, p. 585)	
Beattie and Thomson (2010, p. VII)	IC "refers to the intangible knowledge resources which create company value"	

Source: Author

to describe exactly" and "intangible things have value but do not exist physically—used in business" (Longman Dictionary of Contemporary English, 2012, p. 916). These definitions point towards the challenge that the intangible nature of IC poses: How can a universal definition of a term be established that is "difficult to describe exactly" and thereby subjective?

Nevertheless, as mentioned before, several characteristics that are ascribed to IC are agreed upon by various researchers (Andriessen, 2004; Lev, 2001; Möller & Gamerschlag, 2009):

– IC is non-rival. It can be used in different ways at the same time without a loss of value. For example, money used to buy a computer cannot be used at the same

time to buy another item. In comparison, the database of a company can be used by several employees simultaneously.
- IC benefits from network effects. The more employees share, use and update the database, the more information is available for everyone participating i.e. IC grows with usage.
- The ownership of IC is often difficult to secure. It is impossible for a company to prevent employees from taking company-specific knowledge with them when leaving the company.
- IC has high fixed and low marginal costs. For example, the implementation of a database requires an investment of financial resources and time. However, there are hardly any expenses for an additional user or more frequent access to the data.
- The risk of investing in intangibles is higher than investing in tangibles. A training which creates knowledge but is not applied by employees cannot be used otherwise, while a computer not used by an employee can easily be given to another employee, sold or placed in the canteen and offered to all employees for private use during breaks, for instance.
- Only in few cases does a market for intangibles exist. The experience of an employee regarding a company-unique process is only of value to the particular company and cannot be sold to other organisations. A computer on the other hand could be sold, since there is a market for second hand computers.

Another element common in all definitions is the split of IC into several components, mostly described as forms of capital such as human capital, structural capital and relational capital (Giuliani & Marasca, 2011). Hall (1998) lists and defines all forms of capital, namely human, customer, stakeholder, cultural, relationship, spiritual, organisational, structural, process, and economic capital. He also compared the different concepts of IC, many of which consist of a combination of three forms of capital. One of these trinity concepts of IC (Hall, 1998) is the value platform developed by a group of practitioners: Leif Edvinsson, Hubert St. Onge, Patrick Sullivan, and Gordon Petrash (1996). They defined IC as the sum and interrelation of organisational capital, human capital, and customer capital.

Figure 2.1 illustrates the interrelation through overlapping circles while the triangle shows the knowledge flow. The triangle additionally indicates that the individual forms of capital are not managed individually, but as an entity. According to the value platform, organisations should work towards an increase in interrelationships between the three parts of IC to increase value creation (Tan et al., 2008).

For comparison, Möller and Gamerschlag (2009) also split IC into three forms of capital: human capital, structural capital and relational capital. However, they subdivide structural capital and relational capital into three 'sub-capitals' each. Structural capital consists of innovation capital, process capital and location capital. Relational capital is split into customer capital, supplier capital and investor capital. Only human capital is not divided any further (Möller & Gamerschlag, 2009). Another concept using the division into three components is offered by Lev (2001).

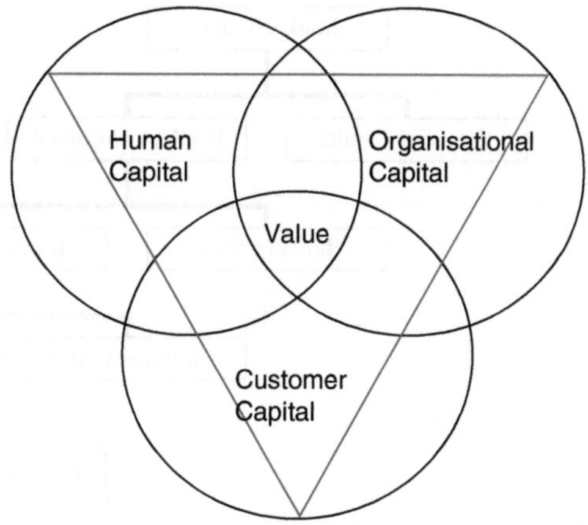

Fig. 2.1 Value platform of intellectual capital (Petrash, 1996)

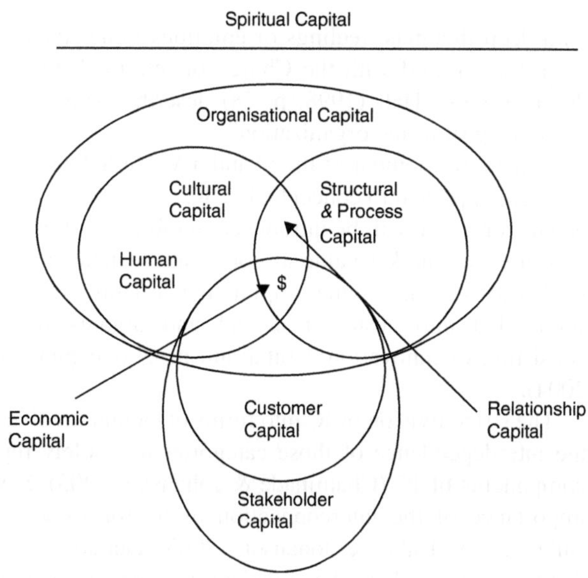

Fig. 2.2 Combination of concepts of forms of capital (Hall, 1998, p. 81)

He divides intangibles into the following by their relation to the generator of the assets: discovery, organisational practices, and human resources.

Hall (1998) illustrates the confusing array of concepts by combining them into one illustration (Fig. 2.2). Figure 2.2 also indicates economic capital as the centre of all capital combinations, since profit is essentially the aim of every firm. Additionally, the relationships between the forms of capital according to their respective definitions are highlighted. For example, cultural capital and human capital are placed in the same circle, since they have similar meaning in relation to the other forms of capital (Hall, 1998). The least defined and used capital is spiritual capital. The Oxford Dictionary offers the following definition for spiritual: "1 connected

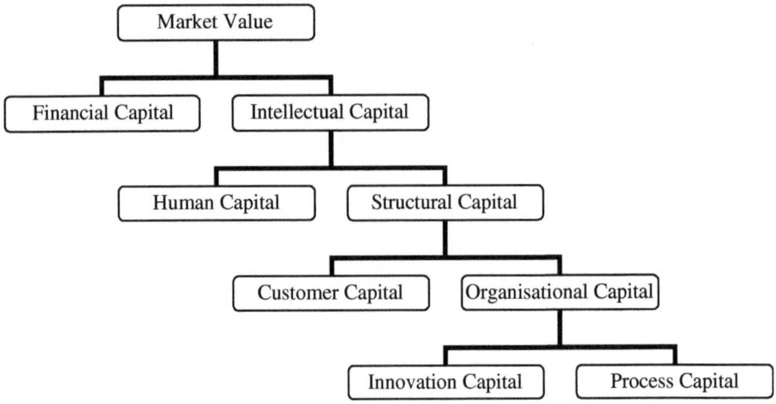

Fig. 2.3 Skandia value scheme (Edvinsson, 1997)

with deep thoughts, feelings or emotions rather than the body or physical things [...] 2 connected with the Church or religion" (Oxford Wordpower Dictionary, 2006, p. 689). Hall (1998, p. 78) describes spiritual capital as "the essence or positive spirit of the organization".

In the development of the Skandia Value Scheme, Edvinsson (1997) chooses a different approach to conceptualise IC (Fig. 2.3). It forms the bases of the Skandia Navigator which will be introduced in more detail in Sect. 2.9.2. Edvinsson (1997) describes the market value as consisting of financial capital and IC. The latter is further divided into human capital and structural capital while structural capital is subdivided into customer capital and organisational capital, with the latter consisting of innovation capital and process capital (Tan et al., 2008; Wingren, 2004).

The strict division of IC into forms of capital involves the danger of overlooking the interdependence of those categories and solely regarding them as individual components of IC (Chaminade & Johanson, 2003). Several researchers stress the importance of the interconnection of IC for value creation (Andriessen, 2004; Bukh, 2003; Bukh & Johanson, 2003; Dumay & Cuganesan, 2011; Giuliani, 2013; Holland, 2004). Nevertheless, the suggested split of IC facilitates the identification process of IC and is thus utilized for this book.

Since the majority of literature on IC is in English, another challenge arises for literature and research in German. A review of the rather limited literature on IC in German also shows that there is not yet an agreement on a single term. The predominant terms used in the German literature are 'Intellektuelles Kapital', which is very similar to IC, or 'Immaterieller Vermögenwert', which is an approximate translation of 'intangible assets' (Alwert et al., 2005). A bigger challenge is the translation of terminology used for concepts, such as the frameworks for IC disclosure introduced in Sect. 2.9, since a word-by-word translation would produce a term that does not align with German grammar (Alwert et al., 2005). Since the author of this book does not speak other languages, no statements can be made to difficulties regarding the term in other languages, but they are speculated to be similar.

A project group funded by the European Commission developed the "Intellectual Capital Statement—Made in Europe (InCaS)". It attempts to offer a common definition for all European countries. The InCaS (2008, p. 7) states: "It [IC] describes the intangible resources of an organisation", in which resources are defined as all tangible and intangible assets a company employs in their business process to execute its value-creating strategy (Barney, 1991; InCaS, 2008). The composition of IC is defined by InCaS (2008, p. 7) as follows:

- *Human Capital* is "what the single employee brings into the value adding processes", including knowledge, experiences and abilities of people.
- *Structural Capital* is "what happens between people, how people are connected within the company, and what remains when the employee leaves the company" such as procedures, cultures, databases, etc.
- *Relational Capital* is "the relations of the company to external stakeholders", including the perceptions that are held about the company.

A recent set of definitions of capitals is provided by the International Integrated Reporting Council (IIRC). They differentiate between six different capitals: three tangible and three intangible capitals. The former are financial capital, manufactured capital, and natural capital while intellectual capital, human capital, social and relationship capital are the intangible capitals. Financial capital describes the monetary resources an organisation uses for the provision of services or manufacturing of goods. Manufactured capitals are those "manufactured physical objects (as distinct from natural physical objects)" (The IIRC, 2013b, p. 11) that organisation can use to produce goods or supply services. Intellectual capital as defined by the IIRC (2013b) includes intellectual property, as well as parts of what the InCaS labelled structural capital e.g. procedures and systems. The definition for human capital is similar in its core meaning to the definition by the InCaS. It is "people's competencies, capabilities and experience, and their motivation to innovate [...]" (The IIRC, 2013b, p. 12). Social and relationship capital is part structural and part relational capital since it includes the relationships within an organisation (structural capital) as well as between an organisation and its external environment (relational capital). Finally, natural capital consists of environmental resources an organisation uses to provide services or manufacture goods, for instance water or air.

Since the InCaS adopted a practice oriented and transnational approach by involving 25 companies from five European countries (InCaS, 2008) and offer a straightforward definition of IC, their aforementioned definition is used for this book. Also, spiritual capital is taken into account as defined by Hall (1998). Additionally, the interrelation of forms of capital introduced by the group of practitioners around Petrash (1996) is utilised for this book as visualised in Fig. 2.4. The outer box indicates intellectual capital as all intangible resources of an organisation. Spiritual capital is part of intellectual capital but since its relationship to the other capitals is not commented on in literature, it is located separately

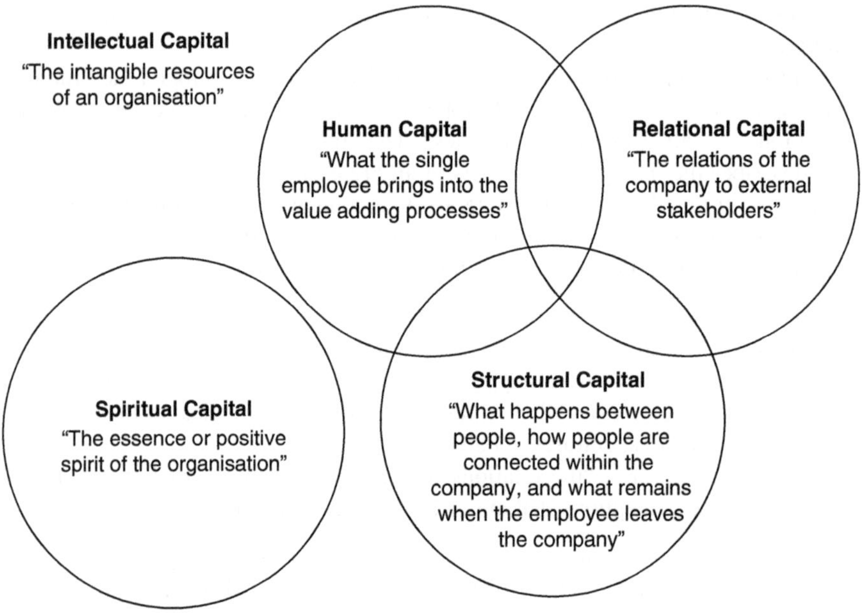

Fig. 2.4 Terms and concept utilized for the current research (Source: Author)

within the outer box. The circles illustrate the other three intangible capitals with their definitions. These capitals are interrelated and thus the circles are overlapping.

2.2 Historical Background of Intellectual Capital

While Bontis (1998, 2001) stated that the first person to mention the term 'intellectual capital' was John Kenneth Galbraith in 1969, the term was actually already used by Edward Thring in his book "Education and School" published in 1864

> "For, in a free country, all classes are working classes, and the superiority of one class to another in the long run depends on the value of their work; and the value of the work depends on the capital, intellectual or other, required before the work can be done; and both intellectual skill and money, in the ordinary course of events, are the result of a mastery over time. Each generation hands over much of its acquired capital to the next. But money differs from intellectual stores in this important particular that it can be passed on at once to a new possessor whereas each man must for himself gain possession of the intellectual capital of past generations." (Thring, 1864, p. 2)

However, only in the early 1980s did the idea of intangible value emerge and the concept of IC gained momentum with the movement towards knowledge- and service-based economies and the recognition of the widening gap between market value and book value of companies (Arvidsson, 2011; Guthrie, 2001). Practitioners were the early driving force behind the concept of IC (Bontis, Dragonetti, Jacobsen, & Roos, 1999; Dumay, 2013).

Two influential practitioners famous for their early research in the area are Leif Edvinsson and Gordon Petrash, working respectively at Skandia and Dow Chemical at the time. Both were looking for a way to explain the hidden value of their particular employer that was not communicated via the traditional financial reporting system (Brennan & Connell, 2000; Edvinsson, 1997, 2013; Petrash, 1996). Through their endeavour, Petrash and Edvinsson pointed out the limitations of communicating information via traditional financial reporting and thus contributed to the quest for a means to address these shortcomings. The result was an overabundance of new approaches to measure IC, all with the purpose of combining financial and non-financial measures that are tied to value creation in a single report (Guthrie, 2001; Petty & Guthrie, 2000). The first supplementary report to a traditional financial statement addressing IC was published in 1994 by Skandia. Guthrie (2001, p. 28) identified the following four developments within the western economies contributing to the growing significance of IC:

- "the revolution in information technology and the information society;
- the rising importance of knowledge and the knowledge based economy;
- the changing patterns of interpersonal activities and the network society;
- the emergence of innovation and creativity as the principal determinant of competitiveness"

Since the late 1990s, IC has been an established topic in academia, in business practice as well as in politics, and a number of large scale projects have been initiated (Guthrie, 2001). Today the topic and importance of IC is recognised on both a national and international level. Examples of national and international projects on IC are the MERITUM project on a European level or the Wissensbilanz—Made in Germany.[1] With the Wissensbilanz, the way of communicating IC in Germany shifted "from reporting of IC as a position to a process view" (Edvinsson, 2013, p. 164). This view was adopted on a European level for the "Intellectual Capital Statement—Made in Europe" (InCaS) project. Another international project is the IIRC, which is currently looking into issues regarding reporting standards today, including the reporting of IC (Edvinsson, 2013). In December 2013 the IIRC presented their integrated reporting (<IR>) framework. Five of these projects will be introduced in Sect. 2.9; for a summary of these examples, see Table 2.2.

As mentioned above, IC and its importance are recognised on an international level. However, Guthrie, Ricceri, and Dumay (2012) conducted a literature review of papers published in the years 2000–2009 which focussed on IC accounting research (ICAR) and found that the "geographical location of the work undertaken"

---

[1]"Wissensbilanz" translated literally into 'balance sheet of knowledge'. It is an approach for IC measurement and reporting developed by a research consortium initiated by the German Federal Ministry of Economics and Labour (Bundesministerium für Wirtschaft und Technologie).

Table 2.2 Summary of examples for national and international large scale projects on IC

Title of project	Developed by	Area of origin
MERITUM project	Research group funded by the EU	France, Spain, Norway, Denmark, Finland, Sweden
Intellectual Capital Statement by the Danish Agency for Trade and Industry	Research group initiated by the Danish Agency for Trade and Industry	Denmark
Wissensbilanz—Made in Germany	Arbeitskreis Wissensbilanz	Germany
Intellectual Capital Statement—Made in Europe	Research group funded by the European Commission	Europe
Integrated reporting <IR>	International Integrated Reporting Council	International

Source: Author

is not equally strong in all regions. Continental Europe was the most active region with 193 papers, followed by Australasia with 74 papers, and North America with 72 papers (Guthrie et al., 2012, p. 74). The authors proposed that "Continental Europe is at the forefront of ICAR because, since the 1990s, European authors, especially Scandinavian countries, have continuously published ICAR articles and books." (Guthrie et al., 2012, p. 74). Additionally, they found that:

> "When we separate Canada and America, a strong presence of Canadian studies is found in contrast to the size and academic population of America, where relatively few studies have been published. We suspect this is because much of the academic American accounting literature is concerned with intangible financial accounting rather than ICA." (Guthrie et al., 2012, p. 74)

Research into IC up to now can be divided into three overlapping levels or steps. The primary aim of the first level was to create awareness of the importance of IC as a value driver (Marr & Chatzkel, 2004; Petty & Guthrie, 2000; Tan et al., 2008). Secondly, it needed to be established that the research into IC is a valid endeavour (Petty & Guthrie, 2000; Tan et al., 2008), followed by the search for suitable methods to measure IC (Dumay, 2013). The subsequent step aims to tie the application of IC to the performance of a company via empirical research (Guthrie et al., 2012; Tan et al., 2008) i.e. to close the gap between theory and practice (Bontis, 2003; Dumay, 2009b). Currently, the focus of research has shifted toward the latter, even though a suitable measurement method has not yet been established, as the discussion in Sect. 2.7 will illustrate. The development towards addressing the theory-practice gap is highlighted by research on publications focusing on IC reporting by Dumay and Garanina (2013). Their analysis shows that the number of papers based on normative research dominated until 2004. Since 2005, empirical research has predominated.

Dumay and Garanina (2013) focussed their review on papers on IC accounting. To check whether the trend towards empirical research is also detectable in various articles on IC, a review was conducted focussing on whether or not an empirical approach was applied. In the Journal of Intellectual Capital, which is specialised for IC in general, 407 papers were published between 2004 and 2015 (third volume), and 143 papers were published in various journals, books, conference proceedings and web pages, as discovered by a Google Scholar search with the search terms ““intellectual capital” and “empirical”” (without citations or patents). The abstracts of all papers from both sources were checked for the approach chosen, and only when no information was available was the paper downloaded and the methodology section read. Of the 143 papers, 19 were either not available online or not available in English or German. One paper was available twice, and for 35 papers, the exact approach was not detectable. 83 papers were based on empirical research and five on research that was not empirical. As for the 407 papers published in the *Journal of Intellectual Capital* during the timeframe considered, 292 were based on empirical research, 106 on non-empirical research, and the remaining nine papers did not consider IC. The comparison of papers based on empirical versus non-empirical research per year is illustrated in Fig. 2.5.

Figure 2.5 highlights that, since 2007, the approach preferred for research on IC is empirical. The spike in 2005 is due to two special issues on “Tiger Brainpower” and “Management Consulting Practices on IC”. It is thus not possible to deduce unambiguously whether the shift to empirical research already happened in 2005. Looking at the data for 2006, there might not have been such a difference in preference without these special issues. A further interesting finding is that only 14 of the 292 papers based on empirical research used interviews and 35 used content analysis, both of which are utilised for the current research.

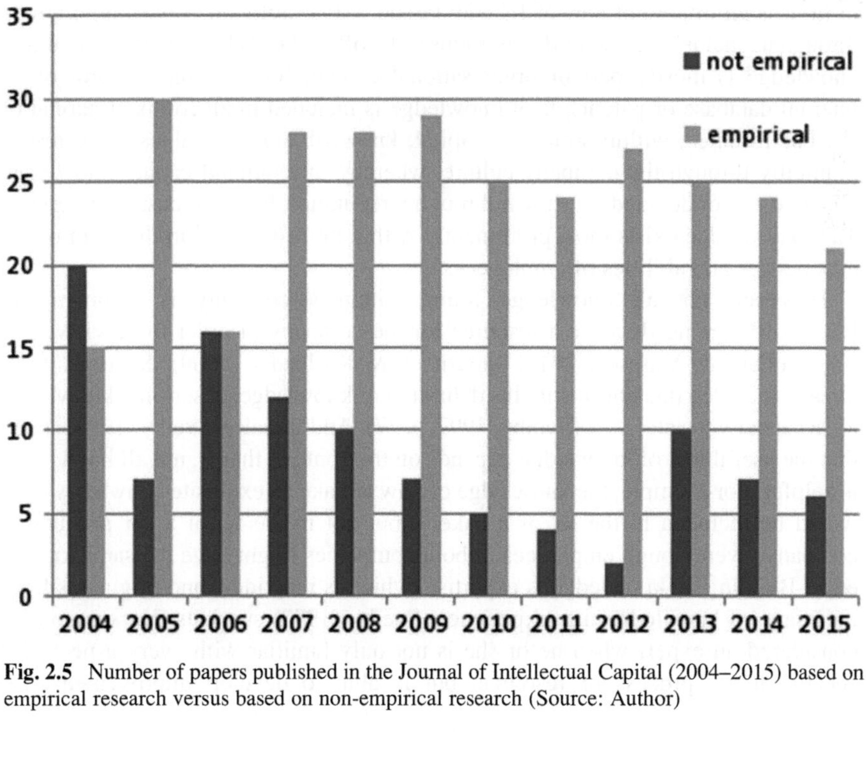

Fig. 2.5 Number of papers published in the Journal of Intellectual Capital (2004–2015) based on empirical research versus based on non-empirical research (Source: Author)

2.3 Related Concepts

Apart from determining the definition and composition of IC, it is necessary to clarify the differences between information, knowledge, and IC to gain a comprehensive understanding of the concept of IC. As Bontis (1998) explains "[. . .] information is the raw material, and knowledge is the finished product" (Bontis, 1998, p. 67). In other words, facts and figures are information: they are of no use whatsoever without any interpretation or analysis. When put into context, information is transformed into knowledge. Knowledge, in turn, is only useful when used and can only grow through communication and discussion. As Edvinsson (2013, p. 167) states: "Knowledge is a social process [. . .]".

In general, there are two types of knowledge: first, codified knowledge that is committed to a storage medium; and tacit (implicit) knowledge (Sullivan, 1998). The endeavour for organisations in regard to those two types of knowledge is to turn as much tacit knowledge into codified knowledge as possible to ensure that it stays with the company, is accessible to its employees and thus shared and built upon. Additionally, companies aim to ensure access to the essential tacit knowledge that cannot be converted, for example by mentoring programs or by keeping retired employees on the payroll as advisors. To accomplish the transformation and consequent effective exploitation of knowledge, a company needs to work towards these objectives actively, since knowledge itself does not change or produce anything, but must be applied to help create value (Andriessen, 2004). Knowledge, in turn, is an important part of IC (Edvinsson, 2013; Sullivan, 1998), highlighted through its inclusion in several definitions of IC offered in Table 2.1. While codified knowledge is mostly part of organisational capital, for example in form of an internal database or patents, tacit knowledge is included in all forms of capital of IC. For instance, within structural capital, knowledge about values is expressed implicitly through the company culture, whereby in relational capital knowledge about customer demands is shown through a reputation for good customer service. Tacit knowledge exists most prominently within human capital in the form of the experiences and abilities of employees.

However, not all knowledge found within a company is automatically IC. Knowledge needs to be a resource for the company in order to be viewed as IC (Giuliani & Marasca, 2011; Mouritsen & Roslender, 2009). Sveiby (1997) already included this notion into his definition of knowledge, describing knowledge as "a capacity to act. [. . .]" (Sveiby, 1997, p. 37). Additionally, Sveiby (1997) stated that the usefulness of knowledge depends on the context, that is, not all knowledge is helpful. For example, the knowledge of how to bake an exquisite strawberry cake would be included in the IC of a bakery, but not in the IC of a car production company, even though employees in both companies might have the same knowledge. Building on knowledge is expertise, which is individual and originates from the usage of knowledge, i.e. experience. Sveiby (1997) suggests that someone is considered an expert when he or she is not only familiar with every aspect of a specific topic, process or resource, but is able to develop improvements for everyone within their area of expertise. Expertise is a highly valuable competitive advantage for any individual since it is impossible to transfer expertise to someone else. Organisations employing an expert need to be aware of the value he or she adds to the IC of the organisation, e.g. by increasing its competitive advantage and therefore chance of survival, and act accordingly.

Another term often associated with IC, especially in the field of accounting, is goodwill. Since there is no universal definition of goodwill, Canibano, Covarsí, and Sánchez (1999) offer two definitions of goodwill, namely as either "the consequence of a firm's above-normal ability to generate future earnings, or as a set of assets controlled by an acquired company but not reported in its financial statements" (Canibano et al., 1999, p. 10). Certain characteristics differentiate goodwill from other assets. Goodwill is always linked to a business or a specific part of a business and cannot be traded separately. Also, the value of goodwill might change day-to-day and is subjective. There is no way to unequivocally link goodwill to the cost incurred during its construction (Gee, 2006). In sum, goodwill is the value which is not included in the financial statement, but generated as a result of a competitive advantage of an organisation or of an individually untradeable asset the organisation uses. While there are similarities to IC, such as the intangible nature and the exclusion from financial statements, goodwill should be regarded as a consequence of IC rather than as a synonym.

2.4 The Accounting Perspective on Intellectual Capital

Since most of the literature is written from the viewpoint of Western culture, the viewpoints presented in this section might not be transferable to other cultures. However, many definitions are accepted internationally and similar challenges may occur. It is obvious that IC is a challenging subject from an accounting perspective. 'Intangible asset' is the term generally accepted within the accounting community and used interchangeably with IC (Möller & Gamerschlag, 2009). Actors within the capital market are aware of the vital role of intangibles for the success and survival of a company. However, due to the high risk associated with investment in intangibles, International Accounting Standards (IAS)/International Financial Reporting Standards (IFRS) requires the expensing of this investment immediately (Lev, 2001). The justification for this approach is the conservatism principle. This principle aims to ensure a realistic, rather than overly positive, picture of the capacity and capability of a company in order to protect investors from possible malinvestment.

According to German law, intangibles that are produced by an organisation, i.e. not bought, cannot be capitalised in the balance sheet unless they are produced for a customer. For example, computer software for internal use cannot be capitalised, but if the same software is developed for a client, it has to be capitalised (Schruff & Haaker, 2009). Intangibles that were bought, and therefore have a monetary value attributed to them and fulfil the criteria for an asset, must be capitalized (Möller & Gamerschlag, 2009; Schruff & Haaker, 2009). However, ignoring future benefits of IC and treating investment in intangibles solely as costs can lead to a comparably skewed picture of the company (Zambon, 2004). Important intangibles, such as brand awareness, motivated and skilled employees, know-how and a company culture supporting innovation, are currently not recognised in the traditional accounting system (Andriessen, 2004; Alwert et al., 2005; Stewart, 1997; Sveiby, 1997).

Two important definitions are stumbling blocks for the recognition of IC in traditional financial reports. A first challenge is the definition of an asset (Vergauwen & Alem, 2005). According to IFRS, assets are "resources an entity controls as a result of past events and from which future economic benefits are expected to flow to the entity" (Frederick, 2009; IPSASB, 2010; Schruff & Haaker, 2009). When applied to intangible assets, there are some difficult requirements within this definition. One of them is the requirement of 'control' of the asset, since a company cannot handle intangibles the same way as tangibles. For example, a table bought by the company belongs to the company and can be used however it sees fit. It is different for the experience and skills of the employees (Vergauwen & Alem, 2005). While the company can exploit these skills and experiences for value creation, the employees are not owned by the company and can leave to join a competitor with very little chance of any preventative measures being taken by the company. In the case of an extra table, the company can decide whether it wants to sell it to a particular organisation or person. Thus, 'control' of intangible assets is only possible in a limited way, leading to the other problematic requirement for the recognition of IC as an asset when examining the definition. The 'future economic benefits' are uncertain (Canibano et al., 1999) due to the limited control over intangible assets and the challenge of their reliable measurement.

Even if the requirements within the definition are met, the classification of 'intangible assets' is the second challenge. According to the International Public Sector Accounting Standards Board (IPSASB), an intangible asset is "an identifiable non-monetary asset without physical substance" (IPSASB, 2010, p. 11). As a result of this definition, intellectual assets are generally categorised as goodwill, as introduced in Sect. 2.3, or as identifiable intangibles i.e. those that can be traded separately. However, to identify one intangible asset separately from all the other intangible assets often proves to be difficult (Canibano et al., 1999; Vergauwen & Alem, 2005).

Another set of challenges are the demands an item has to meet to be recognised on the balance sheet. Reliable measurement of the costs or value of an item and thus the possibility to trade it separately is one of the requirements according to the IPSASB and the IFRS (Canibano et al., 1999; Frederick, 2009). A further recognition criterion is the ownership of or right to an item. In addition to the aforementioned definition according to IFRS, which focuses on "the future economic benefits associated with an asset" (Frederick, 2009, p. 10), the IPSASB states that an asset can originate "from binding arrangements (including rights from contracts or other legal rights)" (IPSASB, 2010, p. 11). These recognition criteria are difficult to establish for an intangible asset. For example, training for employees can have future economic benefits for the company, but it is not certain whether the employees will actually use their new knowledge for the organisation. Again, the cost of training can be calculated precisely most of the time, but the value of the knowledge gained cannot be calculated and the company does not own the knowledge via binding arrangements, contracts, or other legal rights (Frederick, 2009).

Considering the aforementioned definition of the term ‘intangible asset’ by the IPSASB in combination with the definition of an “asset” according to the IFRS, an intangible asset is rather a subset of IC (Caddy, 2000; Guthrie, 2001; Tan et al., 2008) since IC includes more than the term intangible asset encompasses. As a result of the challenges for the recognition of all aspects of IC in the traditional accounting system, the meaningfulness and comparability of financial reports is reduced (Canibano et al., 1999; Frederick, 2009; Gowthorpe, 2009). Consequently, apart from the discussion about the most appropriate term, the debate over the best way to measure and disclose intangibles, and even over a change in traditional financial reporting, is still ongoing.

In 2012 the Deutschen Rechnungslegungs Standards Committee (DRSC) introduced a standard regulating group management reports, the Deutscher Rechnungslegungs Standard (DRS) Nr. 20 (Goebel, 2015). The aim of the standard is to ensure the provision of information regarding the use of the entrusted resources within the reporting period. Further, the information provided is meant to ensure that the reader of a management report can get a realistic idea of the situation of the company, its development, and possible risks and opportunities. According to DRS 20, businesses are required or recommended to include information on IC in their reports (Deutsches Rechnungslegungs Standards Commitee e.V, 2012). Examples for IC explicitly mentioned in DRS 20 are shown in Table 2.3.

Reasons stated in the standard for including information on IC are, for instance, to highlight developments and events that influence the business performance significantly (DRS20/107) and to illustrate sustainability (DRS 20/B28). DRS 20.11 defines sustainability as a concept that aims for a holistic and lasting development of the economic, environmental, and social performance of a company. According to the standard, sustainability can be illustrated by identifying the relationships between operating number and economic, environmental, and social concerns/issues (Deutsches Rechnungslegungs Standards Commitee e.V, 2012).

Table 2.3 IC explicitly mentioned in DRS 20

SC	RC	HC
Organisational structure	Customer satisfaction	Employee turnover
Business procedures	Image	Satisfaction of staff
Internal control systems	Supply arrangements and their insecurities	Employees’ lengths of service
Risk management procedures	Dependencies on individual suppliers, customers, etc.	Professional trainings offered

Deutsches Rechnungslegungs Standards Commitee e.V. (2012)

2.5 Motivation for Intellectual Capital Reporting

So, should an organisation disclose its IC or not? Beattie and Thomson (2010), for example, asked 228 finance directors, human resource specialists, and marketing specialists about their main incentives and disincentives for the disclosure of IC. Combined with the findings of other researchers, some insight into the topic can be gained. In accordance to the different accounting standards of each country, the regulations for the accounting of intangibles in general, and IC in particular, vary. However, there are a couple of generally accepted concepts in this regard. The most fundamentally agreed upon point of view in the accounting literature is the deficiency of the traditional financial accounting practice with respect to IC (Bontis, 2003; Gowthorpe, 2009). Supporting this statement, finance directors who were interviewed for the aforementioned study by Beattie and Thomson (2010) state that the main motivation for disclosure of IC was the correction of the undervaluation of the company, i.e. to provide a more accurate reflection of the actual value of the organisation. Also, the effective management of IC resources and efficient execution of the value creation process are goals of IC disclosure (Beattie & Thomson, 2010).

The main incentive for marketing specialists is the provision of information for stakeholders (Beattie & Thomson, 2010; Mouritsen, Bukh, & Marr, 2004) resulting in better understanding and more accurate assessment (Bontis, 2003; Brüggen, Vergauwen, & Dao, 2009; Petrash, 1996) of services and products by these stakeholders (Bukh, Nielsen, Gormsen, & Mouritsen, 2005). With an increase in transparency, organisations aim for an increase in trustworthiness, thereby affecting the judgement and approval of stakeholders and leading to moral and financial support. However, in the light of the discussion on the effects of IC disclosure, Brüggen et al. (2009) note that "the level of IC disclosure is not related to the level of information asymmetry" but is rather "a matter of common practice in certain industries" (Brüggen et al., 2009, p. 242). In other words, a severely incomplete image of an organisation does not necessarily lead to an effort for more disclosure and transparency. The main influence is the behaviour of an organisation's environment (Brüggen et al., 2009).

Some literature highlights a positive effect on the availability of scarce resources, like the employment and retention of valuable staff, as another incentive for the disclosure of IC. Since the scarcity of highly qualified staff is increasing, this effect is of great importance (Alwert et al., 2005; Zerfaß, 2009). The human resource specialists involved in Beattie and Thomson's (2010) study cited the effects of winning and keeping the trust of their employees as the most important impact of IC disclosure. Additionally, high morale and loyalty of employees was named, as well as the positive effects on the management of a company e.g. a better understanding of the essential resources for further development of the organisation (Guthrie, 2001; Lev, 2001). This led to a more intense focus on the development of IC, including the willingness for necessary investment (Guthrie, 2001).

In direct contrast to the demand for transparency are the increase in the complexity of financial reports and the rising quantity of information that stakeholders are confronted with (Beattie & Smith, 2013; Bukh & Johanson, 2003; Gowthorpe, 2009; Nielsen & Madsen, 2009). The fear of releasing information detrimental to the organisation's competitive advantage is another disincentive (Beattie & Thomson, 2010; Sveiby, 1997; Zambon, 2004).

Petrash (1996), on the other side, states that competitiveness is a motivation for the disclosure of IC: "[...] the better our competition understands their own intellectual assets and the process to manage them, the healthier the competition will be in the future" (Petrash, 1996, p. 365). Another effect of the disclosure of IC in regard to competition is possible network effects, which can result in the predominance of certain product technologies. An example of these effects is provided by Stewart (1991) who describes that the struggle between Video Home System (VHS) and Betamax format for videocassette players. The end result was the demise of Betamax format when the company producing the VHS format shared its technology with others, who then quickly adopted the format and thus created a strong dominance of the market. In summary, the main argument for companies against the disclosure of IC is the chance of competitors gaining insight into valuable corporate trade secrets, and the increasing complexity and quantity of the information provided to stakeholders.

2.6 Challenges of Intellectual Capital Reporting

There are similarities in the challenges of all reporting approaches for intangibles (Bjurström, Catasus, & Johanson, 2003; Johanson, Koga, Skoog, & Henningsson, 2006; Sveiby, 1997; Zambon, 2004). One challenge identified is the lack of a one-size-fits-all approach which would help to make IC comparable versus the need for flexible and adaptable guidelines. Communication is recognized as a challenge as well. The communication of IC is affected by variables, such as the cultural background of the person compiling the report as well as the person reading it, or the experience and expertise of the participating actors (Johanson et al., 2006). Also, a common language for the interpretation of IC disclosure does not exist yet (Bjurström et al., 2003; Zambon, 2004), further complicating communication. Another challenge is to determine unambiguously who the owner of IC is, since most tasks and services in companies are performed by a number of people, often from various departments (Möller & Gamerschlag, 2009; Zerfaß, 2009). The value created by IC or the need for its development can therefore be hard to pinpoint exactly and thus be difficult to report.

An argument taken into account neither by the current measurement methods nor the frameworks for the disclosure of IC, is the idea of IC liabilities, addressed by Caddy (2000). He argues that IC does not necessarily create value but that there is a risk that IC can also bring a loss. An example of a loss of IC is the investment of a company in the training of one of its employees. The training increases the human capital, but when either the new knowledge is not incorporated into the value creation process or the newly trained employees leave the company, the investment is lost. Another scenario would be that the training leads to a great business idea which the company invests in, but due to external circumstances, the idea never makes it to market maturity. Again, the investment into IC does not pay off as expected. Caddy (2000, p. 137) reasons that "there should be a recognized impairment of the organization's current intellectual assets". An argument pointing in a similar direction is stated by several researchers: the increasing complexity of reports might be used to distract readers' attention from unfavourable information or focus their attention merely on the positive effect of IC (Abeysekera, 2006; Dumay, 2003; Gowthorpe, 2009).

The question, however, of how the IC of a company or its investment into IC can be valued, still remains (Zambon, 2004). In this regard, Zambon (2004, p. 159) posed the question whether intangibles should "be recognised as a value within the traditional financial statement" or rather be disclosed via descriptions in the respective section. This question is related to the criticism of the measurement of IC voiced by Dumay and Rooney (2011), further described in Sect. 2.7, who vote for a narrative approach to IC disclosure. In order to discover the possibly hidden IC of a company, Edvinsson (2013) calls for a less reporting-focussed approach and more cross-disciplinary thinking.

Several researchers call for a revision of current reporting standards. Roslender (2004) encourages thinking outside the box instead of following the traditional way of thinking within the field of accounting when it comes to the measurement and reporting of IC. According to him, there is a need for a comprehensive perspective on measurement and reporting which does not necessarily need to be based entirely on numbers, but also on narratives, including the provision of forward-looking information, concentrating on the value creation process (Bukh, 2003; Roslender, 2004). Beattie and Thomson (2010) argue that regulations addressing the whole issue of IC are improbable, since IC is "unique to individual companies and companies are best placed to describe this uniqueness in their own terms" (Beattie & Thomson, 2010, p. XIV). Cultural differences pose another difficulty in the development of a comprehensive perspective on IC and its disclosure. Research by Chaminade and Johanson (2003) indicates that cultural differences influence the introduction of the reporting and management of IC, but no obvious differences in the practice of measuring, managing, and reporting of IC in knowledge-intensive organisations in Europe exists. Several guidelines aim to address these challenges, and the most prominent and current frameworks for the disclosure of IC are introduced in Sect. 2.9.

2.7 Discussion on Intellectual Capital Measurement

In order to report IC, organisations have to know what kind of IC is available in their organisation and how much. Thus, this section presents a discussion on the measurement of IC. Before reasons for the measurement or evaluation of IC can be presented, however, it is necessary to determine the definition of measurement. Andriessen (2004) presents definitions for measurement, value, and valuation. Measurement is "the process of assigning scaled numbers to items in such a way that the relationships that exist in reality between the possible states of a variable are reflected in the relationships between the numbers on the scale" (Andriessen, 2004, p. 408). Since the suggested definition for measurement is predominantly influenced by an accounting viewpoint, but a more comprehensive view is a goal of this book, the term measurement in this book is understood as a tool for the comparison "of something with respect to its embodiment of a certain value" (Andriessen, 2004, p. 18). Value can be understood as "the degree of usefulness or desirability of something, especially in comparison to other things" (Andriessen, 2004, p. 18). In other words, for this book, measurement is defined as a tool for the comparison of things with respect to their usefulness and desirability. This definition permits comparison via figures, narratives, or any other way organisations can think of and does not limit the perspective utilised to either a management or an accounting view.

Nevertheless, the reasons for or against measurement of IC can be attributed to the accounting and management perspectives, comparably to the differentiation of underlying concepts for the definitions of IC presented in Sect. 2.1. From a management perspective, a motivation is not the actual result of the measurement but the process itself. It forces managers to examine and possibly visualise the IC of their company, leading to a better understanding of the resources available (Giuliani & Marasca, 2011; Gowthorpe, 2009; Petrash, 1996; Roslender, 2004). A prevalent rationale for the research on the measurement of IC from a management perspective is expressed in the saying "what can't be measured can't be managed" (Andriessen, 2004; Roos & Roos, 1997; Sullivan, 1998). This truism was confirmed by Marr, Gray, and Neely (2003) to be the basis for measuring IC according to the publications they reviewed. They classified those reasons into the following five categories (Marr et al., 2003, p. 443):

1. to help organizations formulate their strategy;
2. to assess strategy execution;
3. to assist in diversification and expansion decisions;
4. to use these as a basis for compensation; and finally
5. to communicate measures to external stakeholders.

From an accounting point of view, different reasons for the requirement to measure and value IC exist, as already addressed in Sects. 2.1 and 2.4. The existence of hidden value, expressed, for example, in the divergence of the market value and the book value of a company, highlight that certain information is not included in traditional financial reporting (Alwert et al., 2005; Edvinsson, 1997; Petrash, 1996; Zambon, 2004). This missing information leads to an incomplete image of a company and consequently to a decline of the relevance of the traditional financial statements (Alwert et al., 2005; Andriessen, 2004; Beattie & Smith, 2013; Lev, 2001; Möller & Gamerschlag, 2009). Furthermore, the information provided via traditional financial reports is based on historic data. Reporting on IC conversely allows the illustration of the present situation and predictions regarding the future development of an organisation, thereby offering stakeholders, such as potential employees, investors, or suppliers, a better foundation for their decisions in regard to their involvement with an organisation (Bontis, 2003; Möller & Gamerschlag, 2009). Additionally, Keehley and Abercrombie (2008) argue that measurement "can change the way people view performance" by placing "performance into context by providing comparisons" (Keehley & Abercrombie, 2008, p. 41).

Following the statement attributed to Albert Einstein "what can be measured is not always important, and what is important cannot always be measured", or, as Eccles et al. (2002, p. 127) state "Apparently, what's easy to measure isn't important, and what's important isn't easily measured", some researchers call for a different and more critical approach towards the measurement of IC. For Chaharbaghi and Cripps (2006) the ambiguity of IC is the main challenge in regard to its measurement. They propose "to shift the emphasis from measurement to recognition" (Chaharbaghi & Cripps, 2006, p. 31). In a commentary to their paper, Newman states that the current research on IC is based on two assumptions that need to be considered carefully: first, that knowledge can be treated like any tangible asset and secondly, that investments in this asset result in an increase in its availability and consequently lead to an accumulation of wealth (Newman cited in Chaharbaghi & Cripps, 2006).

Dumay (2009a) argues that even with the huge number of measurement methods already in place, none has become prevalent so far and thus suggests that a different approach needs to be adopted. He encourages researchers to take a new perspective on IC and to try to avoid linking the concept to such existing ideals as the traditional accounting system based on the measurement of financial value. Dumay and Rooney (2011) find that, within the scope of their case study, measurement is not necessarily the basis for management. Instead, a narrative report on how the company's IC is used and increased should be presented (Dumay & Rooney, 2011). Beattie and Smith (2013) remind that IC itself is not able to create value; it needs to be used. They suggest that narrative IC reporting offers the possibility to link IC to the business model of a company and thus describe the way IC is used for value creation (Arvidsson, 2011; Beattie & Smith, 2013; Bukh, 2003) and the competitive advantage incurred through its use.

With no best practice for the handling of IC at hand, organisations have to decide individually whether the reasons for the measurement of IC outweigh the arguments against it. When an organisation makes the decision on the measurement of IC, the next choices that the organisation needs to make is whether to disclose its IC and how. Therefore, the next section offers an insight into available communication channels for disclosure, bases for financial communication, and limits on communication, since these topics are the origin of possible IC disclosure methods.

2.8 External Communication of Intellectual Capital

Generally, possible communication channels for financial reporting can be categorised into two groups. One group is titled *personal communication* and includes annual general meetings, roadshows, press conferences, and conferences for financial analysts. The second category is *impersonal communication* such as annual or quarterly financial reports, newsletters, press releases, and advertisements (Kuhnle & Banzhaf, 2006). Today, with the rise of the internet and associated communication channels, organisations have a diverse set of methods they can choose from for their communication, not only for financial information but for their entire corporate communication, such as homepages, blogs, feeds, or social networks. However, the annual report is still the most important medium for the communication of a company's financial situation (Beattie, 2013; Bontis, 2003).

Corporate reporting involves the process of communication between an organisation and outside parties, involving shareholders and stakeholders. Its aim is to communicate the strategy of the organisation and to define and align the tasks that need to be accomplished to reach the organisation's goals (Zerfaß, 2009). An important part of corporate communication is financial communication. Since IC as a factor for value creation, it is often linked to financial reporting alongside traditional factors such as land and machines. Historically, the first regulations regarding financial communication were introduced in the United States of America (USA) as a reaction to the stock market crash on 24th October 1929, also known as Black Thursday. Since then, rules and regulations were developed to ensure comparability and to reduce the possibility of fraud (Kuhnle & Banzhaf, 2006). The latest set of regulations is the IFRS, which aims for a comparability of financial communication and the communication of information relevant to stakeholders to enable them to forecast the company's future economic situation (Kuhnle & Banzhaf, 2006). According to IFRS financial reporting in general should meet the following qualitative characteristics: truthful/reliable, understandable, relevant, and comparable. These characteristics are further defined in Table 2.4.

The annual report consists of four equally important parts: the balance sheet and the income statement, which constitute the financial statements, the notes (Kuhnle & Banzhaf, 2006) and the 'surrounds', i.e. the narratives. Strict regulations exist regarding the form and content of the financial statements. The income statement is supposed to show all receipts and expenditures of the period covered (Kuhnle & Banzhaf, 2006). Assets and liabilities of a company are reflected in the balance sheet, registering the sources and applications of funds (Bachert, 2005; Hirschler, 2012). The purpose of the balance sheet is threefold: documentation of available assets and liabilities, profit assessment on a specific reference date and provision of information to internal and external stakeholders (Bachert, 2005; Hirschler, 2012).

Table 2.4 Principles of orderly accounting according to IFRS

Characteristic	Definition
Truthful/ reliable	Information must be correct (i.e. free from error), comprehensive, cautious and neutral
Understandable	Clear and precise in its language, format and structure, i.e. understandable for the target audience
Relevant	Information should be relevant for the evaluation of the company by and economic decision-making of the target audience
Comparable	A report should be comparable to other companies' reports, as well as to former reports of the company regarding its structure and accounting methods to recognise development trends

Kuhnle and Banzhaf (2006)

However, only items that meet certain criteria can be entered into the financial statement, as described for IC in the previous Sect. 2.4.

The purpose of the notes, the narrative section, is to convey additional qualitative information about the organisation, thus helping to interpret the information provided in the quantitative sections and serving as an additional platform for information that does not fit into the other two parts (Kuhnle & Banzhaf, 2006). According to the IFRS, the following information needs to be provided via the qualitative section (Kuhnle & Banzhaf, 2006; RöverBrönner GmbH & Co KG, n.d.):

- information regarding the basis for the breakdown of the financial report and specific accounting and valuation principles used;
- additional information relevant for understanding the figures in the financial report;
- relevant items that cannot be included in the financial statement.

In brief, supplementary reporting, besides the annual report, is necessary since the latter does not reflect the organisation anymore due to its failure to account for the role of IC (Gowthorpe, 2009; Mourtisen, Bukh, & Marr, 2005) in the value creation process, the evaluation of the company value, and the strategy of an organisation.

While the financial statement and the income statement are subject to strict regulation, the narrative section leaves room for customisation and offers the possibility to include relevant information not represented in the financial statement, such as IC. At the same time, it opens the door for distortion or abuse. Beattie and Jones (1992, p. 291) researched "the use and abuse of graphs of annual reports of UK companies", highlighting that the choice of data shown in the narrative section in form of graphs and the way these graphs are constructed can influence the perception of the company portrayed. They conclude: "This manipulation undermines the neutrality of financial statements, which has long been recognised as an essential requirement of financial reporting" (Beattie & Jones, 1992, p. 301) and thus point out a need for change. As early as 1983, Adelberg also called for change as, in his view, accounting communication is not readable enough. He argued that missing feedback from the audience of accounting communication is the main challenge in this regard (Adelberg, 1983).

As to the question of what and when information should be communicated, limitations of corporate communication need to be considered. These limitations are threefold: *Economic limits* occur due to the cost of preparation and publication of information. *Competitive limits* exist since a company should not release information that would disclose their competitive advantage or company secrets. Last but not least, there are *communicative limits*. Once published, it is hard to take back, rectify, or retract information (Kuhnle & Banzhaf, 2006). A company has to be aware of these limitations and must be careful as to what information it wants to share, how, and with whom. Contradictory statements or withheld information are often uncovered by the audience and lead to a loss of trust in the company (Zerfaß, 2009).

If an organisation decides to disclose its IC regardless of these challenges and discussions, the next challenge arises in the execution, as no best practice for the disclosure of IC yet exists. However, there are a variety of frameworks available. Bukh, Larsen, and Mouritsen (2001) describe these intellectual capital statements (ICS) as tools to illustrate the effects of IC and the activities of the organisation rather than capture its actual value. Nevertheless, an ICS allows stakeholders to gain further insight into a company than traditional financial reports. The aim of these frameworks is to establish comparable measures regardless of the industry, size, or country of the firms analysed (Chaminade & Johanson, 2003) and the establishment of comparable and reliable reports on IC that support financial reports without distorting them (Edvinsson, 1997). As mentioned in Sect. 2.2, IC has now gained attention on national and international levels and therefore, there are a number of frameworks for the measurement and reporting of IC. Those frameworks presented in Sect. 2.9, however, are those most commonly found in literature that focus on external disclosure. They are results of individual, national, and international projects and are presented in chronological order according to their publication date.

2.9 Frameworks for the Disclosure of Intellectual Capital

2.9.1 Intangible Asset Monitor

Sveiby (1997) developed an instrument to measure and report intellectual capital, the Intangible Asset Monitor. It is based on the assumption that any kind of output or generation of assets is a result of human action and is therefore dependent on IC (Brennan & Connell, 2000; Zambon, 2004). Sveiby divides the market value into tangible and intangible assets, and the intangible assets further into three categories: competence of personnel, external structure, and internal structure (Sveiby, 1997), which are similar to the human capital, relational capital, and structural capital

Table 2.5 Example of indicators of intangible assets on basis of the IAM

Perspective	Competence	Internal structure	External structure
Growth & renewal	Number of years in the profession	Investment in information processing systems	Profitability per customer
Efficiency	Proportion of professionals in firm	Sales per support person	Satisfied customer index
Stability	Average age	Ratio of staff employed in the last 2 years	Proportion of big customers

Adapted from Sveiby (1997)

defined by InCaS and presented in Sect. 2.1 of this chapter. Sveiby defines the categories as follows (Zambon, 2004):

- *Competence* is the aptitude to act in diverse situations and includes experience, skills, values, and education, as well as social skills.
- *External structures* are the relationships a company has e.g. with its customers, investors, and suppliers, and also includes the image and brand name.
- *Internal structure* includes organisational assets like processes, legal structure, concepts, patents, and administrative systems. These structures normally belong to the company and stay intact if employees leave.

Each intangible asset defined is measured through the following indicators: growth/renewal (change), efficiency, and stability/risk. A combination of these indicators combined with the categories creates a matrix of nine cells as shown in Table 2.5. For each field of this matrix, indicators are defined (Abhayawansa, 2014; Sveiby, 1997) which enable the company to monitor development and thus discover room for improvement (Zambon, 2004). The matrix of the Intangible Asset Monitor can be utilised as a structured guide on how to manage the intellectual capital of a company (Al-Ali, 2003). Additional positive aspects are the possibility to customise the indicators to fit the respective company, and its focus on sustainability and risks through the 'stability' perspective. On the other hand, the company-specific set of indicators does not allow comparison with other organisations, but only with the measures of previous years of the respective company (Andriessen, 2004).

2.9.2 Skandia Navigator

In 1994, the first intellectual capital report was presented by the Swedish company Skandia, initiated from Edvinsson, who was the Corporate Director of Intellectual Capital at the time (Andriessen, 2004; Edvinsson, 2013; Zambon, 2004). Edvinsson developed the Skandia Navigator (Edvinsson, 1997). The term 'Navigator' was chosen to express the intent to balance several types of information, such as financial, non-financial, past and current performance, as well as expected future development, in a dynamic way (Edvinsson, 1997).

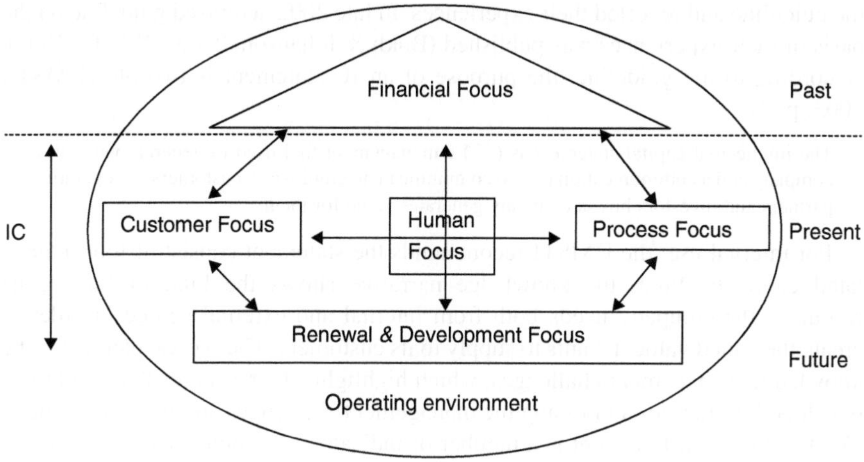

Fig. 2.6 The Skandia Navigator (Edvinsson, 1997, p. 371)

The Skandia Navigator defines six areas of focus (Edvinsson, 1997; Sveiby, 1997; Zambon, 2004) illustrated in Fig. 2.6. The financial focus displays the company's balance sheet and its past, while customer, human and process focus show the intellectual capital of the present. Renewal and development indicate the company's future (Tan et al., 2008). External operational environment is the sixth focus of the Skandia Navigator (Edvinsson, 1997). This time context is a distinct feature of the Skandia Navigator. The segmentation in regard to the time context adds structure to the way intellectual capital is reported; however, all time stages should be viewed as interconnected.

When measuring IC and developing a company's intellectual capital report, the indicators used for the Skandia Navigator allow flexibility. Additionally, the tool can be adapted for different use, for example for performance appraisals of individual employees (Edvinsson, 1997). Unfortunately, the indicators and consequent reports offer no possibility for benchmarking and show no cause-and-effect relationship between the indicators used (Andriessen, 2004).

2.9.3 Intellectual Capital Statement by the Danish Agency for Trade and Industry

The Danish Agency for Trade and Industry initiated a project on IC with the objective of providing Danish organisations the means to strengthen their competitiveness through the management of IC (Frederick, 2009). A guideline resulted from the project which was published in 2000. The Danish Ministry of Science, Technology and Innovation (DMSTI) organised a subsequent project wherein 80 Danish firms of varying size from both the public and private sectors tested the guideline and reported their experiences. In late 2002, a revised guideline on the basis of their experiences was published (Bukh & Johanson, 2003; DMSTI, 2003). According to the guideline, the purpose of an IC statement is twofold (DMSTI, 2003, p. 7):

> The intellectual capital statement is (. . .) a management tool used to generate value in a company and a communication tool to communicate to employees, customers, co-operative partners and investors how a company generates value for them.

For internal use, the DMSTI recommends the statement consist of four interrelated elements. First, the knowledge narrative shows the kind of knowledge resources the company needs both from internal and external source in order to create the added value it wants to supply to its customers. The second element is the knowledge management challenges, which highlights the resources that need to be developed. Initiatives addressing the management challenges are the third element. The fourth and last element is a number of indicators to monitor the initiative. To create a cohesive IC statement, the guideline stresses the importance of the interrelationship of the four elements (Abhayawansa, 2014; DMSTI, 2003; Mouritsen et al., 2004).

In regard to the external IC statement, the guideline does not lay down any mandatory structure. It recommends aligning the design of the statement with the requirements of the target groups to the fullest extent possible, and writing it in a way that is understandable, convincing, and trustworthy. Hence, it needs to be ensured that all important information which shows the reality of the organization is provided. Also, the methods used should be explained and relevant figures provided. The following structure for the IC statement is suggested by the DMSTI (the suggested headlines are formatted in italic). First is an *annual report*, which presents the objectives, challenges and results of the organisation in regard to its knowledge resources. A brief *description of the firm* is offered in the second part. The third part is the *knowledge narrative*. Due to the complexity of this part, the DMSTI recommends focussing on no more than three messages, such as the products, services, and users of the company, its knowledge resources, and a report on management challenges. The fourth part is an overview of the major findings of the statement labelled the *intellectual capital statement model*. *Management challenges,* including initiatives and indicators, as the fifth part, explain the handling and furthering of knowledge resources and how their development is monitored. The statement finishes with the *accounting policies* of the company including the definition of figures used (Bukh & Johanson, 2003; DMSTI, 2003).

Apart from formal recommendations, the DMSTI provides further practical information and suggestions based on the experience of the pilot companies. For example: the amount of resources a company needs for the generation of the first IC statement depends on the existing level of information already available, the experience in regard to knowledge management and the preparation of similar statements, and the type of publication the company chooses for the statement. Also, for the implementation and execution of a project leading to an IC statement within a company, the DMSTI suggest forming a project group consisting of members of various departments and levels from within the organisation (DMSTI, 2003). In general, the guideline offers a basic structure, but leaves lots of room for companies to tailor the statement to their needs and thereby limits its comparability to year-on-year evaluations of the company (Frederick, 2009).

*2.9.4 MERITUM Project and E*KNOW NET Project*

MERITUM (MEasuRing InTangibles to Understand and improve innovation Management) was a project by research groups from France, Spain, Norway, Denmark, Finland, and Sweden. The project was funded by the European Union (EU) and its aim was to develop a common framework for managing and reporting non-financial resources (Frederick, 2009). To achieve this objective, the project was divided into four workflows. First, the intangibles were defined and classified. Secondly, the question of how intangibles can be managed was investigated, followed by a study on the effects of IC on the capital market. Finally, a guideline was developed on how to manage and report IC (Bukh & Johanson, 2003).

According to the guideline, IC is divided into relational, human, and organisational capital (Bukh & Johanson, 2003) and a report on IC should be structured in three levels (Fig. 2.7). Firstly, the firm's vision: How do stakeholders benefit from the company's knowledge production activities, i.e. the value creation and its key factors, and what are the critical intangible resources that need to be acquired or internally developed? Secondly, the firm's resources and activities of

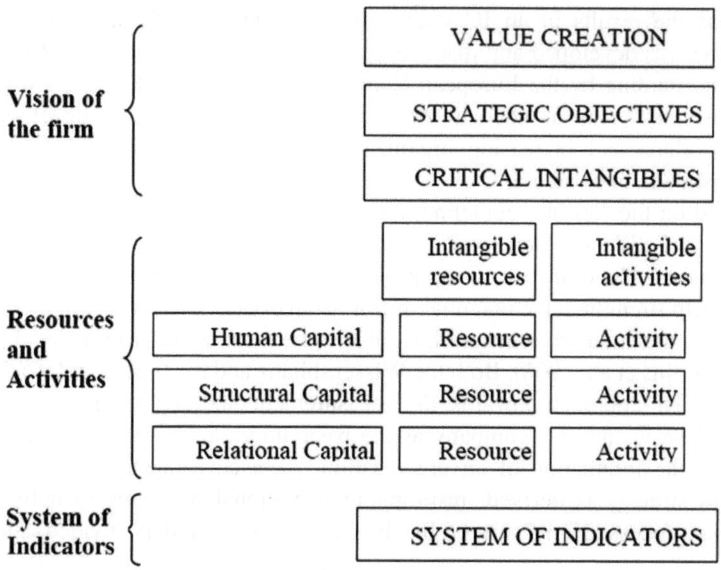

Fig. 2.7 The MERITUM model (Bjurström et al., 2003, p. 7)

the critical intangibles of the firm are stated, as well as its activities in regard to those assets. Thirdly, a set of indicators is set up to measure intangible assets and the impact of important intangibles on strategic objectives of the particular organisation (Bjurström et al., 2003; Johanson et al., 2006).

MERITUM was followed by a project called E*KNOW NET, also funded by the EU. The E*KNOW NET Project is research-oriented and aims to build a platform for exchange and research on IC and intangibles via three objectives. The first objective is to create a virtual network by establishing a link between European and International research centres. A second objective is to investigate if improvement on the guideline is possible and to make the guideline and its results available to more people and groups. Furtherance of the discussion with users is the third objective, in order to identify training shortfalls in the area of IC management (Bjurström et al., 2003; Bukh & Johanson, 2003).

2.9.5 "Wissensbilanz—Made in Germany" and "Intellectual Capital Statement—Made in Europe (InCaS)"

Realising the importance of IC for its economy, the German Federal Ministry of Economics and Labour (Bundesministerium für Wirtschaft und Technologie) initiated a research consortium in 2004, focusing on IC in small and medium sized companies (Abhayawansa, 2014; Mertins, Alwert, & Will, 2006). This "Arbeitskreis Wissensbilanz" developed the "Wissensbilanz—Made in Germany", hereafter referred to as 'Wissensbilanz', a guideline on how to measure IC and to compose the results in an IC statement. Additionally, software supporting the guideline was developed and made available (Alwert, Bornemann, & Will, 2006). After the funding by the European Commission was halted, the "Bundesverband Wissensbilanz" was founded in 2012 with the intent of further developing the Wissensbilanz and increasing organizations' overall awareness of IC and the Wissensbilanz in particular.

Based on the German guideline, the "Intellectual Capital Statement—Made in Europe (InCaS)" was developed by a research project funded by the European Commission. The objective of the project was to provide a management tool that would help strengthen the potential of European organizations through their IC and to enable intra-industry benchmarking of IC statements on a European level (Halim, 2010; Mertins et al., 2006). Both the Wissensbilanz and the European InCaS have a very similar approach towards the measurement and reporting of intellectual capital. The vision of a company as the basic understanding of the firm's raison d'être is the foundation of an organisation. As a consequence of the vision, a business strategy is derived, resulting in operational measures to optimize the business process. IC is part of the business process and is divided into three

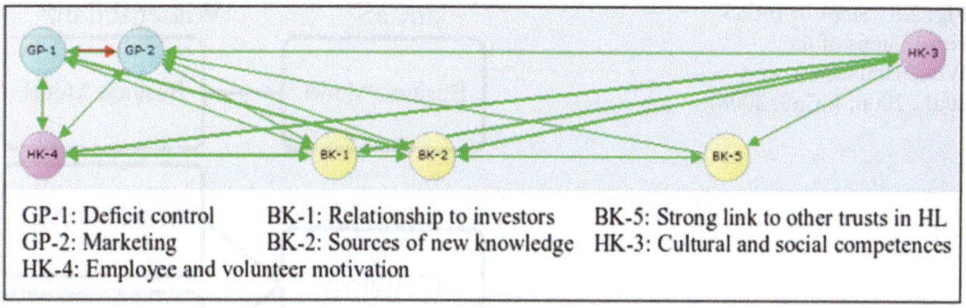

Fig. 2.8 Interdependency of elements visualised with the software of the Wissensbilanz (Blankenburg, 2010)

categories: Human Capital, Structural Capital, and Relational Capital. Through the interrelation of financial and other tangible resources, IC and the knowledge process involved in the business process, business success can be achieved. This business success, in turn, is affected by the business environment through opportunities and risks, and therefore influences the business strategy and even the vision of the company. With the help of the software provided by the Wissensbilanz, interrelations can be visualized.

Figure 2.8 offers an example created by the author of this book for the Gesellschaft zur Beförderung Gemeinnütziger Tätigkeit Lübeck. The abbreviations in the graph are symbols for elements identified as important for the organisation. At the same time the elements are assigned to a capital through the abbreviations and colours used facilitating quick understanding of the interrelations. Elements assigned to structural capital (Geschäftsprozesse (GP)) are marked blue, those ascribed to relational capital (Beziehungskapital (BK)) are coloured yellow, and elements that are part of human capital (Humankapital (HK)) are marked red.

In regard to the implementation of an IC statement, both the Wissensbilanz and the InCaS guideline recommend appointing an external moderator to lead a project team consisting of staff members through the implementation process. The arguments for the use of an external moderator are the moderator's objectivity, experience with the guideline, and detachment from any internal hierarchy (Alwert et al., 2006; InCaS, 2008).

There are only minor differences in the way the InCaS and the Wissensbilanz are designed. While the Wissensbilanz suggests eight steps, the InCaS includes five steps. Nevertheless, the content of the steps in general is the same in both guidelines; only how they break down into individual steps differs as Fig. 2.9 illustrates.

A detailed description of the business model, i.e. a "definition of the value creating model" and a "definition of the business strategy" (InCaS, 2008, p. 9), is the first step in both guidelines. The second step of the InCaS guideline, "IC Analysis", combines the second and third steps of the Wissensbilanz, "Definition of IC" and "Assessment of IC" respectively. Steps four "Measurement" and five

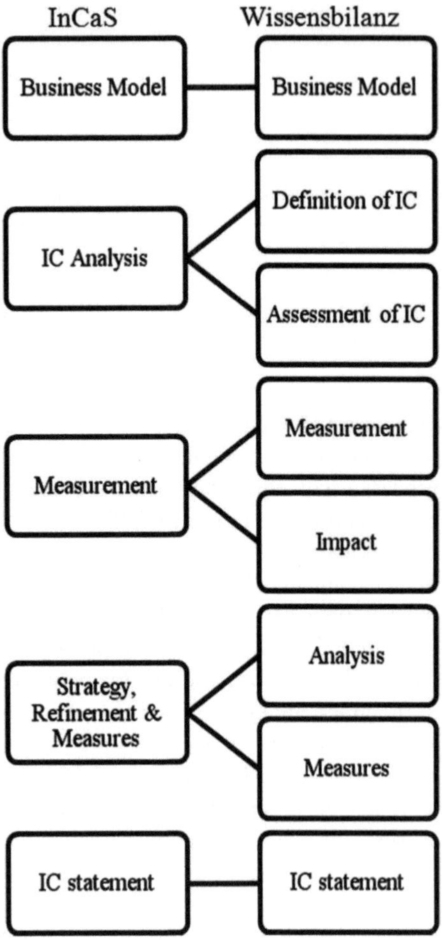

Fig. 2.9 Steps of InCaS versus steps of the Wissensbilanz (Alwert et al., 2006; InCaS, 2008)

"Impact" of the Wissensbilanz are combined as "Measurement" in the InCaS guideline. The fourth step of the InCaS guideline is called "Strategy Refinement & Measures" and merges steps six "Analysis" and seven "Measures" of the Wissensbilanz. Both guidelines conclude with the generation of a more extensive internal ICS report as well as a clear and short external ICS report (Alwert et al., 2006; InCaS, 2008).

Due to the scope of the guidelines, companies have to decide whether the benefits of such an IC statement outweigh the costs. The comparability of the reports of different companies remains challenging due to company specific indicators when measuring IC. However, both guidelines, the Wissensbilanz and

InCaS, are practice related and, with the supporting software, offer manageable and graphic ways to present the IC of an organisation.

2.9.6 *Integrated Reporting <IR>*

In 2012, the Chartered Global Management Accountant (CGMA), a joint venture between the American Institute of Certified Public Accountants and the Chartered Institute of Management Accountants, conducted an international study interviewing 280 chief executive officers. The findings highlight the importance of non-financial information and that the measurement and reporting of these non-financials need to be intensified yet still remain challenging (CGMA, 2012). This challenge, in addition to the merging of various existing standards, is tackled by an alliance of "regulators, investors, companies, standard setters, the accounting profession and NGOs" (The IIRC, 2013b), the aforementioned IIRC.

The IIRC aims to establish an integrated approach and thinking regarding corporate reporting and thus supports the aforementioned argument by Roslender (2004), who promotes a comprehensive perspective on measurement and reporting. Integrated reporting (<IR>) is defined by the IIRC as

> "A process founded on integrate thinking that results in a periodic integrated report by an organization about value creation over time and related communication regarding aspects of value creation" (The IIRC, 2013b)

Three objectives are set by the IIRC to ensure long-term financial stability and success of an organisation: an increase in the quality of information, a holistic perspective on the elements for value creation, and last but not least, an increase in understanding of all these elements. The integrated report which emerges is supposed to provide all relevant information for shareholders to properly evaluate the present and possible future situation of a company (The IIRC, 2013b) in a "clear, concise, connected and comparable format" (The IIRC, 2011, p. 2). These objectives are similar to the requirements for non-financial business reporting defined by the International Corporate Governance Network, which also asserts that business reporting must help "investors understand a company's strategic objectives and its progress towards meeting them" and "reflect the complexities in a contemporary business" (International Corporate Governance Network, 2008, p. 7).

<IR> differs from traditional reporting in various respects. The thinking is holistic rather than in silos; not only is financial capital taken into account, but also different forms of capital and their interdependencies. The focus is past and future-oriented and aims to reveal the strategy for value creation as opposed to focussing on the past. Additionally, integrated reporting increases transparency, is adaptive to the circumstances of the individual organisation, and is clearly and concisely structured. The first international <IR> framework was presented in

Table 2.6 Guiding principles of <IR>

Guiding principle	Resulting content of reporting
Strategic focus and future orientation	Provision of insight into the strategy, its relation to the value creation process in the short, medium and long term, and its use of and effect on various forms of capital
Connectivity of information	Illustration of a holistic picture, showing interrelatedness and dependencies between factors effecting the value creation process
Stakeholder relationships	State key stakeholders and the nature of the relationship
Materiality	Disclosure of information that essentially affect the value creation process
Conciseness	The report should be kept concise
Reliability and completeness	Inclusion of positive and negative material matters, without mistakes
Consistency and comparability	Information presented need to be consistent over time and enable comparison (where necessary for the value creation process)

The IIRC (2011)

December 2013 based on a pilot programme in which over 100 business and more than 35 investor organisations took part.[2] The aim of the framework is to describe the concepts and provide a guideline which can be adapted for any sector. The purpose of <IR> itself is to offer an insight into the value creation process of a company. Generally, an integrated report is based on several guiding principles presented in Table 2.6.

<IR> puts the business model at the centre of value creation. It includes business activities and governance, which in turn consist of risks and opportunities, strategy and resource allocation, performance and outlook. The business model uses all forms of capital to create output with consequences for these forms of capital (Fig. 2.10). The whole value creation process is influenced by the external environment, such as the economic or social conditions or technical developments (The IIRC, 2011). Permanent monitoring and analysis is necessary since value creation is not static and interconnections might change over time (The IIRC, 2013b). The degrees to which organisations use and thus include the individual forms of capital vary. Therefore, they are simply illustrated as one factor in Fig. 2.10 and their interrelationships are not pictured since these differ for each organisation.

The integrated report allows managers to explain the whole value process and the relevance of each factor to the process, which then highlights essential elements for investment or development focus in order to ensure long term success (The IIRC, 2011). For stakeholders, an <IR> approach and report offers a less complex but holistic view, thereby increasing credibility and trust (The IIRC, 2013a).

[2]For a comprehensive lists of the participants, please see http://www.theiirc.org/companies-and-investors/pilot-programme-business-network/ (accessed 14.11.2013) and http://www.theiirc.org/companies-and-investors/pilot-programme-investor-network/ (accessed 14.11.2013).

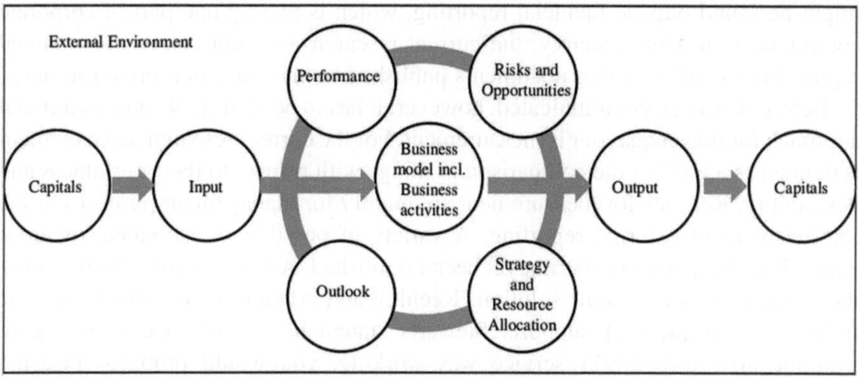

Fig. 2.10 The value creation process based on the IIRC (The IIRC, 2013a)

2.10 Intellectual Capital in Context of the Current Research

Research on IC has taken place in several steps, starting with the creation of awareness, followed by the establishment of the topic within academia, leading to empirical research (Petty & Guthrie, 2000). The latter closes the circle back to the focus on practice that the topic started with. While there has already been quite a lot of research into IC, a remaining challenge in the field is that no common definition for IC exists (Abeysekera, 2006; Alwert et al., 2005; Canibano et al., 1999; Dumay, 2009a). As introduced in Sect. 2.1, the perspectives on IC can be segmented into accounting view and management view, wherein the latter views IC as dynamic and manageable while the former regards IC as static and measureable. For the current research, the management view is adopted and the definition and composition of IC provided by the InCaS project is utilised. According to InCaS, IC is "the intangible resources of an organisation" (InCaS, 2008, p. 7), in which resources are defined as all tangible and intangible assets a company employs in their business process to execute its value-creating strategy (Barney, 1991; InCaS, 2008). IC is composed of human capital, structural capital, and relational capital (InCaS, 2008). Spiritual capital, as defined by Hall (1998) is considered for the current research as well and the concept of interconnection between the forms of capital provided by Petrash (1996) is utilised.

IC is a controversial topic from an accounting point of view for several reasons. The ownership of IC is hard to distinguish clearly, the controlling of IC and its results is challenging (Vergauwen & Alem, 2005), and the economic benefit of IC in the future is unclear (Canibano et al., 1999). The importance of additional information to the quantitative information presented via the traditional financial reporting system is recognised, but at the same time, there is no solution yet as to how to include further information without compromising the transparency and comparability of a financial statement. An alternative for the communication of IC might be found outside financial reporting, which is merely one part of corporate communication. Consequently, the current research does not centre upon annual reports but includes further documents published by the particular organisations.

Before IC can be communicated, however, it has to be identified and a traditional approach for that endeavour is measurement. For the current research, measurement is defined as a tool for the comparison of things with respect to their usefulness and desirability. Reasons for measurement are mainly for management purposes or the improvement of external reporting. A variety of possible measurement methods exists, but a best practice has not yet been established. According to Stewart (1991), there is no one-size-fits-all solution. Keehley and Abercrombie (2008) offer the following example that supports Stewarts statement: "if you were looking to examine how well a 911 service was working, you would probably measure response time to emergency calls—not unit cost" (Keehley & Abercrombie, 2008, p. 43). Consequently, the challenge for companies is to find the measurement method that fits their purpose, i.e. either internal management decision-making or external reporting. Additionally, the measurement method needs to fit the company culture in order to ensure a successful implementation and execution. The following statement by Guthrie (2001) provides a fitting summary of the situation on the measurement of IC:

> "...we are not yet in a position to provide robust and entirely accurate measures and also assign monetary value. However, we are able to assess whether the management of IC is headed in the right direction" (Guthrie, 2001, p. 38)

Apart from the challenge of measuring IC as a basis for disclosure, difficulties in the reporting of IC exist. The fear of handing over information which potentially diminishes the firm's competitive advantage vis-à-vis its competitors is the disincentive stated the most in literature, for example by Sveiby (1997), Bjurström et al. (2003), Zambon (2004), Vergauwen and Alem (2005), Johanson et al. (2006), Brüggen et al. (2009), Beattie and Thomson (2010). Another prominent disincentive is the increasing quantity and complexity of information provided (Beattie & Smith, 2013; Bukh, 2003; Gowthorpe, 2009; Nielsen & Madsen, 2009). Incentives for the disclosure of IC stated in literature are a more accurate reflection of the value of an organisation (Beattie & Thomson, 2010; Bontis, 2003; Brüggen et al., 2009; Petrash, 1996), since traditional financial reports do not fulfil this aim anymore (Bontis, 2003; Gowthorpe, 2009; Mouritsen, Larsen, & Bukh, 2005). The attraction of new and retention of existing employees, as well as a better management of resources due to a better understanding of them, are further incentives. Whether literature states that these incentives and disincentives are also applicable to NPOs is illustrated in Sect. 3.5 and discussed in Sect. 8.2. Additionally, they are taken into consideration for the framework ultimately developed.

In 2001, Guthrie summarized the IC reporting issue as "the biggest challenge by far is establishing a consensus about the need to report, what to report and how to report it" (Guthrie, 2001, p. 37). Currently, there is still no best-practice for the disclosure of IC. Extant reports are criticised for not taking risk and liabilities into account. Furthermore, the discussion on whether IC should be measured and disclosed in the form of numbers or narratives is ongoing, as well as on the appropriateness of a common framework versus individually adapted reports of organisations. Looking at current discussions in the field, Guthrie's statement is still valid.

With the term and concept of IC introduced and an overview on the discussion regarding the measurement and disclosure of IC offered, the first part of the basis for the current research is established which focuses on the disclosure of IC. A literature review on NPOs, their relation to IC in general and the disclosure of IC in particular are introduced in Chap. 3. For three main reasons, it is important to understand IC in the for-profit sector before the non-profit sector is addressed. First, there are hardly any reporting or management theories developed explicitly for the non-profit sector. This holds true for the theories presented in this Chap. 2, as well as for theories on IC. A second reason is that most managers of NPOs know of and draw upon the theories and practices developed for the for-profit sector due to a lack of specific theories and practices for the third sector. Moreover, the curricula in most business schools concentrate on the for-profit sector. If classes on the non-profit sector are offered, they are relatively new. For this reason, content taught may not have impacted actual practices yet. Another reason to gain an understanding of how IC works in the for-profit sector is the fact that NPOs often have to compete with and are compared to for-profit businesses. To gain acceptance, NPOs must therefore meet the standards of for-profit companies. For these reasons, this Chap. 2 does not specifically address the non-profit sector, but a separate, following chapter addresses NPOs. Together, those two parts of the literature review provide a comprehensive literature review on the topic at hand and build a solid theoretical foundation for the current research.

References

Abeysekera, I. (2006). The project of intellectual capital disclosure: Researching the research. *Journal of Intellectual Capital, 7*(1), 61–77. doi:10.1108/14691930610639778.

Abhayawansa, S. A. (2014). A review of guidelines and frameworks on external reporting of intellectual capital. *Journal of Intellectual Capital, 15*(1), 100–141. doi:10.1108/JIC-04-2013-0046.

Adelberg, A. H. (1983). The accounting syntactic complexity formula: A new instrument for predicting the readability of selected accounting communications. *Accounting and Business Research, 13*(51), 163–175. doi:10.1080/00014788.1983.9729749.

Al-Ali, N. (2003). *Comprehensive intellectual capital management*. Hoboken, NJ: Wiley.

Alwert, K., Bornemann, M., & Will, M. (2006). *Wissensbilanz – made in Germany*. Berlin: Bundesministerium für Wirtschaft und Technologie.

Alwert, K., Heisig, P., & Mertins, K. (2005). Wissensbilanzen – Intellektuelles Kapital erfolgreich nutzen und entwickeln. In K. Mertins, K. Alwert, & P. Heisig (Eds.), *Wissensbilanzen – Intellektuelles Kapital erfolgreich nutzen und entwickeln* (pp. 1–18). Heidelberg: Springer.

Andriessen, D. (2004). *Making sense of intellectual capital: Designing a method for the valuation of intangibles*. Oxford: Elsevier.

Arvidsson, S. (2011). Disclosure of non-financial information in the annual report: A management-team perspective. *Journal of Intellectual Capital, 12*(2), 277–300. doi:10.1108/14691931111123421.

Bachert, R. (2005). *Buchführung und Bilanzierung – Controlling und Rechnungswesen in Sozialen Unternehmen*. Weinheim: Juventa Verlag.

Barney, J. (1991). Firm resources and sustained competitive advantage. *Journal of Management, 17*(1), 99–120. doi:10.1177/014920639101700108.

Beattie, V. (2013, April 16). Conversation with Vivien Beattie at BAFA Annual Conference 2013.

Beattie, V., & Jones, M. J. (1992). The use and abuse of graphs in annual reports: Theoretical framework and empirical study. *Accounting and Business Research, 22*(88), 291–303. doi:10.1080/00014788.1992.9729446.

Beattie, V., & Smith, S. J. (2013). Value creation and business models: Refocusing the intellectual capital debate. *The British Accounting Review, 45*(4), 234–254. doi:10.1016/j.bar.2013.06.001.

Beattie, V., & Thomson, S. J. (2010). *Intellectual capital reporting: Academic utopia or corporate reality in a brave new world?* Edinburgh: The Institure of Chartered Accountants of Scotland.

Bjurström, E., Catasus, B., & Johanson, U. (2003). *A European research arena on intangibles (E*KNOW-NET)*. Accessed April 2, 2012, from http://www.pnbukh.com/site/files/pdf_filer/Final_report_WP2.pdf

Blankenburg, K. (2010). *Measuring intellectual capital – Exemplified – Through the preparation of an intellectual capital statement for a non-profit- organisation*. Hamburg: Hochschule für Ökonomie und Management Hamburg.

Bontis, N. (1998). Intellectual capital: An exploratory study that develops measures and models. *Management Decision, 36*(2), 63–76. doi:10.1108/00251749810204142.

Bontis, N. (2001). Assessing knowledge assets: A review of the models used to measure intellectual capital. *International Journal of Management Reviews, 3*(1), 41–60.

Bontis, N. (2003). Intellectual capital disclosure in Canadian corporations. *Journal of Human Resource Costing and Accounting, 7*(1), 9–20. doi:10.1108/eb029076.

Bontis, N., Dragonetti, N., Jacobsen, K., & Roos, G. (1999). The knowledge toolbox: A review of the tools available to measure and manage intangible resources. *European Management Journal, 17*(4), 391–402. doi:10.1016/S0263-2373(99)00019-5.

Brennan, N., & Connell, B. (2000). Intellectual capital: Current issues and policy implications. *Journal of Intellectual Capital, 1*(3), 206–240. doi:10.1108/14691930010350792.

Brüggen, A., Vergauwen, P., & Dao, M. (2009). Determinants of intellectual capital disclosure: Evidence from Australia. *Management Decision, 47*(2), 233–245. doi:10.1108/00251740910938894.

Bukh, P. N. (2003). The relevance of intellectual capital disclosure: A paradox? *Accounting, Auditing and Accountability Journal, 16*(1), 49–56. doi:10.1108/09513570310464273.

Bukh, P. N., & Johanson, U. (2003). Research and knowledge interaction: Guidelines for intellectual capital reporting. *Journal of Intellectual Capital, 4*(4), 576–587. doi:10.1108/14691930310504572.

Bukh, P. N., Larsen, H. T., & Mouritsen, J. (2001). Constructing intellectual capital statements. *Scandinavian Journal of Management, 17*(1), 87–108. doi:10.1016/S0956-5221(00)00034-8.

Bukh, P. N., Nielsen, C., Gormsen, P., & Mouritsen, J. (2005). Disclosure of information on intellectual capital in Danish IPO prospectuses. *Accounting, Auditing and Accountability Journal, 18*(6), 713–732. doi:10.1108/09513570510627685.

Caddy, I. (2000). Intellectual capital: Recognizing both assets and liabilities. *Journal of Intellectual Capital, 1*(2), 129–146. doi:10.1108/14691930010377469.

Canibano, L., Covarsí, M. G.-A., & Sánchez, M. P. (1999). The value relevance and managerial implications of intangibles: A literature review. In *Measuring and reporting intellectual capital, Amsterdam* (pp. 1–74). Paris: Organisation for Economic Co-operation and Development. Accessed August 07, 2012, from http://www.oecd.org/sti/industryandglobalisation/1947974.pdf

Chaharbaghi, K., & Cripps, S. (2006). Intellectual capital: Direction, not blind faith. *Journal of Intellectual Capital, 7*(1), 29–42. doi:10.1108/14691930610639750.

Chaminade, C., & Johanson, U. (2003). Can guidelines for intellectual capital management and reporting be considered without addressing cultural differences? *Journal of Intellectual Capital, 4*(4), 528–542. doi:10.1108/14691930310504545.

Chartered Global Management Accountant. (2012). *Rebooting business: Valuing the human dimension*. New York. Accessed June 25, 2012, from http://www.cgma.org/Resources/Reports/DownloadableDocuments/CGMA_launch_report.pdf

Danish Ministry of Science, Technology and Innovation (DMSTI). (2003). *Intellectual capital statements – The new guideline*. Copenhagen. Accessed August 06, 2012, from www.vtu.dk

Deutsches Rechnungslegungs Standards Commitee e.V. (2012). *Deutscher Rechnungslegungs Standard Nr. 20 (DRS 20)* (pp. 1–56). Accessed November 23, 2015, from www.drsc.de/docs/press_releases/2012/120928_DRS20_nearfinal.pdf

Dumay, J. (2003). An examination of two grand-theories of IC as barriers to the use of IC concepts. In *Proceedings of the 7th International conference on intellectual capital, knowledge management and organisational learning* (pp. 146–154). Reading: Academic Publishing.

Dumay, J. (2009a). Intellectual capital measurement: A critical approach. *Journal of Intellectual Capital, 10*(2), 190–210. doi:10.1108/14691930910952614.

Dumay, J. (2009b). Reflective discourse about intellectual capital: Research and practice. *Journal of Intellectual Capital, 10*(s), 489–503. doi:10.1108/14691930910996607.

Dumay, J. (2013). The third stage of IC: Towards a new IC future and beyond. *Journal of Intellectual Capital, 14*(1), 5–9. doi:10.1108/14691931311288986.

Dumay, J., & Cuganesan, S. (2011). Making sense of intellectual capital complexity: Measuring through narrative. *Journal of Human Resource Costing and Accounting, 15*(1), 24–49. doi:10.1108/14013381111125305.

Dumay, J., & Garanina, T. (2013). Intellectual capital research: A critical examination of the third stage. *Journal of Intellectual Capital, 14*(1), 10–25. doi:10.1108/14691931311288995.

Dumay, J., & Rooney, J. (2011). 'Measuring for managing?' An IC practice case study. *Journal of Intellectual Capital, 12*(3), 344–355. doi:10.1108/14691931111154670.

Eccles, R. G., Herz, R. H., Keegan, E. M., & Phillips, D. (2002). *The value reporting revolution: Moving beyond the earnings game*. New York: Wiley.

Edvinsson, L. (1997). Developing intellectual capital at Skandia. *Long Range Planning, 30*(3), 366–373. doi:10.1016/S0024-6301(97)00016-2.

Edvinsson, L. (2013). IC 21: Reflections from 21 years of IC practice and theory. *Journal of Intellectual Capital, 14*(1), 163–172. doi:10.1108/14691931311289075.

Frederick, W. R. (2009). *Recent developments in intellectual capital reporting and their policy implications* (OECD Education Working Papers, 17). doi:10.1787/227362757626.

Gee, P. (2006). *UK GAAP for business and practice*. Oxford: Elsevier.

Giuliani, M. (2013). Not all sunshine and roses: Discovering intellectual liabilities 'in action'. *Journal of Intellectual Capital, 14*(1), 127–144. doi:10.1108/14691931311289057.

Giuliani, M., & Marasca, S. (2011). Construction and valuation of intellectual capital: A case study. *Journal of Intellectual Capital, 12*(3), 377–391. doi:10.1108/14691931111154698.

Goebel, V. (2015). Intellectual capital reporting in a mandatory management report: The case of Germany. *Journal of Intellectual Capital, 16*(4), 702–720. doi:10.1108/JIC-02-2015-0011.

Gowthorpe, C. (2009). Wider still and wider? A critical discussion of intellectual capital recognition, measurement and control in a boundary theoretical context. *Critical Perspectives on Accounting, 20*(7), 823–834. doi:10.1016/j.cpa.2008.09.005.

Guthrie, J. (2001). The management, measurement and the reporting of intellectual capital. *Journal of Intellectual Capital, 2*(1), 27–41. doi:10.1108/14691930110380473.

Guthrie, J., Ricceri, F., & Dumay, J. (2012). Reflections and projections: A decade of intellectual capital accounting research. *The British Accounting Review, 44*(2), 68–82. doi:10.1016/j.bar.2012.03.004.

Halim, S. (2010). Statistical analysis on the intellectual capital statement. *Journal of Intellectual Capital, 11*(1), 61–73. doi:10.1108/14691931011013334.

Hall, M. L. W. (1998). The confusion of the capitals: Surveying the cluttered landscape of intellectual 'capitals' and terminology. In P. H. Sullivan (Ed.), *Profiting from intellectual capital – Extracting value from innovation* (pp. 76–83). New York: Wiley.

Hirschler, K. (2012). *Bilanzwissen für Führungskräfte*. Wiesbaden: Springer Gabler.

Holland, J. (2004). *Corporate intangibles, value relevance and disclosure content*. Edinburgh: The Institure of Chartered Accountants of Scotland.

InCaS. (2008). *Intellectual capital statement – Made in Europe*. Accessed January 31, 2010, from www.incas-europe.org

International Corporate Governance Network. (2008). *ICGN statement and guidance on non-financial business reporting*, London. Accessed May 27, 2012, from https://circabc.europa.eu/webdav/CircaBC/FISMA/markt_consultations/Library/accounting/Non-financial-reporting/individuals-others/INT_icgn_3_en.pdf

International Public Sector Accounting Standards Board (IPSASB). (2010). *Intangible assets*. New York: International Federation of Accountants.

Johanson, U., Koga, C., Skoog, M., & Henningsson, J. (2006). The Japanese Government's intellectual capital reporting guideline: What are the challenges for firms and capital market agents? *Journal of Intellectual Capital, 7*(4), 474–491. doi:10.1108/14691930610709121.

Keehley, P., & Abercrombie, N. N. (2008). *Benchmarking in the public and nonprofit sectors* (2nd ed.). San Francisco, CA: Wiley.

Kong, E. (2008). The development of strategic management in the non-profit context: Intellectual capital in social service non-profit organizations. *International Journal of Management Reviews, 10*(3), 281–299. doi:10.1111/j.1468-2370.2007.00224.x.

Kuhnle, H., & Banzhaf, J. (2006). *Finanzkommunikation unter IFRS*. München: Verlag Franz Vahlen GmbH.

Langenscheidt Verlag. (2010). In Langenscheidt-Redaktion. (Ed.), *Langenscheidt Universal-Wörterbuch Latein*. Berlin: Langenscheidt Verlag.

Lev, B. (2001). *Intangibles: Management, measurement, and reporting*. Washington, D.C.: Brookings Institution Press.

Longman Dictionary of Contemporary English. (2012). *Longman dictionary of contemporary English* (5th ed.). Harlow: Pearson Longman.

Marr, B., & Chatzkel, J. (2004). Intellectual capital at the crossroads: Managing, measuring, and reporting of IC. *Journal of Intellectual Capital, 5*(2), 224–229. doi:10.1108/14691930410533650.

Marr, B., Gray, D., & Neely, A. (2003). Why do firms measure their intellectual capital? *Journal of Intellectual Capital, 4*(4), 441–464. doi:10.1108/14691930310504509.

Mertins, K., Alwert, K., & Will, M. (2006). Measuring intellectual capital in European SME. In *I-Know'06* (pp. 21–25). Graz, Austria.

Möller, K., & Gamerschlag, R. (2009). Immaterielle Vermögenswerte in der Unternehmenssteuerung - betriebswirtschaftliche Perspektiven und Herausforderungen. In K. Möller, M. Piwinger, & A. Zerfaß (Eds.), *Immaterielle Vermögenswerte – Bewertung, Berichterstattung und Kommunikation* (pp. 3–21). Stuttgart: Schäffer-Poeschel Verlag Stuttgart.

Mouritsen, J., Bukh, P. N., & Marr, B. (2004). Reporting on intellectual capital: Why, what and how? *Measuring Business Excellence, 8*(1), 46–54. doi:10.1108/13683040410524739.

Mouritsen, J., Larsen, H. T., & Bukh, P. N. (2005). Dealing with the knowledge economy: Intellectual capital versus balanced scorecard. *Journal of Intellectual Capital, 6*(1), 8–27. doi:10.1108/14691930510574636.

Mouritsen, J., & Roslender, R. (2009). Critical intellectual capital. *Critical Perspectives on Accounting, 20*(7), 801–803. doi:10.1016/j.cpa.2009.08.004.

Mourtisen, J., Bukh, P. N., & Marr, B. (2005). A reporting perspective on intellectual capital. In B. Marr (Ed.), *Perspectives on intellectual capital* (pp. 69–81). Oxford: Elsevier Butterworth-Heinemann.

Nielsen, C., & Madsen, M. T. (2009). Discourses of transparency in the intellectual capital reporting debate: Moving from generic reporting models to management defined information. *Critical Perspectives on Accounting, 20*(7), 847–854. doi:10.1016/j.cpa.2008.09.007.

Oxford Wordpower Dictionary. (2006). In J. Turnbull (Ed.), *Oxford wordpower dictionary* (3rd ed.). Oxford: Oxford University Press.

Petrash, G. (1996). Dow' s journey to a knowledge value management culture. *European Management Journal, 73*(4), 365–373.

Petty, R., & Guthrie, J. (2000). Intellectual capital literature review: Measurement, reporting and management. *Journal of Intellectual Capital, 1*(2), 155–176. doi:10.1108/14691930010348731.

Roos, G., & Roos, J. (1997). Measuring your company's intellectual performance. *International Journal of Strategic Management, 30*(3), 413–426.

Roslender, R. (2004). Accounting for intellectual capital: Rethinking its theoretical underpinnings. *Measuring Business Excellence, 8*(1), 38–45. doi:10.1108/13683040410524720.

Schruff, L., & Haaker, A. (2009). Immaterielle Werte in der deutschen und internationalen Rechnungslegung. In K. Möller, M. Piwinger, & A. Zerfaß (Eds.), *Immaterielle Vermögenswerte – Bewertung, Berichterstattung und Kommunikation* (pp. 49–72). Stuttgart: Schäffer-Poeschel Verlag Stuttgart.

Stewart, T. A. (1991). Brainpower – How IC is becoming America's most valuable asset. *Fortune Magazine*, 44–60.

Stewart, T. A. (1997). *Intellectual capital: The new wealth of organizations*. New York: Currency Doubleday.

Sullivan, P. H. (1998). Advanced definitions and concepts. In P. H. Sullivan (Ed.), *Profiting from intellectual capital – Extracting value from innovation* (pp. 35–42). New York: Wiley.

Sveiby, K.-E. (1997). *The new organizational wealth* (1st ed.). San Francisco, CA: Berrett-Koehler.

Tan, H. P., Plowman, D., & Hancock, P. (2008). The evolving research on intellectual capital. *Journal of Intellectual Capital, 9*(4), 585–608. doi:10.1108/14691930810913177.

The IIRC. (2011). *Towards integrated reporting – communicating value in the 21st century*. Accessed May 15, 2012, from http://www.theiirc.org/discussion-paper/

The IIRC. (2013a). *Business and investors explore the sustainability perspective of integrated reporting – IIRC pilot programme yearbook 2013*. Accessed December 05, 2013, from http://www.theiirc.org/resources-2/

The IIRC. (2013b). *The international <IR> framework*. Accessed December 10, 2013, from http://www.theiirc.org/international-ir-framework/

Thring, E. (1864). *School and education*. Cambridge: Macmillan.

Vergauwen, P. G. M. C., & Alem, F. J. C. V. (2005). Annual report IC disclosures in The Netherlands, France and Germany. *Journal of Intellectual Capital, 6*(1), 89–104. doi:10.1108/14691930510574681.

Wingren, T. (2004). Management accounting in the new economy: From 'tangible and production-focused' to 'intangible and knowledge-driven' MAS by integrating BSC and IC. *Managerial Finance, 30*(8), 1–12. doi:10.1108/03074350410769191.

Zambon, S. (2004). Intangibles and intellectual capital: An overview of the reporting issues and some measurement models. In P. Bianchi & S. Labory (Eds.), *The economic importance of intangible assets* (pp. 153–184). Hants: Ashgate.

Zerfaß, A. (2009). Immaterielle Werte und Unternehmenskommunikation – Herausforderungen für das Kommunikationsmanagement. In K. Möller, M. Piwinger, & A. Zerfaß (Eds.), *Immaterielle Vermögenswerte – Bewertung, Berichterstattung und Kommunikation* (pp. 23–48). Stuttgart: Schäffer-Poeschel Verlag Stuttgart.

Chapter 3
Introduction to the Non-Profit Sector

Before the issue of IC in NPOs and IC reporting in NPOs are addressed, basic characteristics and distinctions are presented. First, the distinction of the third sector from the other sectors provides an understanding for its characteristics in general. The German third sector and its peculiarities are introduced next, followed by a segmentation of the third sector and types of German NPOs. This introduction to the non-profit sector represents the second half of the review of the literature crucial for the topic of the current research.

3.1 Distinction of the Three Sectors

Society is split into three sectors: the state or public sector; the private sector; and the non-profit sector. The latter is synonymously called the third sector or voluntary sector (Menges, 2004; Wex, 2004). Blankart and Gehrmann (2006) compare the sectors and highlight the main differences, for instance, regarding their main aim or characteristics, their source of funding and the mechanism by which the sector is coordinated (Table 3.1).

The main aim of private sector companies is to make profit. Their sources of funding are profits from the sale of products or services, the credit market and the capital market, and the sector is coordinated by competition (Blankart & Gehrmann, 2006). Public sector organisations are financed via fees, donations, and public grants, etc. and the sector is coordinated through cooperation of the organisations. Drucker (1990) concludes that "The source of its money is probably the greatest single difference between the non-profit sector and business and government" (Drucker, 1990, p. 41). NPOs are defined via a negation, the prohibition of profit distribution (United Nations Department of Economic and Social Affairs, 2003), which is another dissociation from the public sector (Menges, 2004; Wex, 2004). In other words, NPOs are not forbidden and sometimes strive to make

K. Blankenburg, *Intellectual Capital in German Non-profit Organisations*, Contributions to Management Science, DOI 10.1007/978-3-319-62655-0_3

Table 3.1 Comparison of the three sectors

	Private sector	Third sector	Public sector
Characteristics/ aim	Profit	Non-distribution constraint	Equality
Source of funding	Sales of products/services, credit market, capital market	Public grants, fees, donations	Fees, public money
Coordination mechanism	Competition	Cooperation	Hierarchy

Blankart and Gehrmann (2006)

profits, but those can only be used exclusively to further the social goal in contrast to private companies, which aim to maximise their profits (Menges, 2004).

The lines between the sectors are blurry (Ryan, 1999; van Broekhoven, 2008; Wex, 2004) as there are co-operations crossing the sectors and overlapping areas. For example, social enterprises are NPOs due to their social aim, but are also private enterprises as they support their aim by operating a profitable business. The three sectors do not only overlap, but are also interconnected (Salamon & Anheier, 1998; Wex, 2004), since a change in one sector has an effect on the other two sectors. In 2008, the financial crisis hit the private sector. As a consequence, the state was affected by rising unemployment, for example, and intervened via bailouts and programmes to boost the economy, which affected national budget. NPOs were affected by the financial crisis as well. Organisations with a focus on unemployment, housing or poverty prevention were in rising demand while donations of time and money decreased at the same time (Charities Aid Foundation, 2012).

Individual citizens often belong to all sectors at the same time and are thus influenced by all of them (Wex, 2004). For example, a citizen of a specific country is influenced by the decisions of the country's government and the culture embedded in its society. As an employee of a company, the same person is subject to trends and changes of the economy, i.e. the private sector. The third sector affects this person, for example, through the standard of medical support or leisure time facilities available. Conversely, society, as the consolidation of its members, affects the three sectors as well (Wex, 2004). In Germany, a demographic change is imminent. This change is the consequence of a decrease of the birth rate and an increase in life expectancy, with the result being that the number of young people living and working in Germany decreases while the number of elderly people living in Germany increases over time (Berthel & Becker, 2010). As a result, the state loses tax income since the workforce decreases in number while having to pay more pensions. The private sector has to deal with the so-called "war of talents" (Berthel & Becker, 2010) among other challenges, and NPOs have to cater a rising demand in the areas of care of elderly people or poverty prevention as the intergenerational contract securing the pensions in Germany will not be in effect much longer.

Another influence on the amount of donations that NPOs cannot influence is the environment, since donors often focus on specific causes rather than on an organisation (van Broekhoven, 2008). This statement is supported by the 'World Giving

Index' (Charities Aid Foundation, 2012), which found that the willingness to donate is affected by disasters and emergencies (Charities Aid Foundation, 2012; Helmig & Boenigk, 2012). Bekkers and Wiepking (2010, cited by Helmig & Boenigk, 2012, p. 171) identified eight influences on the willingness of people to donate, namely: awareness of need, altruism, psychological benefits, reputation, values, cost and benefits, efficacy and solicitation. NPOs can approach most of these influences or at least address them in their external communication, for example. Further reasons for NPOs to communicate with their environment according to literature are discussed in Sect. 3.5.

Lichtsteiner, Gmür, Giroud, and Schauer (2013) reveal several areas of competition for NPOs: their output market, employees, volunteers, members, donations, government grants, and influence on politics. Not only do NPOs compete with other NPOs, but also with for-profit companies. Looking at the increasing competition between the non-profit sector and the private sector, Ryan (1999) raises the question of whether NPOs are actually fit to compete, taking into account the resources a for-profit organisation can muster versus those of a NPO. This argument is picked up by Pallotta (2013, 2014), who argues that there is a double standard in the way actions leading to value-creation are regarded. The success of a private company is measured based on its revenue. To push this revenue, the firm spends money on marketing, for example, and no stakeholder objects. In contrast, non-profits wanting to increase their income from donations by using marketing to make them and their cause known are regarded as dubious. The same difference in view can be detected in regard to overhead costs. Donors expect that their money is used toward the social goal of the NPO or for the particular project they gave money for. Hence, the overhead costs are to be kept as low as possible while providing excellent service. But what if an investment in overhead costs would increase the ability of the organisation to reach its goals? For instance, purchasing a car to reach more communities, a generator for an office in a project country to ensure a supply of electricity and thus the possibility to work more hours every day, training for staff, or software to make administrative tasks more efficient (Glassman & Spahn, 2012). A private firm is not faced with these expectations at the same level (Pallotta, 2013, 2014). This dichotomy is furthered through the advancement of for-profit organisations into the non-profit sector, leading to structures and processes of NPOs being increasingly compared to those of the private sector. As a result, NPOs need to meet the demands imposed on for-profit businesses as well to show legitimacy, competitiveness and the capability to survive. However, some of these requirements and the developed processes to meet these demands are not as appropriate or efficient for NPOs, and thus make it more challenging (Drucker, 1990; Glassman & Spahn, 2012) for NPOs to compete with for-profit companies.

Nevertheless, the main issue apart from the survival of NPOs is whether the shift towards management orientation and efficiency (Alexander, 1999; van Broekhoven, 2008) and the adaptation to the competitive environment (Ryan, 1999) will hinder NPOs from pursuing their social objectives (Alexander, 1999; Ryan, 1999) "that distinguish[es] them from for-profit organizations" (Ryan, 1999, p. 2). While members of NPOs are often more committed to the cause of the organisation and are thus willing to go the extra mile for their beneficiaries, they have a hard time competing with for-profits on price, which might impact the allocation of government grants (Ryan, 1999). Consequently, NPOs need to present themselves and their achievements differently than private companies by highlighting their differences when compared to for-profit companies, such as commitment, motivation, and their desire to achieve a wider social change as opposed to a short-term solution. IC is part of this approach. Before the perspective of NPOs regarding IC is discussed, the German non-profit sector is introduced, followed by an overview of ways of segmenting the third sector into more homogeneous sections and on types of German NPOs.

3.2 The German Non-Profit Sector

Literature on the third sector in Germany is scarce. An internet search for literature highlights this situation. The search was conducted in May 2014 via Google Scholar, to ensure academically appropriate hits and excluding patents and citations. In total, 25 search terms were utilised (see Fig. 3.1).

All terms were checked for hits with the particular term anywhere in a publication first, and explicitly mentioned in the title of a publication second. The latter is

	number of hits	
Search terms	anywhere within the article	part of title of the article
"Der dritte Sektor" und "Deutschland"	1760	2
"Der 3. Sektor" und "Deutschland"	35	0
"Nonprofit Sektor" und "Deutschland"	1170	0
"Non Profit Sektor" und "Deutschland"	835	0
"Not for Profit Sektor" und "Deutschland"	15	0
"Nonprofit Organisationen" und "Deutschland"	3220	1
"Nonprofit Organisation" und "Deutschland"	1320	0
"Non Profit Organisationen" und "Deutschland"	5460	2
"Non Profit Organisation" und "Deutschland"	3210	0
"Gemeinnützige Organisationen" und "Deutschland"	1970	0
"Gemeinnützige Organisation" und "Deutschland"	1210	0
"Nonprofit Organisations" and "Germany"	954	0
"Nonprofit Organisation" and "Germany"	1840	0
"Non Profit Organisations" and "Germany"	9050	0
"Non Profit Organisation" and "Germany"	9890	0
"voluntary sector" and "Germany"	15800	1
"Not for profit sector" and "Germany"	2620	0
"Nonprofit Organisation"	3310	33
"Non Profit Organisation"	29100	69
"Nonprofit Organisations"	4180	119
"Non Profit Organisations"	23800	231
"third sector"	46000	1370
"3rd sector"	741	5
"non profit sector"	24900	281
"nonprofit sector"	34000	769
	226390	**2883**

Fig. 3.1 Search terms and corresponding hits (Source: Author)

of importance since the mentioning in the title of a publication indicates a focus and not just a possibly short reference of the topic within the publication. A total of 226,390 publications with the term ‘third sector’ or synonyms anywhere within the publication were reported by Google Scholar, which points towards an existing interest in this field. 60,359 publications of these publications mention ‘Germany’ or ‘Deutschland’ at least once. However, only six of these publications included ‘Germany’ or ‘Deutschland’ as part of the title and thus put a specific focus on this country.

The most comprehensive work on the German third sector was done as part of the John Hopkins Comparative Non-profit Sector Project in the late 1980th/early 1990th. Before the third sector in Germany can be introduced, it is necessary to get an idea of the history of the development of the German non-profit sector without going into too much detail. Anheier and Seibel (1993) identify two historically grown principles, namely the principle of self-administration and the principle of subsidiarity, that still influence the third sector in Germany today and are introduced in the following paragraph.

In the aftermath of the Vienna Congress in 1815, *Vereine* (associations) were regarded as a “potential source of political unrest” (Anheier & Seibel, 1993). Associations with a cultural focus such as sports or singing found their way back into everyday life, as did local “associational initiatives . . . aiming for risk protection in shops and improvement of education” (Anheier & Seibel, 1993, p. 5). Thus associations were slowly accepted, even within an autocratic state. This acceptance is a significant difference in the development of the German non-profit sector in comparison to those of other countries where the state and the third sector were regarded as explicitly contrary poles (Anheier & Seibel, 1993). During this time the oldest NPOs still in existence were founded: the German Red Cross in 1863 and the Deutsche Gesellschaft zur Rettung Schiffbrüchiger in 1865. It should be noted that Germany only became a nation-state in 1871, i.e. the organisations were founded during a time when “Germany” was still a confederation of individual states. Both organisations, going back to the early 1860s, are based on the idea that states are at times not able to provide fast and sufficient help. Both organisations still exist today and are well-known for their work.

Starting in 1883, social security legislations passed, based on the idea of collective risk protection (Anheier & Seibel, 1993), which are still valid today in their basic form. The insurances established in the wake of these legislations were designed mainly as self-administered but supervised and controlled by the state. This principle of self-administration thus allowed the emergence of a third sector “in an autocratic society, where the freedom of association had only partly been granted” (Anheier & Seibel, 1993, p. 2). Only in 1948 did the German *Grundgesetz* (GG), the Basic Law, pass, which included the right for all Germans “to found associations and societies”, GG Article 9, with any focus as long as no laws or ethical or moral principles are violated (Anheier & Seibel, 1993).

Another conflict brought about the second principle that shaped the German non-profit sector: the principle of subsidiarity. Going back on a conflict between state, Protestant Prussia in this case, and the catholic church in the 1870s, which led to all Catholic schools being taken over by the state, the Pope stated that "individual compassion and solidarity" takes priority over "state-organized assistance and public welfare programs" (Anheier & Seibel, 1993). In Germany, this principle is apparent in its social policy (finally passed in 1961) wherein the subsidiarity of individual action over social welfare provision by the state is stipulated (Anheier, 1998; Anheier & Seibel, 1993; Priller, Zimmer, Anheier, Toepler, & Salamon, 1999). As a result, all savings have to be depleted before the state steps in to assist with living costs.

The historic development and the principles described created one important characteristic of the German third sector, which is its dichotomy. One the one hand, NPOs exists which have a proximity to the state, especially in the health care and social services areas. They provide services in these areas that were assigned to them by the state and for which they receive payments or funding (Helmig & Boenigk, 2012; Zimmer & Priller, 2007). This type of cooperation is well established within the German third sector and illustrate the importance of government funding for NPOs (Anheier, 1998). On the other hand, organisations focusing on culture, sports and environmental issues for instance are ingrained in civil society, (Zimmer & Priller, 2007), and depend largely on donations and membership fees.

Based on these historic developments, the *Bürgerliches Gesetzbuch* (BGB), the German civil code initiated in 1900, distinguishes in §21 and §22 between economic and ideology- focussed organisations (Anheier & Seibel, 1993; Bundesministerium der Justiz und für Verbraucherschutz, 2002; Wex, 2004) and member-based and non-member based institutions (Anheier & Seibel, 1993), which are further introduced in Sect. 3.3. NPOs are generally seen as supporting the stabilisation of a society through the procurement of norms of a society and the support of conflict avoidance, consequently furthering integration of individuals into the society (Wex, 2004). They choose their social aim voluntarily based on demand, are a voluntary consolidation of people with the same aim (Wex, 2004). An NPO can have several aims if these are not mutually exclusive. Helmig and Boenigk (2012) structured typical aims of NPOs depending on whether they relate to the organisation or to stakeholders (Table 3.2).

The economic importance of the non-profit sector in Germany was researched as part of the John Hopkins Project. It was revealed that the non-profit sector is indeed "a major economic force" (Priller et al., 1999). In 2007, the share of the third sector amounted to more than 4% of the gross domestic product of Germany, and more than 1.8 million paid employees worked for organisations within the third sector (Helmig & Boenigk, 2012). Additionally, no less than 20% of the German population work voluntarily for an NPO (Priller et al., 1999). In 1990, nearly every sport facility in Germany was financed and provided by NPOs as well as every fourth hospital bed (Salamon & Anheier, 1998). All these numbers did not take clerical organisations into account. In sum, the non-profit sector in Germany is not to be underestimated in its importance.

The importance of the third sector is not only valid in today's climate in Germany, but even more so when looking at plans set by Germany for the future.

Table 3.2 Typical aims of non-profit organisations

NPO	NPO sector	Workforce	Donors and members	State
Transparency	Information on the work of the NPO	Acquisition of volunteers	Amount of donations	Financial support
Quality	Comparability with other NPOs	Quality of the work offered to volunteers	Acquisition of new donors	Quality of relationships
Economic efficiency	Development of a network	Motivation of staff	Retention of donors	Knowledge about NPO
Cost minimisation			Donated amount of funds, commodities and time	

Helmig and Boenigk (2012)

Based on the Europe 2020 initiative, working towards less unemployment of young people through provision of means for students and trainees to gain experience in other countries, the creation of new jobs, and minimizing poverty and exclusion in Europe, Germany set the following goals (European Commission n.d.):

- 77% of the population aged 20–64 to be employed
- 3% of GDP to be invested in R&D
- 14% decrease of Greenhouse gas emission (base year 2005)
- 18% of total energy consumption from renewable sources
- less than 10% of children should leave school at an early age
- 42% of the population aged 30–34 years to have successfully completed university or university-like education with an educational level ISCED 1997 (International Standard Classification of Education) of 4–6
- 330,000 fewer people should be at risk of poverty or exclusion

Looking at these topics, essentially unemployment, education, research, environment, poverty and integration, it is apparent that these are all themes discussed and pursued by NPOs. Every topic is even listed among the examples of topics for organisations with the status of *Gemeinnützigkeit* (public benefit status) (see Sect. 3.3 for more details). Hence, the national non-profit sector plays a vital role in the achievement of the goals set and in securing and improving the standard of living in Germany.

3.3 Segmentation of the Third Sector and Types of German NPOs

There are various forms of organisations that are counted among the third sector (KPMG, 2012; Wex, 2004), and several differentiating factors which define them. Five popular approaches to segment the third sector are presented in this section

Table 3.3 Approaches for the segmentation of the third sector

Approaches for segmentation	Characteristics
Shape of support	– Member-based versus non-member based – Principle of congruence versus based on engagement and support
Legal forms	– Foundations – Charitable limited liability companies – Charitable stock corporations – Associations
Sources of funding	Memberships, donations, grants, inheritance, foundation administration, adjudgement of fines, 'supportive business', fundraising
Area of work	Culture and recreation; education and research, health; social services; environment; development and housing; civic and advocacy; philanthropic intermediaries; international; religious congregations; business and professional, unions; not elsewhere classified
Focus of activities	Continuum: social activity versus economic activity

Source: Author

(Table 3.3). The most popular ways to organise non-profit organisations into smaller, clearer, and more manageable segments or categories are presented in this paragraph, starting with the categorisation via the legal status of an NPO.

In Germany, two main groups, non-incorporated organisations and those with legal capacity, can be differentiated. To ensure comprehensibility, only the most common types of organisations are introduced (Zimmer & Priller, 2007). An example of a non-incorporated organisation is the unincorporated foundation, which is structured very similar to a trust having legal capacity, but is not regarded as a juristic person. Consequently, assets of this foundation need to be managed by a juristic person or entity. In contrast to unincorporated foundations, unincorporated non-profit associations are regulated in Germany by the BGB. It implicates that unincorporated non-profit organisations can be brought to trial or bring someone to trial, and the acting management board is individually liable in full (Menges, 2004).

Anheier and Seibel (1993) point out, however, that legal structures are not recommended to segment the German non-profit sector since, for instance, the Paritätischer Wohlfahrtsverband is a non-profit organisation yet also an umbrella for several organisations with different legal structures. Another example is registered associations, which do not have to be non-profit organisations. It is thus challenging to differentiate organisations clearly due to their legal structure. Since the legal structure of an organisation affects its work, common structures are presented in short nevertheless.

There is no legal definition for a **foundation** with legal capacity (*Stiftung*), however, they are characterised by three common features: they need to be purposive, have to have financial or material assets (§82 BGB), and they are not associations or organisation (Menges, 2004). In other words, foundations support a specific social aim through the provision of assets, such as scholarships or funds for specific projects. The law in Germany for foundations was modernised in 2002, is part of the BGB (§80–88), and specified in the laws of the individual counties

(*Bundesländer*). Since 2002, foundations do not have to be authorised anymore but have the capacity to be a subject of legal rights and duties as soon as they fulfil all the legal requirements (Menges, 2004). Foundations can again be separated into sub-forms which are not presented in this paper because the focus of the research is not on foundations. There is no formal register for foundations and consequently no access to even the most basic data such as a reliable number of foundations in Germany, their names, aims, or contact information.

Associations having legal capacity are defined as a union of people working towards a common social goal on a voluntary basis for a certain amount of time, not dependent on certain individual members, consisting of at least seven people at time of the foundation (§56 BGB), having a charter (§57 BGB) and a board (§64 BGB) (Anheier & Seibel, 1993; Menges, 2004). Registered associations gain their legal capacity by registering with a local court. With the registration, associations may attach "e.V.", an acronym for "eingetragener Verein" i.e. registered association, to their name, which differentiates them from non-registered associations. There is no law as to the structure and content of the charter of any association. In Germany, any person who has reached the age of consent can start an association (Menges, 2004). The right to form an association is even stated in the German basic law, which states that: "All Germans shall have the right to form corporations and other associations", found in Article 9 GG.

A less common form for NPOs with legal capacity is **charitable limited liability companies** (*Gemeinnützige Gesellschaften mit beschränkter Haftung*) (Anheier & Seibel, 1993). The form of a charitable limited liability company is subject to the legal requirement of limited companies. According to Menges (2004), the charitable limited company is the preferred form for an NPO consisting of a small and closed group of people, such as workshops employing handicapped people (Anheier & Seibel, 1993). An advantage of this form is that the liability of the members of its board is limited since the organisation is liable with its assets. To start a charitable limited company, its charter needs to be notarized and the organisation needs to be registered in the companies' register (Menges, 2004).

In order to gain the public benefit status (*Gemeinnützigkeit*), an organisation must show several characteristics. It needs to be selfless, exclusive, and provide its service directly (Anheier & Seibel, 1993), i.e. not via a third party. Selfless in this case means that members do not receive any compensation in form of profits or anything similar. Exclusive refers to the aim of the organisation, which has to be *gemeinnützig*, i.e. benefit the public, as mentioned in article 52 of the *Abgabenordnung* (AO), the German Fiscal Code. 25 examples for such aims are stated in Article 52(2) AO including the support of education and research, consumer protection, animal protection, and development assistance. "Direct" as a characteristic required for the public benefit status, refers to the work done towards the aim, which has to be provided by the organisation itself (Anheier & Seibel, 1993).

Apart from the public benefit status, two further statuses are regarded as tax-privileged according to §52–54 AO, namely benevolence (*Mildtätigkeit*) and churchliness (*Kirchlichkeit*). The main difference is in their target group. Public benefit organisations aim to support the general public. Benevolent organisations support individuals and clerical organisations support religious groups. To be accredited with any of the three statuses, the work of the organisation has to be selfless. As per §55 AO, selfless support or work is described as action that does not aim at one's own economic goals, including for example the utilisation of funds solely for statutory purposes and shortly after the funds were raised, the prohibition of distribution of profits to members of an organisation, and not paying high remuneration. Organisations meeting these criteria are exempt from paying corporate income tax as per §5 Körperschaftssteuergesetz (Menges, 2004) and their services are taxed with 7% value added tax instead of 19%. Donations to any tax-privileged organisations, with a few exceptions listed in §9 (2), Körperschaftssteuergesetz, are deducted from taxable income. Additionally, these organisations are turnover tax-exempt according to §4 (18) Umsatzsteuergesetz.

Looking at the different legal forms of NPOs from a financial perspective, an explanation presents itself as to why certain forms are chosen over others in certain circumstances. To start a charitable limited company, the minimum capital, consisting of monetary and material assets, is € 25,000. For a charitable stock corporation, the minimum is € 50,000, and for an association having legal capacity, a minimum is not required. However, since this type of organization often operates only with its gains from interests, it is recommended to start with € 50,000. To start an association having legal capacity, no minimum capital is required but the members of the association must pay a membership fee (Menges, 2004).

Another possibility to characterise NPOs is by their area of work based on the international classification of non-profit organisations (Salamon, 2010). This classification identifies twelve areas of work: culture and recreation; education and research; health; social services; environment; development and housing; civic and advocacy; philanthropic intermediaries; international; religious congregations; business and professional unions; not elsewhere classified (Kong, 2010a; Salamon, 2010; Zimmer & Priller, 2007). Since the majority of organisations can be assigned to more than one of these areas, the approach is not suitable for an unambiguous differentiation, but as a general classification.

Other broad approaches for segmentations are to divide NPOs into organisations following the principle of congruence versus those based on engagement and support (Grossekettler, 2006) or member-based versus non-member based organisations (Anheier & Seibel, 1993). Organisations following the principle of congruence are structured in a way that the beneficiaries of the services the organisation offers are those individuals who bear the costs of this service. Additionally, individuals affected by decisions made by the management of an organisation have the right to democratically vote this management and have thus the means to hold the management responsible for their decisions. Hence, these organisations consist of an exclusive circle of individuals: their members (Grossekettler, 2006). Organisations that base their work on engagement and support follow a different system. In their case, beneficiaries do not bear the costs, but the two groups are mostly unknown to one another (Grossekettler, 2006). Individuals bearing the costs of these organisations can again be divided into continuous donors, members, and occasional donors. This structure has an essential effect on the funding of NPOs compared to those organisations following the principle of congruence, since it offers less planning certainty in regard to funding. As a result, the focus for fundraising of these NPOs is on public grants, financial donations, commodity contributions, and volunteer work (Grossekettler, 2006).

Sources of funding are also a way to segment the third sector (Menges, 2004). The common ways of fundraising are memberships, donations, grants, inheritance, trust administration, adjudgement of fines, and 'supportive business' (KPMG, 2012), further described in the following paragraphs.

Membership subscriptions can be paid via monetary or material contributions. The actual amount an NPO may ask from its members is not regulated. However, if an association, whose work benefits mainly its members, charge membership fees that are too expensive for the average person, the charitable association cannot claim that it is supporting the general good and thus its charity status might be denied (§52 (1) AO).

A **donation** is a voluntary financial or material spending or provision of time and know-how to support a purpose of a charitable organisation, without the expectation of a return service for the benefit of the donor. Material donations are commodities of any kind given voluntarily to an organisation without a payment of any kind in return. The donation of time or know-how for a charitable entity, i.e. voluntary work, is not tax-deductable, since no direct financial expenditure occurs for the donor. Earnings for which an association provides a service, such as the sales of tickets to a fundraiser, are not regarded as donations. There are specialised NPOs with the sole purpose to collect donations for other NPOs, for example for schools, hospitals, churches, museums etc. (Menges, 2004).

Grants from the respective state or the EU are an important source of income for many German NPOs (Salamon, 2010). They are given by a legal person or entity, often tied to requirements or restrictions and to a specific purpose (Glassman & Spahn, 2012; Lichtsteiner et al., 2013).

Inheritances are another way for charitable organisations to receive funds. Several charitable organisations offer and support this type of donation, Plan International Germany, for example (Plan Stiftungszentrum, n.d.), and Unicef Germany. For NPOs, inheritances are exempt from inheritance tax, as long as they are solely used for the charitable purpose.

Trust administration, according to law, is either the investment of funds to earn interest or the renting and letting out of material assets. Both forms are tax-privileged for NPOs. The renting and letting out of property is not allowed to take the form of a commercial operation, such as renting out a ballroom to different parties every weekend (Menges, 2004).

Courts have the possibility to rule that fines be paid to a specific NPO to make amends for a crime committed. To receive such **adjudgement of fines**, NPOs have to be listed with the courts first (Menges, 2004).

The only aim of a '**supporting business**' is to directly support the NPO in reaching its social aim, i.e. the purpose of the business and the aim of the NPO need to complement each other, for example, a shop for goods produced in a project of the NPO to support unemployed women with the profits distributed back to the same project.

Since these ways of funding have a huge impact on the way NPOs are structured and how they work, it is necessary to be aware of these various approaches, but as they are not mutually exclusive, they would also not be a suitable criterion to differentiate German NPOs either. Additionally, the only sources of information on the actual sources of funds are the individual annual reports. Unfortunately, the resources to check all annual reports are not available for the current project and therefore no information on the German third sector in regard to their revenue sources can be provided. Literature states, however, that the most common source of income for German NPOs is the state (Priller et al., 1999).

With the increasing competition with for-profit organisations, the danger of economic goals interfering with social goals of an organisation rises (Crossan and Van Til, 2008; Priller et al., 2012). Priller et al. (2012) established that the main influence on aims and strategies of NPOs in Germany is still a focus on social welfare. However, participants of the study ranked 'economic principles' the second highest influence on their strategies. These results points towards a conflict of the social focus of organisations and the economic demands placed upon them (Priller et al., 2012).

Taking the conflict as a starting point, i.e. the focus on social activity versus economic activity, Crossan and Van Til (2008) developed a continuum that segments the third sector. The continuum expresses the intergradient levels of the social and economic focus of organisations. On the 'social' end of the continuum, the social focus outweighs the economic focus, while the balance is reversed on the commercial focus end of the continuum. In between, there are those organisations that have both a social and an economic focus, usually leaning more towards one or the other. As a result, the continuum is segmented into four parts, two on the non-profit and for-profit side each. The non-profit side is divided into social and social commercial segments whereas the economic part of the continuum is split into commercial social and purely commercial (Crossan & Van Til, 2008). Organisations classified into one of the economic segments are not part of the third sector.

This section of Chap. 3 highlights not only various approaches to segment the third sector, but also the difficulties to find a characteristic that allows a clear differentiation. For the current research, the segmentation chosen by the DZI is followed. The DZI is a non-profit organisation itself. It collects and provides information on German donations soliciting charities (Deutsches Zentralinstitut für soziale Fragen, n.d.). The disadvantages of segmentation based on the source of funding of NPOs are compensated for in the current research through sampling on the one hand, described in Sect. 6.4. On the other hand, since information is provided by the DZI, the necessity to check the individual annual reports is averted. Donation soliciting charities are of special interest for the current research since they depend most on external communication to collect onetime donations as well as to recruit members and long-term regular donors.

3.4 Intellectual Capital in Non-Profit Organisations

In Sect. 3.1, the differences between NPOs and for-profit firms were highlighted, but, there are some similarities as well. Both types of organisations have goals they aim to achieve and are productive systems, i.e. they convert resources into services or products. Also, they are social systems in the sense that they depend on manpower, are dependent on their environment, and the way they work can be explained by internal factors such as their culture or identity (Lichtsteiner et al., 2013). These similarities point at the possibility that theories, approaches, and tools developed for private organisations might be applicable to NPOs to a certain extent. Derived from these similarities, Lichtsteiner et al. (2013) developed the "Freiburger Management Modell" for NPOs based on business economics but adapted accordingly. They highlight that NPOs mainly deliver services which are executed on two levels. On the factual level, the know-how, abilities, and experience of the provider are key for the quality of the service. The key for quality on the communicational level are the behaviours, emotions, and attitudes of the provider and the beneficiary, since their interaction creates either a positive or negative experience (Lichtsteiner et al., 2013).

All these intangible features of service provision lead to two important aspects that NPOs need to cope with. First, services cannot be produced beforehand and stored until they are demanded. Hence, NPOs have to ensure that structures and staff are available whenever necessary and thus cover the fixed costs that incur due to this approach (Lichtsteiner et al., 2013). The second aspect is based on the challenge of getting the service noticed. Since return donors receive only the promise that their donation is put to good use, NPOs need to provide other means than profits or products for stakeholders to validate the trustworthiness of the organisation (Lichtsteiner et al., 2013). Deduced from these challenges and combined with business economics knowledge, Lichtsteiner et al. (2013) developed three areas NPOs need to manage in order to handle today's challenging competitive market successfully: process management, marketing management, and resource management. Looking at these areas, a resemblance with the three capitals of IC, i.e. human capital, structural capital, and relational capital, is noticeable as visualised in Fig. 3.2.

IC is of high importance for NPOs specifically due to the different role of financial capital. NPOs do not have a "conventional bottom line" (Drucker, 1990, p. x) which can thus not be utilised as a measure for success and proper management or for benchmarking (Bronzetti, Mazzotta, Puntillo, Silvestri, & Veltri, 2011; Kong, 2007a, 2007b). IC, however, focuses on non-financial features and thus offers a different perspective (Kong, 2007b, 2008). Several characteristics of IC mentioned in Sect. 2.1 are important for NPOs. For instance, since IC is non-rival, it encourages sharing of IC rather than competing for it. A risk of fierce competition for NPOs is that the initial social aim is lost in the struggle for survival (Alexander, 1999; Ryan, 1999). Sharing IC, on the other hand, increases the availability of IC because it benefits from network effects (Andriessen, 2004; Lev, 2001; Nahapiet &

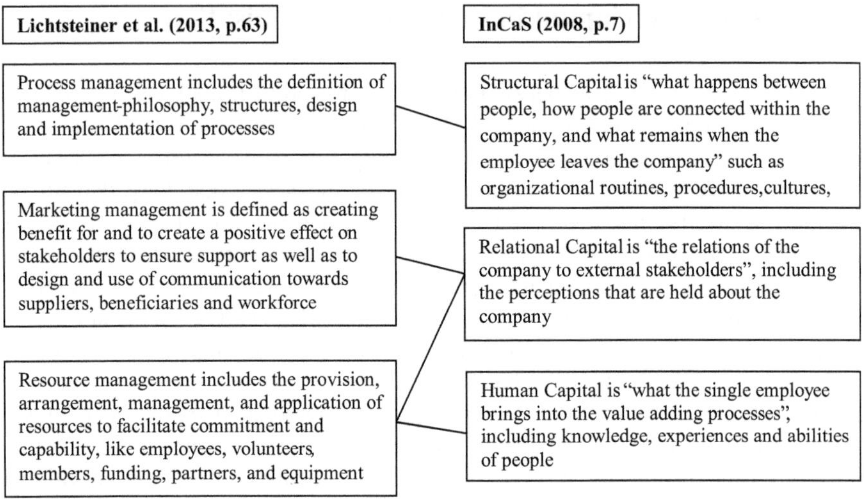

Fig. 3.2 Comparison of IC to statements on crucial factors for the success of NPOs (Source: Author)

Ghoshal, 1998), and the availability of IC in turn is necessary to achieve the social aim (Kong, 2007b; Sillanpää et al., 2010).

Spiritual capital is hardly ever included into models of IC (Hall, 1998), as mentioned in Sect. 2.1. Looking at definitions or descriptions of spiritual capital, it is mostly mentioned in combination with religion (Wortham & Wortham, 2007). Over the years, the religious concept of loving one's neighbour and altruism developed into the concept of 'altruistic individualisation' (Beck & Beck-Gernsheim, 1994). In other words, individuals have to balance the tension between the collective framework determined by society and the demand to develop their own biography. Donating money, goods or services is a conscious decision that depends increasingly on the alignment of the interests of the individual and the aims and actions of the NPO (Hustinx & Lammertyn, 2003; Jüttig, 1998). While there is no monetary return for the donation of time, material or money, individuals might look for an emotional return such as appreciation, approval, belonging or the feeling of doing something 'good' (Jüttig, 1998). Spiritual capital of an NPO might be one important aspect for the decision of individuals to support an organisation as it is a way for supporters to validate their choice. Unfortunately, a comprehensive philosophical and theological discussion on the motivation for giving would go beyond the scope of the current research. Nevertheless, the reasons for individuals to volunteer or donate to an NPO should be researched by the particular organisation to gain insight into the best way of approaching prospective new volunteers or donors.

A facet of spiritual capital is workplace spirituality, which is a highly personal and complex construct (Milliman, Czaplewski, & Ferguson, 2003). It expresses "the effort to find one's ultimate purpose in life, to develop a strong connection to co-workers and other people associated with work" (Milliman et al., 2003, p. 427), as well as consensus of the beliefs and values of the organisation and the individual. Depending on the individual, workplace spirituality does not necessarily include a religious aspect (Milliman et al., 2003). Milliman et al. (2003) defined three dimensions of workplace spirituality for their research: the individual level/meaningful work, the group level/sense of community and the organisational level/alignment with organisation values. Work is experienced as meaningful when the individual enjoys and is energised by his or her work and when work provides "personal meaning and purpose" (Milliman et al., 2003, p. 428). The group level includes aspects of structural capital, since a sense of community is also part of the work climate within an organisation, as is an aspect associated with the organisational level: the "organisation cares about employees" (Milliman et al., 2003, p. 428).

NPOs aim to cater to the needs of a particular group of people, often with restricted funding available (Alexander, 1999; Bronzetti et al., 2011), and "NPOs are focused on efficacy and efficiency of services" (Bronzetti et al., 2011, p. 17). To achieve this aim, the management of structural capital is crucial. Well-conceived processes need fewer resources, and properly maintained databases, for instance, help to stay in contact with donors and to keep track of current the whereabouts and needs of beneficiaries (Kong & Prior, 2008). An advantage of NPOs is that the inclusion of volunteers and members into the management process can lead to helpful innovations or further developed processes due to the different perspectives of members, volunteers, beneficiaries, etc. Another effect of the inclusion of these groups and individuals is their resulting high affinity and loyalty to the organisation as well as a positive organisational culture (Lichtsteiner et al., 2013). Organisational culture is defined as giving every member of the organisation's workforce a common perspective on how to handle information, how decisions are made and what values are pursued. At the same time, it provides the framework for the working environment which in turn effects the satisfaction of the workforce (Marr & Roos, 2005) and thus the workplace spirituality.

Organisational culture, and thus structural capital, both influences and is influenced by human capital (Bronzetti et al., 2011), since the people working for an NPO act according to the organisational culture while shaping it at the same time. The workforce, and thus the human capital of NPOs, is more heterogeneous and complex compared to that of private firms (Bronzetti et al., 2011). It consists of paid employees versus volunteers, full-time versus part-time employees, long term volunteers who support and work for an NPO almost as much as full-time employees versus volunteers who are able to contribute only a few hours a month. The backgrounds of employees and volunteers are heterogeneous as well. Some volunteers have fitting educational and/or professional backgrounds, for instance a graphic designer supporting an organisation in terms of advertising, an IT-specialist creating a homepage in his free time, or an accountant or bank clerk taking on the responsibility of an organisation's reports and accounts. Other people volunteer without having any fitting expertise to offer but because they feel connected to the cause and are motivated by personal experience. Consequently, for the recruitment of volunteers, NPOs need to consider the reason for people to volunteer and types of volunteering. Hustinx and Lammertyn (2003) developed a framework based on sociological modernisation theories to research these motivations and patterns. These theories point towards a development from traditional and collective frameworks for behaviour towards individualistic reflexive behaviour (Hustinx & Lammertyn, 2003). In other words, individuals have to react to a changing society and are responsible for their own biography; society does not dictate a lifestyle or career path anymore (Beck & Beck-Gernsheim, 1994). The motivation of individuals to volunteer thus often depends more on personal interests than on a sense of duty to society or altruism. NPOs need to consider this development not only in their approach to recruiting volunteers, but also in their long-term strategy. Individualistic reflexive behaviour leads people to volunteer based on different reasons, for example to increase their chances for a place at a university or a job, or to find a community they feel they belong to. The number of people who start to volunteer because they identify with the cause of the respective organisation, because it is common in their environment, or because they want to give something back to society, thereby decreases. Also, with the digression from the traditional and collective framework, the number of long-term engagements decreases as well (Hustinx & Lammertyn, 2003). The various backgrounds and especially the differences in motivation for the work prevent homogeneous management of the workforce on the one hand, but grant organisations access to a vast portfolio of knowledge, abilities, and experiences from various areas on the other.

Human capital is unique to every organisation and a competitive advantage (Bronzetti et al., 2011; Jüttig, 1998) if an NPO is able to recognise and exploit it for value creation. At the same time, human capital is a resource for new ideas and innovation, which attract donors and workforce alike (Kong & Prior, 2008). Ideas for improvement, if taken seriously, affect the processes of an organisation and thus its structural capital (Lichtsteiner et al., 2013). Interdependence between human capital and relational capital exists as well in different forms, for instance via internal communication with the workforce or when recruiting volunteers through the image of the NPO or the direct communication with individuals.

Relational capital of NPOs is essential to ensure external funding, support by volunteers, and public trust (Bronzetti et al., 2011; Lichtsteiner et al., 2013). While the latter is important for private businesses as well, volunteers being part of the workforce is a unique feature of the non-profit sector. Also, since the external funding of NPOs includes different aspects than that of for-profit organisations, relational capital is necessary to ensure funding. Relational capital depends a lot on communication. Thus, in the next section, the current status of IC reporting is illustrated followed by a more detailed discussion on reasons for NPOs to disclose their IC. Prior to this, the relationship of IC and the work of NPOs as described in this current section is summarised in Fig. 3.3.

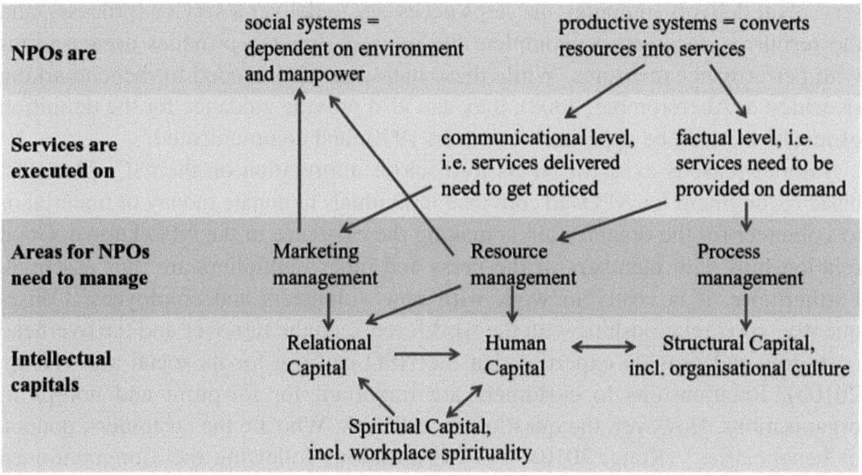

Fig. 3.3 Relationship of IC and the work of NPOs according to literature (Source: Author)

3.5 IC Reporting of Non-Profit Organisations

Currently, the regulations regarding financial statements depend on the form of the respective organisation. According to the BGB §27 (3), §666, §259, and §260, associations and foundations have to provide a report on income and expenditures as well as an inventory. They can, however, choose to prepare a balance sheet and an income statement instead (Bundesministerium der Justiz und für Verbraucherschutz, 2002; KPMG, 2012). Under §63 AO, NPOs have to prove that the requirements for tax shelter due to their charity status are upheld by providing information on the allocation of resources (Bundesministerium der Justiz und für Verbraucherschutz, 1976). Donations have to be recorded providing the time of donation, evidence of appropriate usage, and a copy of the receipt for the charitable contribution. Material donations have to be valued according to their market value at the time they are given to the organisation (Menges, 2004).

According to literature, the third sector is dominated by the demand for transparency and depends even more on trust and social acceptance than the private sector (Drucker, 1990; Glassman & Spahn, 2012; Raynard, 1998; van Broekhoven, 2008). NPOs try to sell something intangible (Drucker, 1990) to a donor who usually does not receive any counter-value (Theuvsen, 2011). Since there are no profits to signal the success of an organisation, achievements need to be illustrated differently (Lichtsteiner et al., 2013). Drucker (1990) states that NPOs need to define and communicate results as well as the efforts undertaken to reach those results. These results should be aimed at reaching the purpose of the organisation. According to Keehley and Abercrombie (2008, p. 28), NPOs connect their purpose to their everyday operation through four main parts: outcomes, outputs, process and inputs. In other words, reflecting on the final aim of an organisation (outcomes), the services it delivers (outputs), the steps necessary to deliver a service (process), and the resources necessary to complete the process (inputs), provides organisations with performance measures. While these measures are intended for benchmarking (Keehley & Abercrombie, 2008), they can also provide guidance for the definition of results that can be appraised (Drucker, 1990) and communicated.

Further reasons exist for NPOs to disclose information on their IC. The most basic requirement for NPOs to convince individuals to donate money or material or to volunteer for the organisation is making the existence of the NPO known. Good relationships with members of the press and other multipliers are thus essential. Furthermore, it is costly to work with new volunteers and employees. Consequently, good relationships with the workforce keep the turnover and the overhead costs low and provide expertise that the NPO can use for its social aim (Kong, 2010b). Relationships to customers are important for for-profit and non-profit organisations. However, the question for NPOs is: Who are the customers, donors, or beneficiaries? (Kong, 2010a) For organisations following the aforementioned principle of congruence, the answer is apparent: the members are the customers. Organisations based on engagement and support are themselves the link between donors and beneficiaries and thus need to foster relationships and communicate in both directions. As highlighted in Sect. 3.1, NPOs face several areas of competition and relational capital can provide an edge over competitors through easier access to resources, for instance (Lichtsteiner et al., 2013).

A further motivation for NPOs to disclose information on their IC is to address the influences on the willingness of people to donate as introduced in Sect. 3.1. In order for people to donate time or money, they need to be aware of the existence of the NPO, its goals and values as well as the resources needed by the NPO. Additionally, people are influenced in their donation decision by the reputation of an NPO and its perceived efficacy (Bekkers und Wiepking, 2010, cited by Helmig & Boenigk, 2012). As mentioned in Sect. 3.1, NPOs can approach most of these influences and address them in their external communication and thus influence their competitiveness in a positive way. Raising the awareness of people that the NPO exists, the needs it addresses, the social change it aims for, and the resources it needs to fulfil its aims are the most essential goals and message behind public relation activities. Also, organisations can use the disclosure of stories of individuals to evoke sympathy for the situation of that person, which can lead to an act of altruism (van Broekhoven, 2008). Information on structural capital in the form of processes and efficacy of the organisation can be addressed in external communication as well. In sum, another motivation for the disclosure of information on IC is a positive influence on the competitiveness of an organisation.

Salamon, Geller, and Newhouse (2012) researched the challenges of the American non-profit sector. They sent out a questionnaire and 731 NPOs responded. The main findings regarding external communication were threefold. First, the communication of the economic contributions of NPOs is important to maintain the support and legitimacy of NPOs. Second, most external stakeholders are either not aware or have merely "a poor grasp of the values that [an] organisation embodies" (Salamon et al., 2012, p. 12). This leads to the effect mentioned in Sect. 3.1 that the willingness to give is influenced by natural disasters and emergencies rather than the work and value of an organisation (Charities Aid Foundation, 2012). Third, the majority of respondents stated that communicating the values of their organisations became increasingly difficult due to the shift in focus of stakeholders towards financial data (Salamon et al., 2012). As a result, the traditional ways of corporate reporting are even less efficient for NPOs than for for-profit companies. They focus on financial measures, leaving NPOs with the challenge to justify their existence and prove their trustworthiness and competitiveness to stakeholders (van Broekhoven, 2008). Competitiveness is another demand of stakeholders that is challenging to prove for both NPOs and for-profit organisations alike, given that IC is not included into the traditional financial reporting despite it being one of the most important communication channels for organisations (Beattie, 2013).

A challenge regarding external communication is the fact that 'NPO' is an umbrella term consolidating a variety of different types of organisations. Therefore, it is difficult to establish a one-size-fits-all approach or best practice for NPOs. Yet there are common values connected with all NPOs which could be used as foundation for the development of a common approach. These values ascribed to NPOs state that they are productive, empowering, effective, enriching, reliable, responsive, and caring (Salamon et al., 2012, p. 4). These common values are all intangible and thus not reflected in publications based on traditional financial reporting. It is important however that NPOs communicate these values and their IC, since they distinguish them from for-profit businesses. Additionally, NPOs should keep the aforementioned influences on the willingness of people to donate in mind, which they can at least address if not use to their advantage.

Comparable to the incentives and disincentives stated in literature for the disclosure of IC in general as introduced in Sect. 2.5, similarities to the incentives for NPOs are noticeable. Due to a limited availability of resources, NPOs need to work as efficiently and effectively as possible. Incentives for the disclosure of information on IC are thus to show stakeholders that the respective organisation is able to manage its resources effectively and execute its value creation process efficiently, as pointed out for organisations in general as well (Beattie & Thomson, 2010). For NPO as service organisations, it is essential to ensure the availability of human capital, such as know-how, experience, and competences, by building a relationship between the organisation and its workforce (Bronzetti et al., 2011). Communicating values, aims, processes etc. are necessary to recruit and retain staff and to foster loyalty. Such a positive effect on the scarce resource of human capital presents another incentive for the disclosure of IC. Last but not least, IC disclosure provides stakeholders with the means to gain a better understanding of the organisation, its value creation processes, and the resources it needs for value creation. According to literature, this information allows stakeholders to validate the trustworthiness of the NPO (Lichtsteiner et al., 2013), leading to approval and support by stakeholders. In sum, the demands of stakeholders need to be answered and the availability of the resources necessary needs to be ensured (Horak & Speckbacher, 2013). Disincentives are not addressed in literature on IC reporting of NPOs. It can be assumed, however, that the increasing scope and complexity of corporate

Table 3.4 Compilation of arguments presented in Sect. 3.5

Context	Finding	Author
German laws & regulations for disclosure by NPOs	Associations and foundations have to provide a report on income and expenditure, and an inventory. They can choose to prepare a balance sheet and income statement instead	Bundesministerium der Justiz und für Verbraucherschutz (2002)
	NPOs have to prove that the requirements for tax shelter status are upheld by providing information on the allocation of resources	Bundesministerium der Justiz und für Verbraucherschutz (1976)
	Donations have to be recorded stating the time when they were donated, evidence of the appropriate usage, and a copy of the receipt for charitable contribution need to be provided	Menges (2004)
Importance of IC for NPOs	Third sector is dominated by high demand for transparency, trust, and social acceptance	Glassman and Spahn (2012), Raynard (1998), van Broekhoven (2008)
	Donors do not receive counter-value	Theuvsen (2011), Grossekettler (2006)
	Good relationship with workforce keeps turnover and overhead costs low, and provides expertise	Kong (2010b), Bronzetti et al. (2011)
	Relational capital can provide an edge over competitors through easier access to resources	Lichtsteiner et al. (2013)
	Information on IC can influence willingness to donate	Bekkers and Wiepking, (2010), cited by Helmig and Boenigk (2012)
	Disclosure of stories of individuals can evoke sympathy and as a result lead to altruism	van Broekhoven (2008)
	Common values of and differentiating factors for NPOs are intangibles (productive, empowering, effective, enriching, reliable, responsible, caring)	Salamon et al. (2012)
	IC disclosure can show effective use of resources and efficient execution of value creation process	Beattie and Thomson (2010)
	IC disclosure provides information necessary for validation of trustworthiness	Lichtsteiner et al. (2013)
Communication challenges	Poor awareness of value of NPOs, Communication of value is increasingly difficult due to focus on financials	Salamon et al. (2012)
Challenges	NPOs cannot use profits to signal success and achievements	Lichtsteiner et al. (2013)
	Who are customers? Members, beneficiaries, donors?	Kong (2010a)

(continued)

Table 3.4 (continued)

Context	Finding	Author
	Willingness to donate is increasingly influenced by natural disaster and not the work and values of NPO	Charities Aid Foundation (2012)
	Focus on financial measures leads to NPOs having to justify their existence and to prove their trustworthiness	van Broekhoven (2008)
Communication	NPOs need to communicate results and efforts undertaken to achieve those	Drucker (1990)
	Communication of economic contributions of NPO is important to maintain support and legitimacy	Salamon et al. (2012)
	Traditional financial report is still one of the most important channels for communication	Beattie (2013)
	NPOs connect their purpose to their every day operation through four main parts: outcomes; outputs; processes; inputs. Reflecting on these provide performance measures	Keehley and Abercrombie (2008)

Source: Author

reporting and the fear of releasing information critical for the competitive advantage are disincentives for NPOs.

In sum, NPOs face serious challenges since for-profit organisations are advancing into their area of work and bringing along the pressure imposed on them. Since NPOs do not work towards a bottom line or produce products, the pressure to show sustainability is hard to meet. Sustainability, however, is one characteristic that encourages investment. For-profit firms also depend on external funding to a certain degree, but since they can also draw on their profit, their situation differs from that of NPOs. In comparing customers of for-profits with those of non-profits, another important difference emerges: individuals who support an NPO financially are not necessarily the same parties who benefit from its work (Grossekettler, 2006), while customers get to use the goods or services they bought. To ensure financial and moral support, external communication of aims and achievements as well as other IC that differentiates NPOs and highlights their uniqueness is essential. Table 3.4 offers a compilation of the arguments presented in this section.

References

Alexander, J. (1999). The impact of devolution on nonprofits. *Nonprofit Management and Leadership, 10*(1), 57–70. doi:10.1002/nml.10105.

Andriessen, D. (2004). *Making sense of intellectual capital: Designing a method for the valuation of intangibles*. Oxford: Elsevier.

Anheier, H. K. (1998). Der Dritte Sektor und der Staat. In R. Graf Strachwitz (Ed.), *Dritter Sektor – Dritte Kraft: Versuch einer Standortbestimmung* (pp. 351–368). Stuttgart: Raabe Verlags-GmbH.

Anheier, H. K., & Seibel, W. (1993). *Defining the nonprofit sector: Germany*. Baltimore, MD: Johns Hopkins Institute for Policy Studies.

Beattie, V. (2013, April 16). Conversation with Vivien Beattie at BAFA Annual Conference 2013.

Beattie, V., & Thomson, S. J. (2010). *Intellectual capital reporting: Academic utopia or corporate reality in a brave new world?* Edinburgh: The Institure of Chartered Accountants of Scotland.

Beck, U., & Beck-Gernsheim, E. (1994). Individualisierung in modernen Gesellschaften – Perspektiven und Kontroversen einer subjektbezogenen Soziologie. In U. Beck & E. Beck-Gernsheim (Eds.), *Riskante Freiheiten: Individualisierung in modernen Gesellschaften* (pp. 10–39). Frankfurt am Main: Suhrkamp Verlag.

Berthel, J., & Becker, F. G. (2010). *Personalmanagement* (9th ed.). Stuttgart: Schäffer-Poeschel Verlag.

Blankart, C. B., & Gehrmann, B. (2006). Der Ditte Sektor in der Europäischen Union: Die Daseinsvorsorge aus ökonomischer Sicht. In H.-J. Schmidt-Trenz & R. Stober (Eds.), *Jahrbuch Recht und Ökonomik des Dritten Sektors 2005/2006 (RÖDS)* (pp. 36–71). Baden Baden: Nomos Verlagsgesellschaft.

Bronzetti, G., Mazzotta, R., Puntillo, P., Silvestri, A., & Veltri, S. (2011). *Intellectual capital reporting practices in the non-profit sector*. Sumy: Virtus Interpress. Accessed July 31, 2012, from http://virtusinterpress.com/IMG/pdf/Sample_Chapter-2.pdf

Bundesministerium der Justiz und für Verbraucherschutz. (1976). *Abgabenordnung (AO)*. Berlin: Bundesministerium der Justiz und für Verbraucherschutz. http://www.gesetze-im-internet.de/ao_1977/

Bundesministerium der Justiz und für Verbraucherschutz. (2002). *Bürgerliches Gesetzbuch* (51st ed.). München: Verlag C.H. Beck oHG im Deutschen Taschenbuch Verlag GmbH & Co KG.

Charities Aid Foundation. (2012). *World giving index 2012*. Accessed February 20, 2014, from https://www.cafonline.org/publications/2012-publications/world-giving-index-2012.aspx

Crossan, D., & Van Til, J. (2008). Towards a classification framework for not-for-profit organisation – The importance of measurement indicators. In *EMED conference: The third sector and sustainable social change: New frontiers for research* (pp. 1–25). Barcelona.

Deutsches Zentralinstitut für soziale Fragen. (n.d.). *DZI Deutsches Zentralinstitut für soziale* Fragen. Accessed February 20, 2014, from http://www.dzi.de/dzi-institut/german-central-institute-for-social-issues/

Drucker, P. F. (1990). *Managing the non-profit organization*. Oxford: Butterworth-Heinemann.

European Commission. (n.d.). *Europe 2020 in Germany*. Accessed December 12, 2013, from http://ec.europa.eu/europe2020/europe-2020-in-your-country/deutschland/progress-towards-2020-targets/index_en.htm

Glassman, D. M., & Spahn, K. (2012). Performance measurement for nonprofits. *Journal of Applied Corporate Finance, 24*(2), 72–77. doi:10.1111/j.1745-6622.2012.00381.x.

Grossekettler, H. (2006). Verbände zwischen Markt und Staat aus finanzwirtschaftlicher Sicht. In H.-J. Schmidt-Trenz & R. Stober (Eds.), *Jahrbuch Recht und Ökonomik des Dritten Sektors 2005/2006 (RÖDS)* (pp. 13–35). Baden Baden: Nomos Verlagsgesellschaft.

Hall, M. L. W. (1998). The confusion of the capitals: Surveying the cluttered landscape of intellectual 'capitals' and terminology. In P. H. Sullivan (Ed.), *Profiting from intellectual capital – Extracting value from innovation* (pp. 76–83). New York: Wiley.

Helmig, B., & Boenigk, S. (2012). *Nonprofit mangement*. München: Verlag Franz Vahlen GmbH.

Horak, C., & Speckbacher, G. (2013). Ziele und strategien. In R. Simsa, M. Meyer, & C. Badelt (Eds.), *Handbuch der nonprofit organisation – Strukturen und management* (pp. 159–182). Stuttgart: Schäffer-Poeschel Verlag Stuttgart.

Hustinx, L., & Lammertyn, F. (2003). Collective and reflexive styles of volunteering: A sociological modernization perspective. *Voluntas: International Journal of Voluntary and Nonprofit Organizations, 14*(2), 167–188. doi:10.1023/A:1023948027200.

Jüttig, D. H. (1998). Geben und Nehmen: Ehrenamtliches Engagement als sozialer Tausch. In R. Graf Strachwitz (Ed.), *Dritter Sektor – Dritte Kraft: Versuch einer Standortbestimmung* (pp. 271–289). Stuttgart: Raabe Verlags-GmbH.

Keehley, P., & Abercrombie, N. N. (2008). *Benchmarking in the public and nonprofit sectors* (2nd ed.). San Francisco, CA: Wiley.

Kong, E. (2007a). A review of the strategic management literature: The importance of intellectual capital in the non-profit sector. In *28th McMaster world congress on intellectual capital and innovation* (pp. 1–26). Hamilton, ON: McMaster University. doi:10.1108/14691930710830864.

Kong, E. (2007b). The strategic importance of intellectual capital in the non-profit sector. *Journal of Intellectual Capital, 8*(4), 721–731. doi:10.1108/14691930710830864.

Kong, E. (2008). The development of strategic management in the non-profit context: Intellectual capital in social service non-profit organizations. *International Journal of Management Reviews, 10*(3), 281–299. doi:10.1111/j.1468-2370.2007.00224.x.

Kong, E. (2010a). Analyzing BSC and IC's usefulness in nonprofit organizations. *Journal of Intellectual Capital, 11*(3), 284–304. doi:10.1108/14691931011064554.

Kong, E. (2010b). Innovation processes in social enterprises: An IC perspective. *Journal of Intellectual Capital, 11*(2), 158–178. doi:10.1108/14691931011039660.

Kong, E., & Prior, D. (2008). An intellectual capital perspective of competitive advantage in nonprofit organisations. *International Journal of Nonprofit and Voluntary Sector Marketing, 13*, 119–128. doi:10.1002/nvsm.

KPMG. (2012). *Rechnungslegung in der Praxis – Bilanzierungs- und Bewertungsfragen nach deutschem Recht bei Non-Profit-Organisationen*, (Homepage). Accessed January 08, 2014, from http://www.kpmg.com/DE/de/Bibliothek/2012/Seiten/Rechnungslegung-in-der-Praxis.aspx

Lev, B. (2001). *Intangibles: Management, measurement, and reporting*. Washington, D.C.: Brookings Institution Press.

Lichtsteiner, H., Gmür, M., Giroud, C., & Schauer, R. (2013). *Das Freiburger Management-Modell für Nonprofit Organisationen* (7th ed.). Bern: Haupt Verlag.

Marr, B., & Roos, G. (2005). A strategy perspective on intellectual capital. In B. Marr (Ed.), *Perspectives on intellectual capital* (pp. 28–41). Oxford: Elsevier Butterworth-Heinemann.

Menges, E. (2004). *Gemeinnützige Einrichtungen*. München: Deutscher Taschenbuch Verlag.

Milliman, J., Czaplewski, A. J., & Ferguson, J. (2003). Workplace spirituality and employee work attitudes: An exploratory empirical assessment. *Journal of Organizational Change Management, 16*, 426–447. doi:10.1108/09534810310484172.

Nahapiet, J., & Ghoshal, S. (1998). Social capital, intellectual capital and the organizational advantage. *Academy of Management Review, 23*(2), 242–266.

Pallotta, D. (2013). The way we think about charity is dead wrong. *TED*. Accessed August 5, 2014, from http://www.ted.com/talks/dan_pallotta_the_way_we_think_about_ charity_is_dead_ wrong#t-93138

Pallotta, D. (2014). Why can't we sell charity like we sell perfume? *The Wall Street Journal*. Accessed August 5, 2014, from http://online.wsj.com/news/articles/SB10000872396390444017504577647502309260064#

Plan Stiftungszentrum. (n.d.). *Plan Stiftungszentrum*. Accessed July 8, 2015, from http://www.plan-stiftungszentrum.de/vererben/

Priller, E., Alscher, M., Droß, P. J., Paul, F., Poldrack, C. J., Schmeißer, C., et al. (2012). *Dritte-Sektor-Organisationen heute: Eigene Ansprüche und ökonomische Herausforderungen*. Berlin. Accessed May 07, 2014, from www.wzb.eu/org2011

Priller, E., Zimmer, A., Anheier, H. K., Toepler, S. & Salamon, L. M. (1999). Germany: Unification and change. In *Global civil society: Dimensions of the nonprofit sector* (pp. 99–118). Baltimore, MD: The John Hopkins Center for Civil Society Studies. Accessed March 24, 2012, from http://scholar.google.com/scholar?hl= en&btnG=Search&q=intitle:Global+Civil+Society+Dimensions+of+the+Nonprofit+Sector#4

Raynard, P. (1998). Coming together. A review of contemporary approaches to social accounting, auditing and reporting in non-profit organisations. *Journal of Business Ethics, 17*, 1471–1479.
Ryan, W. P. (1999). The new landscape for nonprofits. *Harvard Business Review, 77*(1), 127–136.
Salamon, L. M. (2010). Putting the civil society sector on the economic map of the world. *Annals of Public and Cooperative Economics, 81*(2), 167–210.
Salamon, L. M., & Anheier, H. K. (1998). Dritter Sektor und Zivilgesellschaft – Globale Entwicklungen. In R. Graf Strachwitz (Ed.), *Der Dritte Sektor und der Staat. Versuch einer Standortbestimmung* (pp. 13–22). Stuttgart: Raabe Verlags-GmbH.
Salamon, L. M., Geller, S. L., & Newhouse, C. L. (2012). *What do nonprofits stand for? Renewing the nonprofit value commitment*, Baltimore, MD. Accessed December 16, 2012, from http://ccss.jhu.edu/publications-findings?did=389
Sillanpää, V., Lönnqvist, A., Koskela, N., Koivula, U., Koivuaho, M., & Laihonen, H. (2010). The role of intellectual capital in non-profit elderly care organizations. *Journal of Intellectual Capital, 11*(2), 107–122. doi:10.1108/14691931011039633.
Theuvsen, L. (2011). Professionalisierung des Nonprofit-Managements durch Governance-Kodizes: Eine Analyse der Transparenzwirkung. In A. Langer & A. Schröer (Eds.), *Professionalisierung in nonprofit management* (pp. 131–149). Wiesbaden: VS Verlag für Sozialwissenschaften.
United Nations Department of Economic and Social Affairs. (2003). *Handbook on nonprofit institutions in the system of national accounts*. New York: United Nations. Accessed September 03, 2014, from www.adm-cf.com/jhu/pdfs/UN_Handbook/UN_Handbook_Master31May2000.pdf
van Broekhoven, R. A. (2008). *Engaging Donors' Trust*. Accessed February 20, 2014, from http://www.icfo.org/ICFO-Publications
Wex, T. (2004). *Der Nonprofit-Sektor der Organisationsgesellschaft* (1st ed.). Wiesbaden: Deutscher Universitäts-Verlag.
Wortham, R. A., & Wortham, C. B. (2007). Spiritual capital and the 'good life'. *Sociological Spectrum, 27*(4), 439–452. doi:10.1080/02732170701335053.
Zimmer, A., & Priller, E. (2007). *Gemeinnützige Organisationen im gesellschaftlichen Wandel* (2nd ed.). Wiesbaden: VS Verlag für Sozialwissenschaften.

Chapter 4
Methodology

> "Methods are the means whereby one collects and analyses data. Methodology refers to the philosophical issues which underlie those methods" (Guthrie, Petty, Yongvanich, & Ricceri, 2004, p. 417, cited by Dumay & Cai, 2015).

This methodology chapter highlights the underlying considerations of the current research. It starts with a presentation of the research objectives and research questions, followed by an introduction of the research philosophy applied. Next, the influences of the researcher are discussed and finally a reflection on ethical implications offered.

4.1 Research Aims and Research Questions

The three aims of the current research emerged from personal experience gained by working for an NPO, literature review, and conversations with practitioners working for various types of NPOs. The first aim of the current research is the development of a framework for the disclosure of IC by German NPOs. The objective of this framework is to help organisations to provide the information demanded and necessary to stay competitive and survive, which is imperative for their work towards a social aim.

Another aim is to add a non-profit perspective to the literature on IC disclosure, since IC is mainly researched from a for-profit perspective yet (Guthrie, Ricceri, & Dumay, 2012). The third aim is to contribute to literature on IC disclosure by German NPOs. IC is recognised as competitive advantage (Kong, 2010; Kong & Prior, 2008; Sillanpää et al., 2010) and thus as essential for the survival of any organisation, including NPOs. By highlighting these competitive advantages NPOs can attract new donors, investors, and other stakeholders, ultimately enabling organisations to put a stronger focus on achieving their social goals instead of spending time and resources on worrying about financial aspects. However, there is

K. Blankenburg, *Intellectual Capital in German Non-profit Organisations*,
Contributions to Management Science, DOI 10.1007/978-3-319-62655-0_4

no empirical research on IC disclosure of German NPOs so far. To gain a comprehensive insight into the topics these two aims address, the status quo of the current knowledge and discussions in these fields are established first. Secondly, it is researched whether NPOs are aware of the term and its concept, and whether IC is already disclosed. Thirdly, the current ways of IC disclosure of NPOs in Germany is established as well as possible reasons for German NPOs to disclose their IC. The research questions are thus:

1. Are German NPOs aware of the term IC and its concept?
2. Is IC currently disclosed by German NPOs?
3. How is IC currently disclosed by German NPOs?
4. What are the reasons for NPOs to disclose information on their IC?

4.2 Research Philosophy

The view on IC taken on for the current research is the management perspective, as highlighted in Sect. 2.10. IC is regarded as a possible competitive advantage and organisations are not seen as isolated, but as interacting with their environment. The philosophical position adopted is that of realism. Realism regards reality as "quite independent of the human mind" (Saunders, Lewis, & Thornhill, 2009, p. 114) and is composed of two types. While "direct realism says what you see is what you get" (Saunders et al., 2009, p. 114), critical realism assumes that we not only see and sense objects, but also process what we see. As a result, it is only possible to understand a phenomenon if we take its context into account. Context, i.e. the social world and its structures, is socially constructed and has several levels which influence the understanding of a phenomenon (Denzin & Lincoln, 2011; Saunders et al., 2009).

Adopting this critical realist perspective, the current research assesses the approach to IC and its disclosure on different levels. A basic assumption adopted is that organisations develop their processes over a period of time. While individuals and stakeholder groups influence processes and their further development in the long run, these processes are independent from the individuals executing them. This is a rather objectivist view of the nature of reality (Saunders et al., 2009). The organisational level is researched through the content analysis of various documents an organisation publishes. Since there are different individual authors of these documents over the years and possibly for various parts of the documents, similarities in the way IC is expressed illustrate the perspective adopted on the organisational level. The individual level is inquired via interviews with representatives of the organisations. Lines between the organisational and individual level cannot be drawn distinctively since the information provided and views expressed by interviewees are influenced by the perspectives of their respective organisation. Nevertheless, differences between the views expressed during the interviews and those detected within the documents point towards their differences. Taking both levels into account, a more comprehensive picture of the reasons for NPOs to disclose or not disclose their IC emerges.

4.3 The Influence of the Researcher

According to Mayring (1996), research is not an objective registration of characteristics of an object but an interaction of the researcher and the subject. Through this interaction, the subjective perspectives change (Mayring, 1996). Additionally, prior knowledge influences the researcher and thus his or her approach to preparation, execution, analysis, and interpretation. Witzel and Reiter (2012) differentiate knowledge into everyday knowledge, contextual knowledge, research knowledge, and sensitising knowledge.

Everyday knowledge includes personal perspectives on topics, for example formed by behaviour or views of family members or friends of the researcher (Witzel & Reiter, 2012). The current research is influenced by a positive view on the work of NPOs and their support due to positive experience with the involvement in NPOs and/or events to support NPOs within a private context. Contextual knowledge is "the objective context of the problem" (Witzel & Reiter, 2012, p. 41) researched, such as organisational rules or relevant legislation. This type of knowledge supports the recognition of objective versus subjective statements during an interview (Witzel & Reiter, 2012). Research knowledge builds through literature review of available scientific literature on the particular topic which equips the researcher with specialized knowledge on the one hand. On the other hand, research knowledge poses the danger of bias through the views of the researchers who wrote the documents reviewed, and through popular approaches described frequently in literature affecting objectivity (Witzel & Reiter, 2012).

For the current research, it needs to be acknowledged that a positive view on IC and its effects exists, based on a combination of prior work experience and the literature review conducted. However, due to the recognition of this notion, the question of whether NPOs are of the same opinion is therefore called into question and investigated first. Sensitising knowledge is characterized by two qualities: "a *general relevance to the problem* and [. . .] a higher *distance* to the problem [italic formatting in original text]" (Witzel & Reiter, 2012, p. 45). In other words, it points out possible directions for research and promotes the revision and development of existing understandings. Sensitising knowledge defines the framework of the problem researched but does not provide the actual substance. For problem centred interviews, "all prior knowledge [. . .] should be used in such a sensitising way" (Witzel & Reiter, 2012, p. 46). The result of treating prior knowledge as recommended by Witzel and Reiter (2012) and conducting interviews accordingly is a mix of deductive and inductive approaches to a researched phenomenon which overcomes possibly biased prior knowledge of the researcher. Furthermore, researchers do not only have an effect on the data collected, but also on the people they interact with. Therefore, an ethical reflection of the project is essential, which, for the current project, is presented in the next section.

4.4 Ethical Reflection

Researchers always interact with other people, such as other researchers, students and/or practitioners, and their rights and interests need to be respected (Creswell, 2009; Saunders et al., 2009). Every contact with other people can have an influence on these individuals or their environment in a direct or indirect way. Saunders et al. (2009, p. 185) summarise that the most important common ethical issues of concern:

- privacy of possible and actual participants;
- voluntary nature of participation and the right to withdraw partially or completely from the process;
- consent and possible deception of participants;
- maintenance of the confidentiality of data provided by individuals or identifiable participants and their anonymity;
- reaction of participants to the way in which you seek to collect data, including embarrassment, stress, discomfort, pain and harm;
- effects on participants of the way in which you use, analyse and report your data [. . .];
- behaviour and objectivity of [. . .] the researcher.

Likewise, these ethical concerns are addressed in the requirements that are important for the current research, namely the "Guideline for Ethical Research" by the University of the West of Scotland (UWS) and the demands by the Hamburg University of Applied Sciences (HAW Hamburg). The "Guideline for Ethical Practice in Research and Scholarship" published by the University Ethics Committee of the UWS approaches the issue of "ethical principles guiding research with human subjects" (University Ethics Committee, 2016, p. 4), which is similar in its requirements to the demands by the HAW Hamburg, expressed via their application form (Ethikkommission des Competence Center Gesundheit der HAW Hamburg, 2014). The UWS guideline is based on four principles: 'benefits and harms', 'autonomy, veracity and informed consent', 'justice and inclusiveness', and 'privacy and confidentiality'.

The principle labelled 'benefits and harms' discusses the "balance between benefits and risks" (University Ethics Committee, 2016, p. 6). While research should be beneficial and a contribution to knowledge, protecting participants of research projects from harm (non-maleficence) is of highest importance. Maleficent behaviour can be physical as well as psychological. While the former rarely occurs in research focussing on economics but rather in medical studies, the latter might be caused by "embarrassing or sensitive questions" (Ethikkommission des Competence Center Gesundheit der HAW Hamburg, 2014, p. 2) that can appear in any empirical research. The second part of this principle, beneficence, includes the appeal to do research that is useful, i.e. contributes to theory and/or practice.

The beneficence of the current research is twofold. One the one hand it addresses an underrepresented topic in literature and thus contributes to theory. On the other hand, the research contributes to practice by taking the voices and current practices of practitioners into account, and by the development of a framework for practice as the final result from this project. 'Autonomy, veracity and informed consent', the third principle, requests researchers to respect the "right of all individuals to determine their own course of action" (University Ethics Committee, 2016, p. 4). Hence, deception of participants needs to be prevented and an informed consent of participants obtained (University Ethics Committee, 2016). An informed consent can be obtained via the presentation of a participant information sheet prior to an interview, for instance (Ethikkommission des Competence Center Gesundheit der HAW Hamburg, 2014). Also, consent needs to be voluntarily given and the participants need to be competent, i.e. need to be of age and mentally able to grasp possible effects of the research for themselves (Ethikkommission des Competence Center Gesundheit der HAW Hamburg, 2014). A further principle is 'justice and inclusiveness' stating that "There should be fairness and equity for all research participants. There are particular obligations to those who are potentially vulnerable" (University Ethics Committee, 2016, p. 5). Last but not least the principle of 'privacy and confidentiality' relates to the insurance of the confidentiality and anonymity of data (Ethikkommission des Competence Center Gesundheit der HAW Hamburg, 2014; University Ethics Committee, 2016).

Following the guidelines for ethical research by the universities, several ethical considerations need to be made for the current research project: the effect an interview might have on the interviewees, data protection and anonymity. Effects on people interviewed were not expected. Participants were fully briefed about the nature and aims of the research when first contacted via telephone. All persons contacted were adults. They were asked to take part as experts in their field, and no personal problems were thematised and no sensitive personal information was asked for. There was no pressure on anyone to participate and no payment for participation was offered. Every person approached and interested received a written information sheet in German. The document provided information regarding the research project and data protection measures put into place. Interviewees were explicitly briefed on the voluntary nature of participation, that interviews were purely business related and did not ask for sensitive business or personal information, and that participants had the right to refuse to answer question without explanation or consequences. Every interviewee was additionally informed of his/her right to withdraw at any stage of the project. This information was presented prior to every interview. Interviews did not start before all questions from the interviewee regarding the project, including data protection, etc., were answered to his/her satisfaction. The interviewer did her best to stay non-judgemental and to respect the privacy of the interview respondents at all times. Other students, researchers and participants were always treated respectfully. Quotes and the work of other used for the literature review or any other part of this research project are identified as such without exception.

All participants gave their explicit consent to state and identify the organisation they represent. While some respondents agreed to the use of their own names, some wish to remain anonymous. Hence, whenever mentioned within this document, the latter are identified as "representative" of their respective organisation without giving further information that might lead to their identification. Since the interviews were conducted in German, the translation to English limits the recognition of individuals further.

Data protection and confidentiality of the data and information provided are ensured through several measures. All personal data and all information provided are used exclusively for research purposes. Personal data, notes, the audio recordings of all interviews and their transcripts are stored on a password protected personal laptop and a copy was saved on an external hard drive in case of theft or technical failure of the laptop. The laptop and the external hard drive are stored in the author's home and not accessible by anyone else. Audio recordings and personal data are deleted as soon as possible.

Ethical approval for the project was granted by the HAW Hamburg in September 2012 and by the UWS in December 2012.

References

Creswell, J. W. (2009). *Research design: Qualitative, quantitative, and mixed methods approaches* (3rd ed.). Thousand Oaks, CA: SAGE.

Denzin, N. K., & Lincoln, Y. S. (2011). The discipline and practice of qualitative research. In N. K. Denzin & Y. S. Lincoln (Eds.), *The Sage handbook of qualitative research* (pp. 1–17). Thousand Oaks, CA: SAGE.

Dumay, J., & Cai, L. (2015). Using content analysis as a research methodology for investigating intellectual capital disclosure: A critique. *Journal of Intellectual Capital, 16*(1), 121–155. doi:10.1108/JIC-04-2014-0043.

Ethikkommission des Competence Center Gesundheit der HAW Hamburg. (2014). Antrag auf Stellungnahme der Ethikkommission des Competence Centers Gesundheit.

Guthrie, J., Petty, R., Yongvanich, K., & Ricceri, F. (2004). Using content analysis as a research method to inquire into intellectual capital reporting. *Journal of Intellectual Capital, 5*(2), 282–293. doi:10.1108/14691930410533704.

Guthrie, J., Ricceri, F., & Dumay, J. (2012). Reflections and projections: A decade of intellectual capital accounting research. *The British Accounting Review, 44*(2), 68–82. doi:10.1016/j.bar.2012.03.004.

Kong, E. (2010). Analyzing BSC and IC's usefulness in nonprofit organizations. *Journal of Intellectual Capital, 11*(3), 284–304. doi:10.1108/14691931011064554.

Kong, E., & Prior, D. (2008). An intellectual capital perspective of competitive advantage in nonprofit organisations. *International Journal of Nonprofit and Voluntary Sector Marketing, 13*, 119–128. doi:10.1002/nvsm.

Mayring, P. (1996). *Einführung in die qualitative Sozialforschung* (3rd ed.). Weinheim: Psychologie Verlags Union.

Saunders, M., Lewis, P., & Thornhill, A. (2009). *Research methods for business students* (5th ed.). Harlow: Pearson Education.

Sillanpää, V., Lönnqvist, A., Koskela, N., Koivula, U., Koivuaho, M., & Laihonen, H. (2010). The role of intellectual capital in non-profit elderly care organizations. *Journal of Intellectual Capital, 11*(2), 107–122. doi:10.1108/14691931011039633.

University Ethics Committee. (2016). *Guideline for ethical practice in research and scholarship*. Accessed June 18, 2014, from http://www.uws.ac.uk/uploadedfiles/flexible_page_content/about_uws/overview/university_ethics/guidelines%20for%20ethical%20practice%20in%20research%20and%20scholarship%20-%20refreshed%20september%202016.pdf

Witzel, A., & Reiter, H. (2012). *The problem-centred interview*. London: SAGE. Accessed February 25, 2014, from http://www.qualitative-research.net/index.php/fqs/article/view/1132/2519

Chapter 5
Theoretical Framework for Intellectual Capital Reporting of NPOs

In literature, no theoretical approach for researching the disclosure of IC has become prevalent so far. Two papers reviewed theories used in combination with content analysis to analyse the disclosure of IC. Guthrie, Petty, Yongvanich, and Ricceri (2004) focused their review on IC disclosure in annual reports and on stakeholder theory and legitimacy theory. The latter can be used to explain why organisations voluntarily publish information, while combination of content analysis and stakeholder theory can be used to deduce whether stakeholder groups are "controlling certain aspects of an organisation" (Guthrie et al., 2004, p. 284). They conclude that both theories are "compatible with the use of content analysis techniques" (Guthrie et al., 2004, p. 290). More recently Dumay and Cai (2015) analysed 110 papers on intellectual capital disclosure for which content analysis was applied as research method. Of the papers within their sample, 48 used specific theory for their analysis or included them in their literature review. The theories most frequently used were agency theory, legitimacy theory, resource-based view, and stakeholder theory. These theories are introduced in the following sub-sections in light of IC reporting of NPOs to facilitate a transparent and comprehensible choice of a theory applied for the analysis of the current research. Additionally, since legitimacy theory is part of institutional theory, and resource-based view and resource dependency theory are based on the same assumptions, these theories are presented as well.

5.1 Agency Theory

Agency theory is an economic theory which views the firm as a nexus of contracts. It is based on the belief that the parties involved behave opportunistically and in self-interest to minimise their own risks (Eisenhardt, 1989; Göbel, 2002). Information is regarded as "a purchasable commodity" (Eisenhardt, 1989, p. 59), leading to information asymmetries between the parties if the information is not equally accessible to both. Information asymmetries can have several causes, like the

K. Blankenburg, *Intellectual Capital in German Non-profit Organisations*,
Contributions to Management Science, DOI 10.1007/978-3-319-62655-0_5

differences between know-how of two people, or conflicting goals within a work relationship (Eisenhardt, 1989; Göbel, 2002). For instance, an employer expects his or her employees to fulfil their assigned tasks in the best quality within the shortest amount of time possible. A conflict possible in this scenario can arise due to the goals of the two parties for instance. While the employer's goal is the maximisation of products produced for the lowest possible costs, the employee aims at a comfortable pace of production and the highest possible salary, for instance (Göbel, 2002).

Sveiby (1997) describes information asymmetries for companies rather graphically. He compares the market-to-book ratio of companies, which expresses the differences of the value of a company expressed in its financial report and its perceived value, taking possible future earnings into account (Sveiby, 1997), to an "iceberg, bobbing up and down as investors change their views about what might be going on under the surface" (Sveiby, 1997, p. 4). The disclosure of additional information by an organisation increases the knowledge of stakeholders about the firm (Arvidsson, 2011), i.e. reduces information asymmetries, increases transparency and decreases the perceived risk. Risks for people donating time or money to NPOs are, for instance, that the goals proclaimed are not those worked towards, that most of the money donated is not used for the social cause but spent differently, and that the approach of the organisation has side effects on other people or the environment which were not taken into account. In brief, a decrease in information asymmetries is an important reason for for-profit as well as non-profit organisations to engage in disclosure of supplementary information. Thus, the link to the motivation for IC reporting is the belief that the reporting of additional qualitative information is a means of overcoming the information asymmetries between an organisation and its stakeholders and thus increasing transparency (Kuhnle & Banzhaf, 2006) and decreasing the perceived risk.

5.2 Stakeholder Theory

Several definitions exist for stakeholders and a collection of these definitions of the term is presented by Reed et al. (2009). A popular definition describes stakeholders as actors who are either affected by or have an interest in an organisation or an issue at hand (Brugha & Varvasovszky, 2000; Freeman & McVea, 2001; Reed et al., 2009), as well as individuals or groups who "have an active or passive influence" on the organisation (Varvasovszky & Brugha, 2000, p. 341). As a result, the active management of stakeholders is essential for the success of an organisation (Freeman & McVea, 2001). The concept of stakeholders and their influence is not new. According to Post, Preston, and Sachs (2002), the idea of the "central contribution of 'interconnectedness' among diverse actors to business success" (Post et al., 2002, p. 6), and therefore the idea of stakeholders, was already pointed out in 1918. For this book, the following definition of stakeholder is constructed based on the aforementioned definitions: Stakeholders are individuals or groups who are affected by an organisation or who have an influence on the survival of an organisation in a positive or negative way. This definition includes the widespread view that the long-term success of a company, product or policy depends on the support of internal and external stakeholders (Brugha & Varvasovszky, 2000; Post et al., 2002; Reed et al., 2009).

Figure 5.1 is based on the target groups of financial reports, since, as mentioned above, traditional financial reporting is still one of the most important communication channels for organisations (Beattie, 2013). The segmentation is based on the approach presented by Kuhnle and Banzhaf (2006). However, the categorisation of target groups starts one level above their suggested segmentation of target groups into 'professional members of the financial community' and 'other stakeholders'. Also, those stakeholders listed by Raynard (1998) are taken into account. Consequently, the target group is split into shareholders and stakeholders first. The latter are in turn separated into professional members of the financial community on the one side, which is further divided into multipliers and institutional investors, and other stakeholders on the other side. The other stakeholders are subdivided into external and internal stakeholders, both divided further into individual stakeholder groups. The original segmentation by Kuhnle and Banzhaf (2006) seems to indicate a strict separation between the shareholders and the stakeholders, as well as the individual stakeholder groups. In practice, most stakeholder groups have points of contact and thus form a network (Post et al., 2002). Furthermore some members even belong to more than one group (Raynard, 1998). However, for reasons of simplicity, the interrelationships between the groups are not visualised in Fig. 5.1.

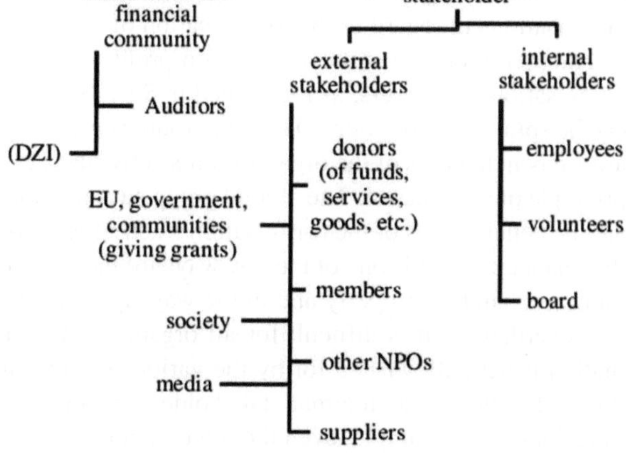

Fig. 5.1 Target groups of a financial report of NPOs (based on Kuhnle & Banzhaf, 2006; Raynard, 1998)

For NPOs, the shareholders labelled as professional members of the financial community hardly exist. There are no financial analysts yet who cover NPOs, banks hardly ever give loans, and no venture capital firm will consider investing in an NPO. Auditors might be named under this label and the DZI. It can be questioned however, if the DZI is a "professional member of the financial community". Looking at the internal and external stakeholders, the unique characteristics of NPOs need to be considered and donors and volunteers explicitly mentioned, since both are essential for NPOs.

While the segmentation presented offers a rough overview on stakeholders of NPOs, organisations need to be careful to take account of every possible group in the analysis of their stakeholders (Post et al., 2002). The main reason for organisations of any kind to conduct a stakeholder analysis is therefore to discover the specific interests of stakeholders, their influence on the success or failure of an organisation (Post et al., 2002), and their relationships to one another. Organisations have to take these interests into account in their management decisions, strategy, or planned action, and in preparation of their corporate reporting. The Chrysler Corporation, for example, initiated a collaboration with their suppliers to achieve cost reductions (Post et al., 2002) and thus ensured their support. In contrast, Shell experienced a prominent case of underestimating one of its stakeholder groups, the non-business stakeholders. After news of the decision by Shell to dispose of the oil storage terminal 'Brent Spar' by sinking it in the North Sea became public, environmentalists called for a boycott of Shell petrol stations and a lot of people followed suit, creating enormous pressure on the company. This case highlights as well that circumstances can change who the most critical stakeholder is (Post et al., 2002). Possible changes in the importance of identified stakeholders complicate the management of stakeholder relationships (Post et al., 2002) and increase the possibility of conflicting interest of stakeholders (Reed et al., 2009). Apart from the challenge of identifying all stakeholders, another difficulty arises for corporate reporting from the fact that the larger the scope of the groups into which stakeholders are segmented, the more heterogeneous their aims, interests, and opinions become. It can be expected that a weaker consensus on the information required exists within the groups. Thus smaller NPOs might have an advantage over bigger organisations in regard to the identification of stakeholders.

Another unique feature to the non-profit sector is the heterogeneity of the organisation's members, as mentioned in Sect. 3.3. In the case of NPOs, members can be split into two groups. The first group pays membership fees and its members are the beneficiaries of the organisation's activities, i.e. the organisation follows the principle of congruence. The second group pays membership fees but non-members are the beneficiaries of the organisation's activities (Lakes, 1998). In the latter case, the financial report is one of the few ways for these members to check whether their money is handled properly and in the way signalled beforehand.

Nevertheless, it is difficult for all organisations alike to recognise what information is actually wished for by the various groups targeted (Kuhnle & Banzhaf, 2006). Employees as internal stakeholders are interested in different information than donors for example, even though both are concerned about the survival of the organisation albeit for different reasons. Individuals donating funds are looking for data and information signalling that their donations are utilised to reach the social goal of the NPO, while employees are also interested in the stability of their jobs. Additionally, individuals can choose to be stakeholders of several organisations at the same time (Lakes, 1998) and thus be influenced by the behaviour of other NPOs. Open but structured discourse with stakeholders can thus lead to acceptance and even an understanding of the views and decisions of the NPO (Raynard, 1998).

Consequently, the amount of information given by organisations, the information wished for and the information asked for by interested groups do not necessarily match (Kuhnle & Banzhaf, 2006). Parsons (2002) researched the impact of the amount of information disclosed and its effect on donors' willingness to give. Her research suggests that more information does not lead to more or higher donations but does have a positive effect on a few individuals, mainly those who had donated to the particular NPO before. Parsons (2002) attributes this lack of interdependence to her low sample size. Nevertheless, this leads back to the aforementioned argument of Adelberg (1983) that feedback is necessary for effective communication. Hence, organisations need to check whether their chosen segmentation of stakeholders is both comprehensive and detailed enough.

When an organisation acquires knowledge about what information it needs to disclose exactly in order to satisfy its stakeholders, still the most effective and efficient way to report this information needs to be identified. Efficient in this case refers to the highest possible cost/benefit ratio. According to Kuhnle and Banzhaf (2006), the following questions have to be answered to address the issue of effective and efficient corporate communication: exactly what information is provided to whom, via which channel, when and at what intervals, and should stakeholders be offered supplementary service. The latter could be to support stakeholders in gaining access to information and processing it further (Kuhnle & Banzhaf, 2006), for example, with the aim to foster the relationship with stakeholders and to ensure proper handling of the information. In sum, stakeholder theory is closely connected to relational capital. It states that the success of an organisation depends on the relationship of an organisation with its stakeholders and the communication between them.

5.3 Legitimacy Theory

Suchman (1995, p. 574) defines legitimacy as "a generalized perception or assumption that the actions of an entity are desirable, proper or appropriate within some socially constructed system of norms, values, beliefs, and definitions." This definition is based on the idea that certain behaviour, strategy or procedure is regarded as legitimate if a group or groups of stakeholders accept it as such, independent of the perception of individuals.

Organisations have diverse reasons to seek legitimacy. Some want to ensure continued acceptance by signalling predictability, trustworthiness, and stability.

Fig. 5.2 Types of legitimacy (adopted from Suchman, 1995)

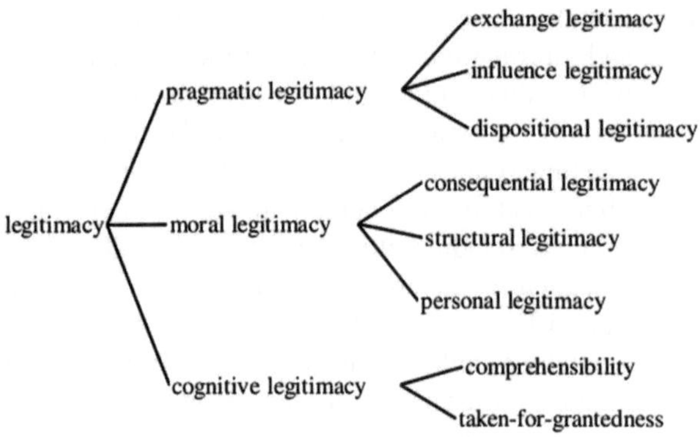

Other organisations seek to gain either active support or acceptance without interference from its stakeholders (Suchman, 1995). The latter reason highlights the connection to stakeholder theory (Guthrie et al., 2004). The way legitimacy is approached and perceived differs in all cases, which might explain the challenge in finding a generally agreed upon definition. To facilitate a structured examination of legitimacy, Suchman (1995) introduced the pragmatic, moral, and cognitive types of legitimacy which he divided further (Fig. 5.2).

Pragmatic legitimacy originates from catering to the needs and/or views of stakeholders (Suchman 1995; Theuvsen, 2011) and is thus linked to stakeholder theory. Pragmatic legitimacy can be separated further into exchange legitimacy, deduced from the expected value of the organisation's actions for the individual, influence legitimacy, originating from the believe that the actions of the organisations have a positive effect on larger interests, and dispositional legitimacy, emerging from signalling the same value system and interests of the organisation and its stakeholders (Suchman, 1995).

Moral legitimacy is based on the perception that the actions of the organisation are generally the right thing to do in opposition to expected benefits for individuals or groups. This type of legitimacy reflects the value system of the environment in which the organisation is embedded. Again, moral legitimacy can be separated. Consequential legitimacy is based on the accomplishments of an organisation, procedural legitimacy on the positive value put on the procedure the organisation utilises, structural legitimacy reflects the "rightness" of systems and structures, and personal legitimacy is based on individual leaders representing an organisation (Deephouse & Suchman, 2008; O'Dwyer, Owen, & Unerman, 2011; Suchman, 1995).

The third type of legitimacy, *cognitive legitimacy*, which "operates mainly at the subconscious level" (O'Dwyer et al., 2011, p. 36). It originates either from comprehensibility, i.e. the availability of believe systems to explain and understand the organisation, its strategies and actions. Alternatively, cognitive legitimacy stems from a "taken-for-grantedness", which is the hardest and most powerful form of legitimacy to attain. Cognitive legitimacy expresses the view that there is no other way to attain an objective than through the respective organisation and its approaches. The presented types of legitimacy cannot be strictly separated in practice (Deephouse & Suchman, 2008; O'Dwyer et al., 2011; Suchman, 1995).

In context of IC, legitimacy can be linked to all three forms of capital. However, relational capital has the strongest link, detectable in the aforementioned definition of legitimacy and based on the idea that legitimacy is dependent on the perception of others, which in turn is part of relational capital.

Closely connected to the legitimacy theory are the concepts of status and reputation. While again various definitions exist, Deephouse and Suchman (2008) offer the following definitions based on several sources from literature. They describe status as an "agreed-upon and accepted ordering or ranking of social actors" (Deephouse & Suchman, 2008, p. 59) based on affiliation to at least one group with typical value systems and best-practices. Reputation is described as a common expectation of how the organisation is going to act or perform deduced from former behaviour (Deephouse & Suchman, 2008, p. 60).

The three concepts of legitimacy, reputation, and status show various similarities. They are all intangible, subjective, and based on external social perception, and value conformity. However, some distinctions exist. While legitimacy expresses conformity with the best-practice, status sorts groups or organisations hierarchically based on behaviour displayed so far, and thus separates actors. Reputation "involves an explicit extrapolation from past to future behaviour" (Deephouse & Suchman, 2008, p. 61) and distinguishes actors, but does not rank them. The definitions of the three concepts of legitimacy, status, and reputation are summarised in Table 5.1. The immediate goals are the establishment and maintenance of trust and credibility through seemingly rational behaviour. A prominent example of the importance of legitimacy and reputation is the case of Unicef Germany. When Unicef Germany was publicly confronted with rumours about mismanagement of donations in 2007, the decrease in reputation, trust, and legitimacy lead to the cancellation of 10% of the regular donors (Diehl, 2008) and to the resignation of the chairperson as well as the managing director (Theuvsen, 2011; Wilke, 2008). In the first 4 months after the news broke, Unicef Germany raised six million euro less than anticipated (Diehl, 2008). One of the first measures of the

Table 5.1 Summary of definitions of legitimacy, status, and reputation

Concept	Definition	References
Legitimacy	"A generalized perception or assumption that the actions of an entity are desirable, proper or appropriate within some socially constructed system of norms, values, beliefs, and definitions."	Suchman (1995, p. 574)
Status	An "agreed-upon and accepted ordering or ranking of social actors".	Deephouse and Suchman (2008, p. 59)
Reputation	A common expectation about how the organisation is going to act or perform deduced from former behaviour.	Deephouse and Suchman (2008, pp. 60–61)

Source: Author

board of Unicef was to promise better financial control and more transparency for donors (Theuvsen, 2011).

5.4 Institutional Theory

Before institutional theory as such and its importance for the topic of the current research is presented, it is necessary to ensure a common understanding of the term institution. An institution can be understood as a large association, or a cultural or structural rule-like practice or obligation, for instance the handshake, marriage, or voting (Jepperson, 1991). For this book, the following definition provided by Scott (2013) is utilized:

> "Institutions comprise regulative, normative, and cultural-cognitive elements that, together with associated activities and resources, provide stability and meaning to social life." (Scott, 2013, p. 56)

Regulative elements are rules, sanctions, and laws; normative elements of institutions are values and expectations of structures and processes for example; cultural-cognitive elements are shared understandings (Palmer, Biggart, & Dick, 2008; Scott, 2013). These elements can be either found separately or, in practice, often more than one can be detected in an organisation (Greenwood, Oliver, Sahlin, & Suddaby, 2008). Scott (2013) additionally points out that institutions only exist through human interaction. Money, for instance, is just printed paper until people start to attach value to it and to use it accordingly, and the IFRS is just words on paper until people acknowledge its existence and start acting in accordance therewith. Generally, the purpose of institutions is to "provide stimulus, guidelines, and resources for acting as well as prohibitions and constraints on actions" (Scott, 2013, p. 58). For example, the healthcare system of a country can influence inhabitants by only providing financial aid in case of an illness if certain precautionary measures can be proven—providing a stimulus for looking after oneself.

With the term institution clarified, institutional theory is introduced in the following paragraph. A comprehensive literature review on organisational institutionalism is not attempted but the most important developments and definitions for this research project are going to be provided. Greenwood et al. (2008) phrase the main question of institutional theory as "why and with what consequences do organizations exhibit particular organizational arrangements that defy traditional rational explanation?" (Greenwood et al., 2008, p. 31).

In comparison to the traditional view of humans behaving in a strictly rational manner, institutional theory is sceptic towards this assumption. This scepticism did not change with the development from the old to the new institutional theory (Göbel, 2002; Powell & DiMaggio, 1991). Additionally, both approaches agree that organisations are not isolated, but in a relationship with and thus affected by their environment (Powell & DiMaggio, 1991). The environment influences the rules and expectations of the way organisations operate, which lead to pressures on every organisation to follow these laws, rules, and rule-like expectations. This pressure to appear rational is more intense for organisations whose output cannot be linked to their processes and "whose outputs are difficult to evaluate" (Greenwood et al., 2008, p. 4). As a result, organisations conform to the rules and expectations of their institutional contexts—they become isomorphic with them—to ensure social approval, legitimacy, and consequently survival (Greenwood et al., 2008; Meyer & Rowan, 1977).

Powell and DiMaggio (1991) attribute the start of new institutionalism in organisational theories to John Meyer and Brian Rowan, who published their paper "Institutional Organizations: Formal Structure as Myth and Ceremony" in 1977. In this publication, Meyer and Rowan (1977) state that prevailing theories until that point in time assumed that "the coordination and control of activity are the critical dimensions" (Meyer & Rowan, 1977, p. 342) for the success of companies while "in practice, formal structures actually coordinate and control work" (Meyer & Rowan, 1977, p. 342). Put differently, formal structures are the critical dimensions. Additionally, while the old as well as the new institutionalism agree that institutionalisation limits the rationality of organisations, they regard different sources as the reasons for these limitations. The old approach identifies conflicting interests within an organisation as the main limitation for rational action; the new approach argues that the main limitations are a result of internal structures grown over time and legitimacy dictating structures (Powell & DiMaggio, 1991).

Institutional theory was criticised for viewing the interrelationship between organisations and their institutional context too much as a one-way street. While the effect of the institutional context on an organisation was acknowledged in research, the other direction, i.e. the influence of organisations on their institutional context, was not sufficiently taken into account. This critique leads to another difference between old and new institutional theory. The former regards organisations as "embedded in local communities" (Powell & DiMaggio, 1991, p. 13), leading to organisations complying with their environment but keeping their individual character through the conservation of their unique structures. By contrast, the new institutional theory regards companies as embedded in their field, sector or society, which influence organisations in a less obvious way by causing the institutionalisation of organisational forms, rules, and structures. This type of influence leads to homogeneity of organisations (DiMaggio & Powell, 1983; Powell & DiMaggio, 1991) with few individual characteristics, and the pressure on organisations to utilize those processes considered rational by the field or society in which the organisation is embedded in order to increase its legitimacy, regardless of whether the practice is the most efficient one for the specific organisation (Meyer & Rowan, 1977).

In summary, institutionalisation and isomorphic pressures offer an explanation as to why organisations behave similar in certain matters. The aims of organisations are trust and consequently legitimacy, which organisations try to gain through conforming with best-practices that are in turn considered rational behaviour (Deephouse & Suchman, 2008). For example, small NPOs are not legally bound to prepare an annual report (KPMG, 2012) but some prepare and publish an annual report nevertheless. A reason for this behaviour might be isomorphic pressure from other NPOs or competing for-profit businesses. Results of this behaviour are comparability on the one hand and homogeneity on the other. The communication of IC can help NPOs to distinguish themselves from other organisations and secure social acceptance at the same time by signalling conformity.

5.5 Resource-Based View

Beattie and Smith (2013) state the resource-based view is "the basis of the IC field" (Beattie & Smith, 2013, p. 245). Firm resources are defined by Barney (1991) as "strengths that firms can use to conceive of or implement strategies that improve its efficiency and effectiveness" (Barney, 1991, p. 106). He segments firm resources into three groups: physical resources, which include raw materials and equipment, human capital resources, and organisational capital resources (Barney, 1991). Comparing the latter to the concept of IC, organisational capital resources consist of structural capital and relational capital. The key issue behind the resource based view of the firm is how sustained competitive advantage develops and how it can be maintained. To this end, Barney (1991) defined sustained competitive advantage as a strategy for value creation that is neither used nor easy to copy by other organisations. For a resource of an organisation to be considered a competitive advantage, it needs to fulfil four characteristics (Barney, 1991). The resource needs to be valuable for the organisation, rare, imperfectly imitable, and it should not be possible to substitute the resource (Barney, 1991). IC fits all these characteristics. The expertise and network of an organisation, for example, are unique and nearly impossible to copy exactly, since they often depend on the history of an organisation, a particular process, or an individual. Even if the individual starts to work for another organisation using his expertise in the same way, creating the same value is hardly possible due to differences in company culture and environment (Barney, 1991).

To establish the most important resources of an organisation, the significance of each resource for the value creation process needs to be identified. A positive side effect of the evaluation of the value creation process is an increased understanding of it, which in turn influences the management of resources. Effective management can ensure the existence of the right amount and right quality of resources, which the efficient execution of the value creation process depends on (Kong, 2007). The management of resources connects all departments of an organisation, whether it is a for-profit or non-profit organisation. NPOs however, need to manage additional resources such as volunteers, donors, and donations. Another difference between for-profit and non-profit organisations is the way resources are procured. Most NPOs do not have the funds to purchase new equipment but need to find a donor or sponsor, and volunteers cannot be attracted via a competitive remuneration package, for instance (Lichtsteiner, Gmür, Giroud, & Schauer, 2013). However, volunteers provide knowledge and experience. Expertise as described in Sect. 2.3 is hard to link to profits directly but is nevertheless a highly competitive advantage and, as such, imperative for survival (Lichtsteiner et al., 2013).

Due to the challenge NPOs face in securing resources (Langer & Schröer, 2011), it is essential for these organisations to use their available resources as effectively and efficiently as possible to keep costs low. In other words, NPOs cannot just work towards their aims without restrictions, but also need to economise the available resources (Lichtsteiner et al., 2013; Pfeffer & Salancik, 2003). If an organisation is neither effective nor efficient, it will cease to exist. High effectiveness in working towards their goal but low efficiency will create resource problems, since more resources are used than are available in the long term (Lichtsteiner et al., 2013). Resources are often taken for granted within an organisation (Barney, 1991) but the external communication of unique resources, such as IC, is essential to highlight the ability to successfully face the competitive environment. For NPOs, signalling the proper handling of resources is imperative. On the one hand, as mentioned in Sect. 3.5, the tax shelter status of organisations depends on the information. On the other hand, donors and volunteers want to be sure that the money and time they donate is used in a considerate way towards the social aim.

5.6 Resource Dependency Theory

The main difference between the resource based view of the firm and resource dependency theory is, while the former pays more attention as to the demand defined internally, the latter focuses on external influences and how organisations obtain their resources (Hillman, Withers, & Collins, 2009). Resource dependency theory regards organisations not as isolated, but as interacting and dependent on their environment with their survival reliant on the effective acquisition and maintaining of resources (Pfeffer & Salancik, 2003). Survival with respect to the interdependence of an organisation with its environment is uncertain until possible actions of the parties with which an organisation interacts are detected or managed (Hillman et al., 2009). Actions, highlighted in literature for an organisation to diminish these uncertainties and dependencies, are mergers or vertical integrations, joint projects, change or adaptation of the size composition of the board of directors, attempts to influence external conditions through political means, and executive succession (Hillman et al., 2009; Pfeffer & Salancik, 2003). Uncertainties are also the basis for the power distribution within a company as well as with stakeholders. Depending on the level of importance of a resource a party is contributing or controlling, this party has corresponding power to influence the success of an organisation (Hillman et al., 2009; Lichtsteiner et al., 2013; Pfeffer & Salancik, 2003). This power in turn affects organisational behaviour. Pfeffer and Salancik (2003) state four sources for control over resources: possession of resources, access to resources, control of the use of a resource, and the possibility to influence or implement rules or regulations regarding the former three sources of control. Organisations attempt to minimise the control of external parties by maximising their own power within their environment. Since the resources NPOs depend upon are mainly intangible, establishing the four sources of control is more important for their survival and more challenging for them than it would be for businesses dependent on tangibles.

5.7 Theoretical Framework for the Motivation of Intellectual Capital Disclosure of NPOs

In the end, each of the presented theories provides valuable answers to the question as to what motivates NPOs to disclose their IC. Table 5.2 offers an overview on the key perspective of the theories (inspired by An, Davey, & Eggleton, 2011, based on Meyer & Rowan, 1977; Freeman & McVea, 2001; Greenwood et al., 2008; Hillman et al., 2009; Kuhnle & Banzhaf, 2006; Pfeffer & Salancik, 2003; Powell & DiMaggio, 1991; Reed et al., 2009; Suchman, 1995; Sveiby, 1997).

At first glance, the reasons for the disclosure of IC in the five theories differ. Based on agency theory, it can be concluded that the disclosure of IC decreases information asymmetries, leading to transparency and trust. Stakeholder theory indicates that IC can be used to signal accountability and conformity with the interests of stakeholders. This pressure to conform is the reason for organisations to communicate and to communicate the way they do, since the goal of organisations is to achieve and maintain legitimacy. Considering legitimacy theory and institutional theory, IC disclosure can show norm congruency and rational behaviour. According to the resource-based view, IC can be used to signal a competitive advantage and, consequently, the ability to survive and be successful. Last but not least, resource dependency theory claims that organisations are interactive and therefore need to communicate with their environment to acquire and maintain resources.

However, various links exist between the theories presented as well. Agency theory is based on the notion of opportunistic behaviour and that a decrease in information asymmetries between an organisation and its financial stakeholders increases transparency and decreases risks (Arvidsson, 2011; Kuhnle & Banzhaf, 2006), thereby making an organisation more attractive for investment. As mentioned in Sect. 2.5, there is no relationship between the level of information asymmetry and the level of IC reporting (Brüggen, Vergauwen, & Dao, 2009, p. 242). Nevertheless, financial stakeholders are one group considered by stakeholder theory, which is concerned with identifying the relevant stakeholders of an organisation to ensure appropriate internal and external communication (Post et al., 2002) and ultimately their support.

Since society is a stakeholder of NPOs as well, and stakeholder groups are part of society, a link exists between stakeholder theory and legitimacy theory which is based on the idea that organisations depend on the approval of their actions by society. Legitimacy theory is regarded as overlapping with institutional theory

Table 5.2 Summary of theories and their reason for IC disclosure of NPOs

	Agency theory	Stakeholder theory	Legitimacy theory	Institutional theory	Resource-based view	Resource dependency theory
Key concepts	Self-interest, information asymmetries, nexus of contracts	Stakeholder management, accountability, stability	Organisational legitimacy, accountability, norm congruency	Institutionalism/ Isomorphism, appearing rational	Effective and efficient resource management	Interdependencies with environment; production of power effects organisational behaviour
Organisations interact with	Financial stakeholders (i.e. shareholders, debt holders)	Stakeholders	Society	Society	Suppliers of (tangible and intangible) resources	External environment
Aim of organisations	Profit maximisation, shareholder value maximisation	Stakeholder support	Acceptance, support	Stability, conformity, and legitimacy	Competitive advantage	Management of interdependencies, increase of own power
Organisations depend on	Financial support (share capital and debt capital)	Stakeholder support (labour, buying goods and services, etc.)	Social approval and support	Social acceptance	Availability of resources, suppliers	Management of interdependencies, to minimise uncertainty to increase legitimacy and independence
Reasons for an NPO to disclose information on IC	To paint a comprehensive picture of the NPO and consequently increasing transparency and trust that an investment is advisable	To show that the NPO respects the non-financial interests of its stakeholders and integrates those values into its work	To ensure a positive perception of the NPO and its work	To signal conformity while distinguishing itself from other organisation in a positive way	To signal proper handling of resources and a competitive advantage to ensure support of suppliers	To illustrate uniqueness, effectiveness and efficiency in the absence of a product, signalling a competitive advantage

Source: Author

(Deephouse & Suchman, 2008), which focuses on the conformity of organisations. Institutional theory is based on the assumption that organisations interact with their environment and therefore experience a pressure to conform to the laws, rules, and expectations of this environment, regardless of whether it is the most rational way for them individually (Greenwood et al., 2008). Conforming behaviour signals stability and legitimacy, both of which are values important for stakeholder support. A question to be considered is whether the groups or individuals that are not stakeholders but part of the external environment are actually relevant for organisations, since, looking at the definition, they are neither affected by nor have an influence on the organisation in any way. As soon as they become affected by an organisation or gain influence on it, they would automatically be regarded as stakeholders.

Stakeholder support in turn affects the availability of resources for an NPO. This notion is based on the resource based view, which states that organisations depend on resources, and on resource dependency theory, which highlights the importance of their environment to obtain these resources. This dependency creates power, which affects the behaviour of organisations. On the one hand, organisations have to meet the demands of influential stakeholders to the best of their ability to ensure their access to resources. At the same time, organisations themselves try to ensure the highest possible level of control of these resources to reduce the power of their environment on their behaviour, and thus, uncertainty.

Resource dependency theory states that the environment of a company is comprised of information that is interpreted by the respective organisation, such as consumer behaviour, activities of competitors and of the state, satisfaction and motivation of employees, etc. This information is then used to facilitate the constant availability of resources essential for survival and success (Pfeffer & Salancik, 2003).

These linkages described are also visualised in Fig. 5.3, wherein the lines link a theory to its aim or the signal it wants to achieve, while the arrows illustrate results or dependencies. Each theory has a colour to facilitate a better understanding. Box sizes do not hold any meaning.

A basic aim that these six theories have in common is survival of the organisation, and one feature is regarded as important in this regard by all theories alike: communication. This is due to the perception that organisations do not exist in isolation and thus, survival depends on interaction (Pfeffer & Salancik, 2003; Powell & DiMaggio, 1991). Agency theory claims that a reduction of information asymmetries increases the attractiveness of an organisation (Kuhnle & Banzhaf, 2006) for investors and customers alike. To achieve a decrease in information asymmetries, the communication of information is essential. Legitimacy theory builds upon the idea of stakeholder theory, stating that processes or actions, for example, are regarded as legitimate if one or more stakeholder groups accept them as such (Elsbach & Sutton, 1992), i.e. if the organisation gains approval. Hence, an organisation needs to communicate with its internal and external stakeholders, and efficient communication results in positive effects for organisations and their stakeholders alike. For organisations, costs can be reduced through effective

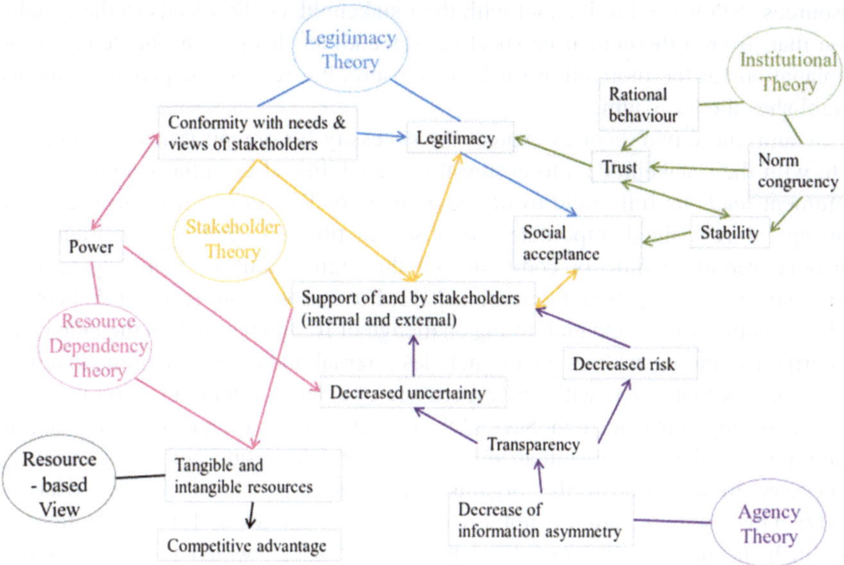

Fig. 5.3 Links between the theories (Source: Author)

communication which, for stakeholders, decreases the complexity of reports and increases the appearance of transparency and appreciation, potentially leading to legitimacy.

Institutional theory states that organisations that conform to the expectations of society and behave accordingly are regarded as rational and thus gain legitimacy (Greenwood et al., 2008; Meyer & Rowan, 1977). Due to rising competition from the private sector, the pressure on NPOs to provide comprehensive information enabling comparability between organisations from both sectors has increased. This pressure is part of the institutional context in which NPOs operate and emanates from their network context, i.e. their structural and relational capital. As a result, NPOs need to decide whether they comply with the expectations and thus clear the way for them to institutionalise. Yet again, organisations need to communicate with the parties they interact with, but in this case, to signal conformity or independence in order to gain approval.

Two aims or necessary steps emerge as the centres within this net of links: support of and by stakeholders and social acceptance. Both are linked to several theories and to one another as well. Support of and by stakeholders is attributed to stakeholder theory, it focuses on the support of groups or individuals who are affected by an organisation or who have an influence on the survival of an organisation in a positive or negative way, as defined in Sect. 5.2. Social acceptance, on the other hand, is attributed to institutional theory and legitimacy theory, which take the entire external environment into account. Another link to be considered is that both support of stakeholders and social acceptance are resources based on the aforementioned definition by Barney (1991) and, to acquire these resources, NPOs need to interact with their stakeholders. This leads to the conclusion that, from a theoretical perspective, stakeholder theory is at the centre of an explanation for the motivation for IC disclosure, but resource dependency theory establishes the basic aim.

In sum, these two theories express the necessity for organisations to communicate with their stakeholders to ensure the availability of essential resources. This argument leads us full circle to the beginnings of IC. As stated in Sect. 2.2, the concept of IC gained importance because practitioners realised that traditional financial reporting did not communicate the entire value of their organisation (Brennan & Connell, 2000; Edvinsson, 2013; Edvinsson & Sullivan, 1996; Petrash, 1996). In other words, the underlying challenge of IC and research in the field of IC is partly accounting related, which includes internal and external communication.

A concept that aligns with the importance of external communication is corporate reporting, introduced in Sect. 2.8. The aims of corporate reporting are to communicate the strategy of an organisation and to define and align the tasks necessary to accomplish the organisation's goals to outside parties (Zerfaß, 2009). This communication is not a one-way street and a way for organisations to establish the needs and demands of their stakeholders, which is at the basis of stakeholder theory. If stakeholders are ignored the organisation would be made aware of their negligence, as the example of Shell presented in Sect. 5.2 shows. According to Abhayawansa (2014), frameworks for disclosure of intellectual capital, like those presented in Sect. 2.9, which were developed during the second stage of IC research "are driven by an assumed demand for IC information from capital market participants" (Abhayawansa, 2014, p. 137). This statement highlights the recognised importance of stakeholders and their power over organisations, which in inherent in stakeholder theory.

For NPOs, Fletcher, Guthrie, Steane, Roos, and Pike (2003) focussed their research "on determining its (intangible) value from a stakeholder perspective" (Fletcher et al., 2003, p. 507), acknowledging the importance of stakeholders. Bronzetti, Mazzotta, Puntillo, Silvestri, and Veltri (2011), writing about IC reporting practices in the non-profit sector, build upon stakeholder theory as well, as visible in their statement that it is important "to properly answer to the different stakeholders' expectations within the organizations mission and values" (Bronzetti et al., 2011, p. 17).

A recent project in the accounting field is based on both the stakeholder theory and the resource dependency theory: integrated reporting by the IIRC, introduced in Sect. 2.9.6. While not explicitly stated their arguments for the necessity of integrated reporting includes views of these theories:

> "It makes visible an organization's use of and dependence on different resources and relationships or "capitals" (...) and the organization's access to and impact on them. Reporting this information is critical to:
>
> - a meaningful assessment of the long-term viability of the organization's business model and strategy;
> - meeting the information needs of investors and other stakeholders; and
> - ultimately, the effective allocation of scarce resources." (The IIRC, 2011, p. 2)

A regulation supporting the focus on both stakeholder theory and resource dependency theory as well is the DRS 20, which aims to ensure the provision of information regarding the use of the entrusted resources within the reporting period (Deutsches Rechnungslegungs Standards Commitee e.V., 2012). This aim is also reflected in the requirement for the tax shelter status of NPOs which is dependent on the provision of information on the allocation of resources (KPMG, 2012). Additionally, van Broekhoven (2008) argued that donors and volunteers want to be sure that the money and time they donate is used in a considerate way towards the social aim. Hence, NPOs need to inform their stakeholders on how resources are used and what they are needed for in relation to value creation. These examples of the use of stakeholder theory and resource dependency theory for research into accounting of IC documented in literature, together with the link to the origins of IC and the relationship to the other theories highlighted in this section, form a strong case to address the research questions, utilising these two theories as the theoretical framework for the analysis of the data collected and described in Sect. 6.5.

References

Abhayawansa, S. A. (2014). A review of guidelines and frameworks on external reporting of intellectual capital. *Journal of Intellectual Capital, 15*(1), 100–141. doi:10.1108/JIC-04-2013-0046.

Adelberg, A. H. (1983). The accounting syntactic complexity formula: A new instrument for predicting the readability of selected accounting communications. *Accounting and Business Research, 13*(51), 163–175. doi:10.1080/00014788.1983.9729749.

An, Y., Davey, H., & Eggleton, I. R. C. (2011). Towards a comprehensive theoretical framework for voluntary IC disclosure. *Journal of Intellectual Capital, 12*(4), 571–585. doi:10.1108/14691931111181733.

Arvidsson, S. (2011). Disclosure of non-financial information in the annual report: A management-team perspective. *Journal of Intellectual Capital, 12*(2), 277–300. doi:10.1108/14691931111123421.

Barney, J. (1991). Firm resources and sustained competitive advantage. *Journal of Management, 17*(1), 99–120. doi:10.1177/014920639101700108.

Beattie, V. (2013, April 16). Conversation with Vivien Beattie at BAFA Annual Conference 2013.

Beattie, V., & Smith, S. J. (2013). Value creation and business models: Refocusing the intellectual capital debate. *The British Accounting Review, 45*(4), 234–254. doi:10.1016/j.bar.2013.06.001.

Brennan, N., & Connell, B. (2000). Intellectual capital: Current issues and policy implications. *Journal of Intellectual Capital, 1*(3), 206–240. doi:10.1108/14691930010350792.

Bronzetti, G., Mazzotta, R., Puntillo, P., Silvestri, A., & Veltri, S. (2011). *Intellectual capital reporting practices in the non-profit sector*. Sumy: Virtus Interpress. Accessed July 31, 2012, from http://virtusinterpress.com/IMG/pdf/Sample_Chapter-2.pdf

Brüggen, A., Vergauwen, P., & Dao, M. (2009). Determinants of intellectual capital disclosure: Evidence from Australia. *Management Decision, 47*(2), 233–245. doi:10.1108/00251740910938894.

Brugha, R., & Varvasovszky, Z. (2000). Stakeholder analysis: A review. *Health Policy and Planning, 15*(3), 239–246. doi:10.1093/heapol/15.3.239.

Deephouse, D. L., & Suchman, M. C. (2008). Legitimacy in organizational institutionalism. In R. Greenwood et al. (Eds.), *The Sage handbook of organizational institutionalism* (pp. 49–77). London: SAGE.

Deutsches Rechnungslegungs Standards Commitee e.V. (2012). *Deutscher Rechnungslegungs Standard Nr. 20 (DRS 20)* (pp. 1–56). Accessed November 23, 2015, from www.drsc.de/docs/press_releases/2012/120928_DRS20_nearfinal.pdf

Diehl, J. (2008). Die Unicef-Krise: Hilfswerk sucht Hilfe. *Spiegel Online*. Accessed February 20, 2014, from http://www.spiegel.de/politik/deutschland/unicef-krise-hilfswerk-sucht-hilfe-a-536641.html

DiMaggio, P. J., & Powell, W. W. (1983). The iron cage revisited: Institutional isomorphism and collective rationality in organizational fields. *American Sociological Review, 48*, 147–160.

Dumay, J., & Cai, L. (2015). Using content analysis as a research methodology for investigating intellectual capital disclosure: A critique. *Journal of Intellectual Capital, 16*(1), 121–155. doi:10.1108/JIC-04-2014-0043.

Edvinsson, L. (2013). IC 21: Reflections from 21 years of IC practice and theory. *Journal of Intellectual Capital, 14*(1), 163–172. doi:10.1108/14691931311289075.

Edvinsson, L., & Sullivan, P. (1996). Developing a model for managing intellectual capital. *European Management Journal, 14*(4), 356–364. doi:10.1016/0263-2373(96)00022-9.

Eisenhardt, M. (1989). Agency theory: An assessment and review. *The Academy of Management Journal, 14*(1), 57–74.

Elsbach, K. D., & Sutton, R. I. (1992). Acquiring organizational legitimacy through illegitimate actions: A marriage of institutional and impression management theories. *Academy of Management Journal, 35*(4), 699–738. doi:10.2307/256313.

Fletcher, A., Guthrie, J., Steane, P., Roos, G., & Pike, S. (2003). Mapping stakeholder perceptions for a third sector organization. *Journal of Intellectual Capital, 4*(4), 505–527. doi:10.1108/14691930310504536.

Freeman, R. E., & McVea, J. A. (2001). *A stakeholder approach to strategic management*. Charlottesville, VA. doi:10.2139/ssrn.263511.

Göbel, E. (2002). *Neue Institutionenökonomik*. Stuttgart: Lucius & Lucius Verlagsgesellschft mbH.

Greenwood, R., Oliver, C., Sahlin, K., & Suddaby, R. (2008). Introduction. In R. Greenwood et al. (Eds.), *The SAGE handbook of organizational institutionalism* (pp. 1–46). London: SAGE.

Guthrie, J., Petty, R., Yongvanich, K., & Ricceri, F. (2004). Using content analysis as a research method to inquire into intellectual capital reporting. *Journal of Intellectual Capital, 5*(2), 282–293. doi:10.1108/14691930410533704.

Hillman, A. J., Withers, M. C., & Collins, B. J. (2009). Resource dependence theory: A review. *Journal of Management, 35*(6), 1404–1427. doi:10.1177/0149206309343469.

Jepperson, R. (1991). Institutions, institutional effects, and institutionalism. In W. Powell & P. DiMaggio (Eds.), *The new institutionalism in organizational analysis* (pp. 143–163). Chicago: The University of Chicago Press.

Kong, E. (2007). The strategic importance of intellectual capital in the non-profit sector. *Journal of Intellectual Capital, 8*(4), 721–731. doi:10.1108/14691930710830864.

KPMG. (2012). *Rechnungslegung in der Praxis – Bilanzierungs- und Bewertungsfragen nach deutschem Recht bei Non-Profit-Organisationen*, (Homepage). Accessed January 08, 2014, from http://www.kpmg.com/DE/de/Bibliothek/2012/Seiten/Rechnungslegung-in-der-Praxis.aspx

Kuhnle, H., & Banzhaf, J. (2006). *Finanzkommunikation unter IFRS*. München: Verlag Franz Vahlen GmbH.

Lakes, B. (1998). NPO im Spannungsfeld von Solidarität und Wettbewerb. In R. Graf Strachwitz (Ed.), *Dritter Sektor – Dritte Kraft: Versuch einer Standortbestimmung* (pp. 447–462). Stuttgart: Raabe Verlags-GmbH.

Langer, A., & Schröer, A. (2011). Professionalisierung in nonprofit management. In A. Langer & A. Schröer (Eds.), *Professionalisierung in nonprofit management* (pp. 9–31). Wiesbaden: VS Verlag für Sozialwissenschaften.

Lichtsteiner, H., Gmür, M., Giroud, C., & Schauer, R. (2013). *Das Freiburger Management-Modell für Nonprofit Organisationen* (7th ed.). Bern: Haupt Verlag.

Meyer, J. W., & Rowan, B. (1977). Institutionalized organizations: Formal structure as myth and ceremony. In W. W. Powell & P. J. DiMaggio (Eds.), *American Journal of Sociology, 83*(2), 340–363.

O'Dwyer, B., Owen, D., & Unerman, J. (2011). Seeking legitimacy for new assurance forms: The case of assurance on sustainability reporting. *Accounting, Organizations and Society, 36*(1), 31–52. doi:10.1016/j.aos.2011.01.002.

Palmer, D., Biggart, N., & Dick, B. (2008). Is the new institutionalism a theory? In R. Greenwood et al. (Eds.), *The SAGE handbook of organizational institutionalism* (pp. 739–768). London: SAGE.

Parsons, L. M. (2002). *The impact of financial information and voluntary disclosure on contributions to not-for-profit organizations: A field-based experiment*. Houston, TX: University of Houston.

Petrash, G. (1996). Dow' s journey to a knowledge value management culture. *European Management Journal, 73*(4), 365–373.

Pfeffer, J., & Salancik, G. R. (2003). *The external control of organizations*. Stanford: Stanford University Press.

Post, J. E., Preston, L. E., & Sachs, S. (2002). Managing the extended enterprise – The new stakeholder view. *California Management Review, 45*(1), 6–28.

Powell, W. W., & DiMaggio, P. J. (1991). Introduction. In W. W. Powell & P. J. DiMaggio (Eds.), *The new institutionalism in organizational analysis* (pp. 1–38). Chicago, IL: The University of Chicago Press.

Raynard, P. (1998). Coming together. A review of contemporary approaches to social accounting, auditing and reporting in non-profit organisations. *Journal of Business Ethics, 17*, 1471–1479.

Reed, M. S., Graves, A., Dandy, N., Posthumus, H., Hubacek, K., Morris, J., et al. (2009). Who's in and why? A typology of stakeholder analysis methods for natural resource management. *Journal of Environmental Management, 90*(5), 1933–1949. doi:10.1016/j.jenvman.2009.01.001.

Scott, W. R. (2013). *Institutions and organizations* (4th ed.). Thousand Oaks, CA: SAGE.

Suchman, M. C. (1995). Managing legitimacy: Strategic and institutional approaches. *Academy of Management Review, 20*(3), 571–610.

Sveiby, K.-E. (1997). *The new organizational wealth* (1st ed.). San Francisco, CA: Berrett-Koehler.

The IIRC. (2011). *Towards integrated reporting – communicating value in the 21st century*. Accessed May 15, 2012, from http://www.theiirc.org/discussion-paper/

Theuvsen, L. (2011). Professionalisierung des Nonprofit-Managements durch Governance-Kodizes: Eine Analyse der Transparenzwirkung. In A. Langer & A. Schröer (Eds.), *Professionalisierung in nonprofit management* (pp. 131–149). Wiesbaden: VS Verlag für Sozialwissenschaften.

van Broekhoven, R. A. (2008). *Engaging Donors' Trust*. Accessed February 20, 2014, from http://www.icfo.org/ICFO-Publications

Varvasovszky, Z., & Brugha, R. (2000). How to do (or not to do)... A stakeholder analysis. *Health Policy and Planning, 15*(3), 338–345. doi:10.1093/heapol/15.3.338.

Wilke, B. (2008). Die "UNICEF-Krise" – Lehren, Chancen und Risiken für das deutsche Spendenwesen. In *Spenden-Siegel FORUM 2008*. Berlin: Deutsches Zentralinstitut für soziale Fragen (DZI). Accessed February 20, 2014, from http://www.dzi.de/spenderberatung/das-spenden-siegel/spenden-siegelforum/spenden-siegelforum-2008/

Zerfaß, A. (2009). Immaterielle Werte und Unternehmenskommunikation – Herausforderungen für das Kommunikationsmanagement. In K. Möller, M. Piwinger, & A. Zerfaß (Eds.), *Immaterielle Vermögenswerte – Bewertung, Berichterstattung und Kommunikation* (pp. 23–48). Stuttgart: Schäffer-Poeschel Verlag Stuttgart.

Chapter 6
Methods

The comprehensive introduction to the methods applied ensures transparency, replicability of the means as well as reliability and plausibility of the findings produced through these utilised methods. Hence, with the underlying methodology presented in Chap. 4, the methods applied are discussed in this chapter. The research approach is introduced first, highlighting the motivation for the approaches chosen. Next, problem centred expert interviews are introduced in Sect. 6.2, with content analysis in Sect. 6.3 including the approach utilised for the current research described. Next, the sample used for the current research is developed and introduced in Sect. 6.4. Section 6.5 offers insight into the approach used for data collection. The approach to analysing the data collected is provided in Sect. 6.6. To this end, the software utilised is introduced first and descriptions of the approaches to analysing the documents and interviews offered. Thereafter, basic considerations for the analysis are presented. Finally, in Sects. 6.7 and 6.8, the building of the coding frame is illustrated and the approach to coding selected material is described, respectively.

6.1 Research Approach

Dumay and Cai (2014) reviewed papers on the disclosure of intellectual capital that used quantitative or qualitative content analysis as a research methodology with three major findings. Their first finding is that the majority of researchers utilising content analysis focus on the analysis of publicly listed companies' annual reports. Reviewing the articles regarding their recommendations for future research, most articles called for a larger sample size, extended longitudinal studies, and focus on other jurisdictions (Dumay & Cai, 2014). Second, the use of more sources than just annual reports is recommended, since an approach including several sources of data

K. Blankenburg, *Intellectual Capital in German Non-profit Organisations*,
Contributions to Management Science, DOI 10.1007/978-3-319-62655-0_6

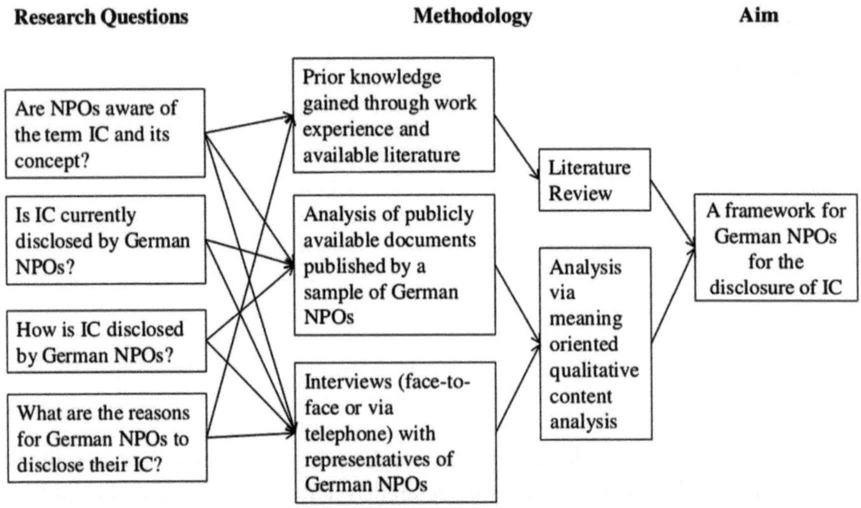

Fig. 6.1 Systematic methodological approach to research questions (Source: Author)

and mixed methods for analysis allow a validation of data and findings (Brüggen, Vergauwen, & Dao, 2009; Denzin & Lincoln, 2011; Dumay & Cai, 2014). Finally, Dumay and Cai (2014) state that IC research is most important if it is significant for practice. To answer this call, a mix of inductive and deductive approaches was applied for the current research (Fig. 6.1). This mixture of qualitative research involving inductive and deductive approaches ensures the reliability and validity of the findings (Mayring, 1996).

Prior knowledge gained through experience by working for a German NPO and informal conversations with former colleagues (during private meetings), combined with findings from prior literature, pointed towards a lack of knowledge of the term IC and the concept of IC by German NPOs. To investigate whether this finding holds true in practice and to enquire how NPOs actually disclose their IC, a qualitative content analysis of publicly available documents published by nine German NPOs was conducted. Also, an interview guide for interviews was developed on the basis of the literature review. Interviews were chosen as the appropriate research method, as open questions allow for narrative answers and thereby balance the possibly biased prior knowledge of the researcher (Witzel, 2000). Problem-centred expert interviews were conducted face-to-face or via telephone to validate the lack of knowledge of IC in practice and to gain deeper insight into the everyday approach to the disclosure of IC by German NPOs. For the analysis of the interviews and the documents a meaning-oriented content analysis was conducted which is further introduced in Sect. 6.3. In short, the recommendation by Dumay and Cai (2014) is answered through the use of problem-centred expert interviews and a qualitative content analysis of several publications by NPOs. Both approaches are introduced and discussed in the next sections.

6.2 Problem-Centred Expert Interviews

Interviews are a method for collecting linguistic data. They always entail subjective views, offering insights into the reasons for behaviour, structures, or processes, for example, that cannot be detected by observation or the review of documents alone (Mayring, 1996). There are various characteristics to differentiate forms of interviews. Based on the degree of freedom of the interviewee, open and closed interviews can be distinguished. An open interview offers the interviewee the possibility to convey his or her own perspective or story on a topic. The disadvantages of open interviews are the danger of the interviewee digressing from the subject, the accumulation of a large amount of data, and the difficulty of comparing the stories provided. A closed interview, in contrast, limits responses to pre-set answers which the interviewee can choose from (Mayring, 1996), thereby making the answers more comparable but lacking the depth of open questions (Saunders, Lewis, & Thornhill, 2009).

Depending on the degree of freedom of the interviewer, structured, semi-structured, and unstructured interviews can be differentiated. Structured interviews are based on a questionnaire that is worked through systematically, corresponding to closed interviews from the interviewee perspective (Mayring, 1996). Again, this type of interview offers a good comparability of answers but lacks depth (Saunders et al., 2009). An unstructured interview is the opposite approach to the structured interview. It is based on few pre-set questions to encourage the natural development of a story by the interviewee or a conversation between the interviewee and the interviewer (Mayring, 1996). The advantages and disadvantages are the same as those of open interviews mentioned above. A semi-structured interview is based on a pre-set list of questions that operate as a guideline for the interviewer. However, semi-structured interviews attempt to keep the conversation as open as possible to allow for subjective answers and the development of the interviewee's own line of arguments (Mayring, 1996). Using an interview guide does not necessarily mean that the questions have to be asked the same way or the in same order in every interview. Even if questions are asked in completely the same way, chances are high that different interviewees will understand the questions in different ways (Rosenthal, 2008). Hence, semi-structured interviews are a middle ground between structured and unstructured interviews. Another advantage of semi-structured interviews is the possibility to adapt questions to the terminology used by the interviewee, again supporting subjective statements and storytelling (Rosenthal, 2008). Additionally, the interviewer can react to statements or the specific situation with appropriate questions while still keeping the conversation focused on a particular topic through the pre-established interview guide (Mayring, 1996; Saunders et al., 2009). The approach of problem-centred semi-structured interviews theoretically balances the necessity of open questions and directing the discussion (Mayring, 1996; Witzel, 2000). However, the challenge remaining is to find the right balance between, on the one hand, openness and as little influence on the interviewee as possible, and the level of structure of the interview on the other (Gläser & Laudel, 2010).

The focus of an interview is another characteristic with which to differentiate forms of interviews. For instance, problem-centred interviews focus on one problem, while in-depth interviews or narrative interviews focus on the detailed story of the interviewee (Mayring, 1996). For the current research, problem-centred expert interviews were conducted. Problem-centred interviews aim for an unbiased approach to individual views on a particular topic (Witzel, 2000) with the intent of connecting prior knowledge with practical knowledge to thus gain a better understanding of a problem (Witzel & Reiter, 2012). According to Witzel and Reiter (2012), problem-centred interviews are an appropriate approach when research focuses on a specific topic, the approach to a specific topic, or when the reasons for a certain behaviour and view is enquired (Witzel & Reiter, 2012). Also,

> "the research question has to correspond to an everyday problem in the perspective of *practical knowledge* [italic in original text] that the respondent can articulate and also has an interest in dealing with" (Witzel & Reiter, 2012, p. 5)

Various definitions and explanations exist for who might be labelled an 'expert' (Bogner & Menz, 2009a; Rosenthal, 2008). As defined in Sect. 2.3, an expert is someone who is not only familiar with every aspect of a specific topic, process, or resource but is able to develop improvements for everyone within the area of expertise (Sveiby, 1997). Bogner and Menz (2009a) describe three common possible approaches for identifying experts. First, the voluntaristic approach which is based on the idea that every person is an expert of his or her own life, corresponding to the aforementioned definition. However, this approach was criticised for being too broad (Bogner & Menz, 2009a). The second approach identified is the constructivist approach, which can be differentiated into methodological-rational and social-representational approaches. The former is based on the idea that, to a certain degree, expertise is the construct of the researcher (Bogner & Menz, 2009a). In other words, an expert is defined as such by the researcher based on the person's experience in the usage of their particular knowledge that is valuable for the research in question (Meuser & Nagel, 2009). In this case, the identification of an expert is based more or less on objective factual knowledge (Bogner & Menz, 2009a). According to the social-representational approach, a person is designated an expert by society, visible, for instance, through a title. A focus on the sociology of knowledge is the foundation for the third approach identified which differentiates between common knowledge, expertise through research, and expert knowledge through daily routine (Bogner & Menz, 2009a). In the end, Bogner and Menz (2009a) recommend turning away from the approaches they identified and to look for the social relevance of a person's expertise instead. They suggest that an expert has in-depth knowledge in a specific area upon which he or she acts in a relevant way. Put differently, an expert has process knowledge, technical knowledge, and expert knowledge and is characterised by his or her ability to influence his or her field of expertise significantly.

Another approach to identifying experts is based on the segmentation of expert interviews, which can be segmented into explorative and systematising expert interviews. Explorative expert interviews serve to gain an initial understanding of a topic and to structure the topic area. Systematising expert interviews aim to extract in-depth theoretical and practical experience gained within the area of interest (Bogner & Menz, 2009a). In this case, the expert is the owner of specific expert knowledge that is otherwise not accessible. This expert knowledge is usually investigated via an interview based on a pre-set list of questions (Bogner & Menz, 2009a), i.e. semi-structured interviews. The current research utilises systematising expert interviews to gain a deeper insight into the level of NPOs' awareness of the term IC and its concept, the way IC is disclosed, the reasons for and against IC disclosure, and how IC is disclosed.

Semi-structured interviews are suitable for expert interviews. Most individuals who are asked to participate in an interview as experts have a specific idea of how an interview is going to proceed. In the business context, the common communication process includes giving answers to questions without going into too much detail as the explanation of details requires too much time (Trinczek, 2009). Trinczek (2009) highlights that beginning an expert interview with managers by asking them to explain as much as possible about a topic is not a successful strategy. However, experts might open up more during the interview and offer comprehensive stories after they have realised that the interview is not a common communication process. Therefore, a semi-structured interview is recommendable for expert interviews in a business context as it offers a guideline of questions while providing the possibility for extensive narration (Trinczek, 2009).

Whichever approach is chosen to identify experts, an assumption that always needs to be reviewed critically is the belief that experts provide objective information. Experts might disclose subjective experiences or opinions based on their individual world view (Bogner & Menz, 2009b; Witzel & Reiter, 2012). Also, increasing job specialisation has resulted in more experts, but at the same time, has reduced the expertise one person can accumulate in a particular area (Bogner & Menz, 2009b). For instance, it is not possible today to be an expert in information technology anymore since too many areas have evolved within this field. As a result, experts might not be aware of every detail of their probably vast and growing area of expertise (Bogner & Menz, 2009b) and researchers need to question the information they receive from experts (Bogner & Menz, 2009b). As a consequence for the current research, a qualitative content analysis of publicly available documents as well as the interviews was conducted and the findings compared afterwards to establish their validity.

6.3 Content Analysis

Content analysis aims to extrapolate meaning from material. The material reviewed is multifaceted, as it can include texts, movies, audio recordings, art, constructions, etc. (Mayring, 1996). Content analysis is often differentiated into quantitative and qualitative content analysis (Gläser & Laudel, 2010; Kuckartz, 2012; Mayring, 1996; Schreier, 2012). Quantitative content analysis is based on the idea that a correlation exists between the importance of an issue and the frequency of appearance of certain codes within the text (Guthrie, Petty, Yongvanich, & Ricceri, 2004; Krippendorff, 2004). These codes are developed by building a closed coding system first, followed by a segmentation of the text in question into units to be analysed. Next, the text is checked for relevant information, and finally this information is assigned to one of the codes established in step one (Gläser & Laudel, 2010). While quantitative content analysis is very structured and thus provides transparency and reliability, its main critique is that it underestimates the context of a text (Gläser & Laudel, 2010).

Qualitative content analysis, in contrast, aims to consider the complexity of the content of the material. It reduces data, shifting the focus from the individual level to the macro level (Schreier, 2012). Commonly qualitative content analysis is a systematic approach that follows several steps. While there are some differences in the degree of detail of these steps, the overall approach is similar. The following steps are suggested by Schreier (2012, p. 6):

1. "Deciding on your research question
2. Selecting your material
3. Building a coding frame
4. Dividing your material into units of coding
5. Trying out your coding frame
6. Evaluating and modifying your coding frame
7. Main analysis
8. Interpreting and presenting your findings"

Smith and Taffler (2000) differentiate content analysis into form-oriented analysis and meaning-oriented analysis. The former is predominantly quantitative, focussing on word counts and explicit information. Meaning-oriented analysis, in comparison, is qualitative and focuses on the implicit meaning of a text (Smith & Taffler, 2000). The lines between these two forms of content analysis as well as between meaning-oriented content analysis and discourse analysis are indistinct (Merkl-Davies, Brennan, & Vourvachis, 2014). A distinctive difference between content analysis and discourse analysis, however, is the way language is perceived. Discourse analysis regards language as reflecting and constructing social reality. Content analysis on the other hand views "language as a tool for description [. . .] and as a medium for communication" (Merkl-Davies et al., 2014, p. 13) which is the perspective of the current research and the reason for consequently conducting content analysis. A qualitative, i.e. meaning-oriented, focus is utilized since the literature review and prior experience point towards IC not necessarily being expressed explicitly.

Mayring (1996) identifies three possible intended outcomes of qualitative content analysis. One aim is to reduce the available material to its main content through abstraction, thereby creating a realistic portrayal of the material. Another aim is explication, i.e. individual parts of the text such as terms or sentences are clarified and interpreted. The third aim is to either create a profile of the text or to judge the text based on designated criteria, both of which are achieved by filtering certain aspects from a text (Mayring, 1996). The chosen aim affects the development of categories for coding, which is a central aspect of any content analysis. For qualitative content analysis, coding is not predetermined, but developed while reading the relevant texts (Mayring, 1996; Merkl-Davies et al., 2014), i.e. it takes an inductive approach. Since the lines between the approaches are blurry (Merkl-Davies et al., 2014), certain aspects of quantitative content analysis can be included into the qualitative approach. Mayring (1996) recommends the following course of action for the development of categories. First, the research question, the theory and the subject matter are defined. Next, criteria for categories need to be selected deductively, taking the subject and the aim of the analysis into account. Armed with these criteria, the text is read carefully, line by line. When a passage in the text fits the defined criteria for a category, a category is constructed. Other passages fitting into this category are added. Passages that do not fit the particular category are used to build new categories if they fit the criteria for categories generally defined in the beginning. After up to half the material is processed this way, the categories found are revised and a fix set of categories defined. Based on these categories, all material is processed, evaluated and interpreted.

Gläser and Laudel (2010) criticise the approach introduced by Mayring for taking less than half of the material into account when developing categories, not allowing further development during the coding, and adjusting the categories to the material and removing theory-driven categories in the process (Gläser & Laudel, 2010). Based on their critique, Gläser and Laudel (2010) developed the approach by Mayring (1996) further. Their basic idea is that text contains information and is not part of the information itself. Therefore, instead of developing categories and coding material, Gläser and Laudel (2010) recommend defining variables to extract information from the text, i.e. to break away from the original material. Instead of replacing theory-driven categories as Mayring (1996) recommends, Gläser and Laudel (2010) suggest complementing them.

Gläser and Laudel's (2010) approach for a qualitative analysis follows five main steps (see Fig. 6.2). First, preliminary considerations are developed, such as the research question, a theoretical analysis of the subject matter i.e. the literature review, and the definition of variables. These variables are based on the literature review and assumptions on causal dependencies. The next step is preparation, which is content-related on the one hand and related to the methodology on the other. Content-related preparation for the qualitative content analysis includes the development of a search-grid based on the literature review and other preliminary considerations in order to ensure that all relevant information to answer the research question is recognised within the text analysed. If the material to be analysed was compiled empirically, the experiences in collecting the data are considered as well (Gläser & Laudel, 2010). For example, if a view or fact is mentioned during the interviews that was not perceived during the literature review, this view or fact is included into the search-grid from the beginning. In short, as part of the content-related preparation, all available knowledge is utilised to optimise the preparation for extraction. As part of the methodological preparation, the relevant material and the units of analysis are established, such as texts, particular chapters or paragraphs

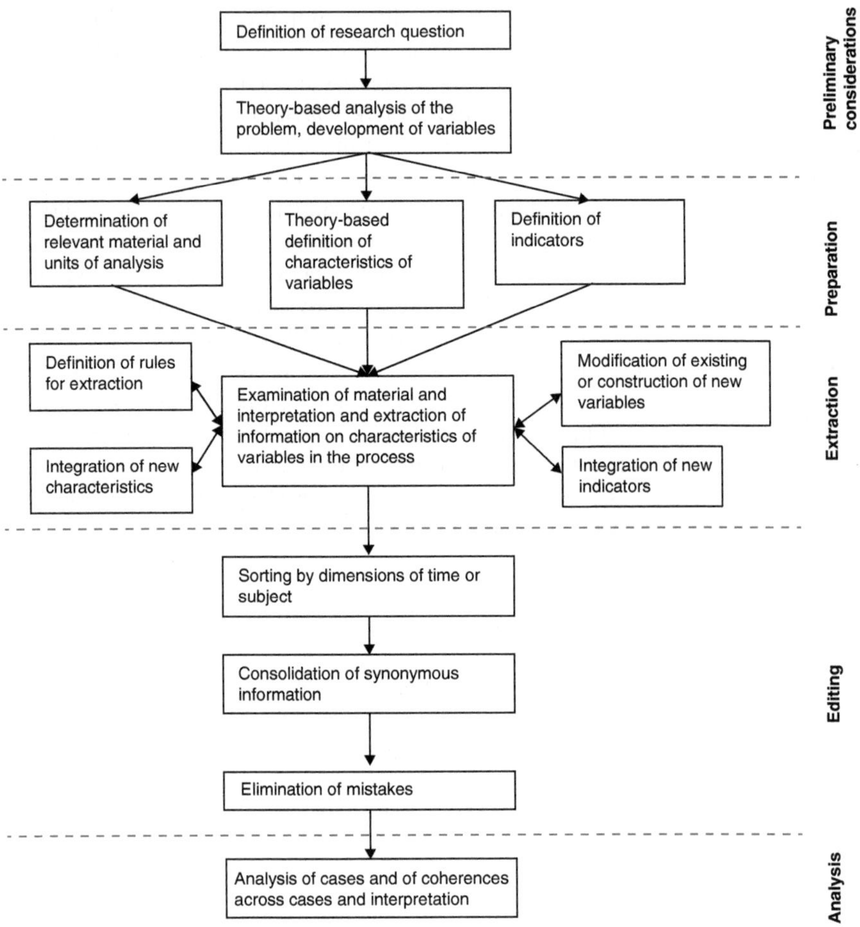

Fig. 6.2 Process of qualitative content analysis as per Gläser and Laudel (2010)

of texts, or sentences. Additionally, characteristics of variables are defined more closely based on a prior literature review (Gläser & Laudel, 2010).

Extraction is the third step, which starts with reading the material to establish whether any relevant information is included in the particular document and what variable this information fits to. The search grid and the characteristics of variables, developed in step two, act as decision guidance. If information can be assigned to more than one variable, extraction rules need to be defined to ensure a transparent and consistent approach. In case relevant information cannot be assigned to any defined variable, a new variable is constructed. Relevant information is extracted from the original material, and the original material is abandoned. It needs to be ensured that the original material and the extracted information are numbered consecutively to ensure that the reference is not lost in case it needs to be reconstructed (Gläser & Laudel, 2010).

The following fourth step is editing of the information collected. This step includes consolidating synonymous information, correcting mistakes and structuring the information based on its content. If necessary, the consolidation can take place several times to reduce the material further. Every step during the consolidation of information is to be saved and recorded separately to ensure transparency. Also, cases and coherences across cases are identified in reference to the research question (Gläser & Laudel, 2010). The last step is the analysis and interpretation of the information in order to answer the empirical research questions. To this end, the assumptions on causal dependencies made in the first step are analysed, for instance, by looking for similarities and differences within the collected information as well as for unexpected information (Gläser & Laudel, 2010).

For the present research, the approaches by Mayring (1996), Gläser and Laudel (2010), and Schreier (2012) were used to define the steps followed for analysis:

1. Basic considerations
    a. Definition of research question
    b. Development of assumptions based on literature review
    c. Selection of relevant material
    d. Definition of units of analysis
2. Building of coding frame
3. Coding of selected material and modification of coding frame
4. Analysis
5. Interpretation

Basic considerations included the research questions, assumptions based on the literature review as well as the selection and collection of relevant material and the definition of the units of analysis. To build the coding frame, main categories were defined and codes assigned to each category. These categories and codes were based on the research questions, the assumptions presented in step one as well as observations made while collecting material. In other words, the coding frame consists of deductively as well as inductively developed variables. In the next step, the selected material was read carefully and coded. If information could not be assigned to any of the defined variables, a new code was constructed. When a unit could be assigned to more than one variable, the definition of those codes needed to be checked and modified if necessary. If such a case occurred, any information coded with the code in question needed to be checked and the proper use of the further defined code verified. The analysis differed slightly for documents and interviews. Thus, they were analysed independently and later compared in the analysis process. Section 6.6 offers a more detailed insight into the approach to analysis taken for the current research. The interpretation was based on the findings established during the analysis and answers the research questions.

Several limitations common to qualitative content analysis needed to be considered. One limitation was subjectivity (Abeysekera, 2006; Guthrie et al., 2004). Krippendorff (2004, p. 81) stated that "data are always the products of chosen procedures and are always geared toward particular ends". Steenkamp and Northcott (2007) identified that

> "Content analysis data are therefore made, rather than discovered, by the researcher. They result from the procedures the researcher has chosen to answer questions concerning the phenomena explored in given texts." (Steenkamp & Northcott, 2007, p. 13)

Merkl-Davies et al. (2014), describing meaning-oriented content analysis, recommended that at least two researchers perform the coding to minimise the danger of bias. As it was not possible to follow this recommendation for the current research, several measures were taken instead: A work group of three PhD-Students was established to spot check the coding that each member of the group carried out for her book. Further, the quality measures for coding based on recommendations by Miles and Huberman (1994), as described in Sect. 5.3, were adhered to. Additionally, the qualitative content analysis of the documents and the interviews, independent from one another, allow for validation of the findings by comparing these findings afterwards. Finally, the following quality criteria stated by Merkl-Davies et al. (2014) were observed (Table 6.1). To ensure qualitative soundness in qualitative research, it has to be transferable to other contexts, dependable in the sense that other researchers are able to repeat the research, and

Table 6.1 Overview of quality criteria for meaning-oriented text analysis approaches

	Definition	Strategies to satisfy [quality] criterion
Credibility	The extent to which the findings are congruent with reality	– Purposeful sampling – Prolonged engagement with text and context by means of repeated close reading – Establishing plausible case that patterns in the meaning of text are constitutive of reality in some way
Transferability	The extent to which findings can be applied to other context	– Purposeful sampling – Providing detailed ('thick') description of the case to allow reader to judge what other contexts may be informed by the findings
Dependability	The ability of other researchers to repeat the work, if not necessarily to gain the same results	–Preceding the analysis by repeated 'close reading' of text by multiple researchers – Showing consistency in interpretation, i.e. same phenomena always matched with the same constructs, by providing a detailed account on how coding decisions were made, e.g. by means of annotated text excerpts (systematic approach)
Confirmability	The extent to which the result of text analysis can be confirmed or corroborated by the reader	– Tying together text analysis and findings in such a way that reader is able to confirm adequacy of findings (transparency)

Merkl-Davies et al. (2014)

confirmable by the reader in regard to the results (Merkl-Davies et al., 2014). The latter was accomplished by providing the greatest level of transparency possible for approaches used, sampling, and the coding processes.

Furthermore, qualitative research has to conform to reality. Content analysis in general is based on the perspective that language is as a tool for description. Within quantitative content analysis, text is regarded as expressing pre-existing reality and valid for every reader. Quantitative content analysis on the other hand, recognises that a text is not necessarily explicit in its meaning and thus understanding of the meaning can differ. To ensure that qualitative research conforms to reality for the reader, the process of analysing a document needs to be illustrated in detail (Merkl-Davies et al., 2014).

Another facet relating to quality that needed to be considered was that the reliability of documents differs. Official records, such as deed registration, registrations of birth, or death certificates are regarded as reliable and unbiased. Newspaper articles, on the other hand, need to be analysed (Mayring, 1996) while contemplating the type of newspaper, its ownership structure, and possible aim of the individual article, for example. When analysing the content, the source needs to be considered as well as the desired impact of the material (Mayring, 1996). For the current research, only documents were analysed that were produced and published by the organisations and that were meant for their stakeholders. The incentive for NPOs to bias their documents was high. However, the aim of the current research was to establish whether NPOs report IC at all, the medium used, and whether quantitative or narrative forms are preferred. In this case, the means through which NPOs described their IC or the message they wanted to convey is of secondary importance.

A facet of disclosure not included in any of the content analysis approaches introduced is graphical disclosure or visual rhetoric, even though "visual forms such as graphs, tables and pictures have been found to provide an immediate and effective means of disclosure" (Beattie & Thomson, 2007, p. 143). Davison (2014) presents an approach to visual rhetoric in accounting. First of all, pictures, graphs, tables, etc. can be divided into the image on the one hand, and their linguistic message i.e. words, such as those in a product label, logo, or caption, on the other. The image expresses a denoted and a connoted message at the same time. For example, a picture of a money box in the form of a pig denotes a porcelain figurine in form of a pig with a slot at the top and a possibility to open the figurine. The connoted message is that of saving, economizing, making provisions, and possibly even security and childhood. Both messages are "inextricably intermingled" (Davison, 2014, p. 13) and form the actual message. Visual rhetoric is far more complex than the aforementioned facets, and the possibility of distortion (Bonga & Jegers, 2009) and abuse (Beattie & Jones, 1992) needs to be considered. For the current research, the theory of denoted and connoted messages (Davison, 2014) is not used to analyse the actual messages as the objective is to determine whether IC is expressed through visual disclosures at all. In other words, photos, graphs, and tables in the documents are checked for expressions of IC but are not analysed further. Future research on both visual rhetoric and the bias of IC descriptions would be interesting and complement the information generated with the current research.

6.4 The Sample

6.4.1 Foundation of the Sample

Currently, there is no requirement for all German NPOs to centrally register anywhere. Consequently, there is no comprehensive list of NPOs in Germany. The most extensive reliable source for NPOs in Germany is the DZI. As mentioned in Sect. 3.3, the DZI offers advisory service to people who want to donate money to NPOs (Neff, 2014). For this cause, the DZI collects data and assesses donation-soliciting NPOs to ensure that the aim proclaimed by the organisations is actually worked towards and that the money donated is used accordingly (Deutsches Zentralinstitut für soziale Fragen, n.d.). Since 2004, all German donation-soliciting NPOs can apply for the DZI Spenden-Siegel, a seal-of-approval. Before 2004, only organisations with "social, particularly humanitarian caritative goals" (Deutsches Zentralinstitut für soziale Fragen, 2011) were able to apply.

With the Spenden-Siegel, NPOs commit to a goal-oriented, economical, and effective application of funds, meaningful and audited financial reporting, clear, true, open, and objective/factual promotion and public relations, effective supervision, and transparency towards the public (Deutsches Zentralinstitut für soziale Fragen, 2011). The Spenden-Siegel is not accredited to every organisation that applies, but NPOs need to fulfil specific criteria, namely (Deutsches Zentralinstitut für soziale Fragen, 2011):

- have either a legal capacity or definite non-incorporated NPOs (see Sect. 3.3 for differentiation), obey the law and respect the human rights
- have their own name, decision-making structure, public image, account and accounting
- follow their own charter or terms of reference, which state the aim and area of activity as well as structure and task of all entities clearly
- is recognised as tax-privileged according to German law
- is located in Germany
- is at least two years old
- collects more than 25,000 € donations per year.

The criteria the DZI applies to assess an organisation are based on experience gained through over 90 years of advisory service. Questions asked and concerns raised regularly by people who contacted the advisory service of the DZI were taken into account (Neff, 2014). Also, the idea of a Spenden-Siegel in general was not developed by the DZI but was adopted from other organisation in various countries like Switzerland, the Netherlands, the USA, and Sweden (Neff, 2014).

In addition to the organisations accredited with the Spenden-Siegel, another 110 organisations are listed on the DZI homepage. These NPOs are not necessarily less efficient or less trustworthy. They simply either did not apply for the Spenden-Spiegel or do not provide the same amount of information compared to those with the Spenden-Siegel (Neff, 2014). This reduced transparency makes them less comparable and therefore unsuitable for the current research project.

As illustrated in Sect. 3.3, the German non-profit sector is heterogeneous and includes organisations of various legal forms with different sources of income and employment structures and diverse areas of work. To establish common themes regarding the handling of IC, maximum variation sampling is applied for the current research. This type of sampling starts with the identification of various characteristics of possible organisations for the sample (Saunders et al., 2009). Hence, in a first step, the data provided by the DZI on the 241 NPOs accredited with the Spenden-Siegel were collected and transferred to an Excel sheet. Due to specific tax laws for organisations run by the church, 21 organisations labelled with the tax status 'clerical' are not taken into account for the sample, leaving 220 organisations. The resulting list provided a good overview on the data available and offered the means to arrange, sort, and filter data easily.

Sampling was based on the following basic assumption on the handling of IC of NPOs:

- Location of the NPOs does not make a difference in the way IC is perceived or disclosed
- Long-standing organisations have strong structures and are less able to react to change
- Small NPOs are likely to be less professionalised, i.e. one person takes on several roles, while in bigger NPOs, tasks are more departmentalised
- NPOs mainly composed of volunteers disclose IC differently than those NPOs consisting of employees
- NPOs with international branches face different standards and demands than those based and working solely in Germany
- There is a connection between the fundraising performance of NPOs and their approach to the disclosure of IC, since the reporting of IC effects fundraising.

Consequently, the criteria utilised for sampling are: longevity, size and composition of workforce, revenue, level of internationality, fundraising performance, and location. Each criterion is illustrated further in the next sections, followed by a description of the resulting sample.

6.4.2 Longevity

First, the organisations were sorted by year of foundation. It was noticeable that there was a break in the number of foundations of NPOs between 1914 and 1949, i.e. the First and Second World Wars. Additionally, the data shows that the foundation of NPOs started again slowly after World War II. To gain a more detailed overview of the number of NPOs founded after 1948, the 220 NPOs are converted into a bar chart illustrating the number of foundations per year (Fig. 6.3). It is detectable that the average number of foundations of 1.7 per year increased

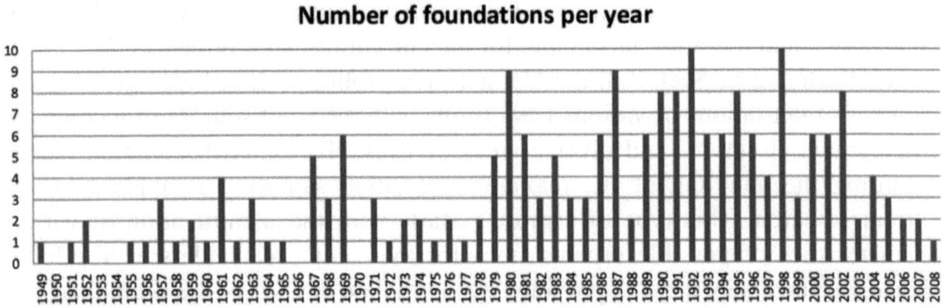

Fig. 6.3 Number of foundation of NPOs in Germany per year (Source: Author; based on Deutsches Zentralinstitut für soziale Fragen, n.d.)

after 1978 to 5.3 organisations per year. Literature does not provide reasons for the peaks and declines of foundations of NPOs. Nevertheless, a probable reason for this increase is that the German Abgabenordnung, regulating the tax status of organisations including resulting rights and obligations, was revised and passed into German law in 1976 and exempted non-profit organisations from paying income tax and value added tax on their ideational focused work (Brixius, 2011). Another peak is due to the reunification of Germany in 1989. Possible reasons for the decline of foundations after 2002 might be the dotcom-bubble that burst in 2000, which led to fewer funds available for donations, and the Enron scandal in 2001, which created doubt and mistrust. As aforementioned, these reasons are not researched and thus the actual reasons might be different. Since the NPOs considered for the sample are those listed with the DZI, a simple reason could be a decline in the uptake of new organisations into their database for internal reasons.

6.4.3 Size and Composition of Workforce

In the case of the current research, size pertains to an organisation's number of employees and volunteers. Looking at the size based on the number of employees and volunteers, 52 German NPOs do not report any employees and 18 organisations state that no volunteers are active for them. The highest number of employees stated is 14,781 and 33,769 volunteers, both reported by the same NPO and thus the largest German NPO from this perspective. Five NPOs report more than 600 employees and 16 organisations report more than 600 volunteers. Less than ten volunteers are reported by 96 NPOs and less than ten employees by 134 NPOs. Both at the same time, i.e. less than ten employees and less than ten volunteers, are reported by 57 organisations. The seven smallest German NPOs according to the data collected by the DZI report two people working for them, either two employees and no volunteers, two volunteers and no employees, or one of each.

6.4.4 *Revenue*

When using the reported total revenue as a measure, German NPOs can be segmented into three broader groups or ten smaller groups (Fig. 6.4). The broader groups are NPOs reporting a total revenue per year of less than 500,000 Euros (500k), between 500k and five million (mio) Euros, and those reporting more than five million Euros. 59 German NPOs report more than five million Euros total revenue per year, 77 organisations report between 500k and five million Euros total revenue per year, and 84 German NPOs report a total revenue of less than 500k Euros per year. The latter group can be divided into five smaller groups using increments of 100k. This segmentation shows that 40 German NPOs report total revenue of less than 200k Euros per year.

6.4.5 *Level of Internationality*

Catering to the assumption that NPOs with international branches face different standards and demands than those working solely in Germany, the NPOs were segmented further by their national versus international focus. 53 organisations work solely in Germany and the other 167 organisations work internationally. Based on the information provided on their individual homepages, the 167 NPOs working internationally were divided further. 72 of these 167 NPOs focus on raising funds to support existing projects in various countries or help those partners with projects on-site. The other 95 organisations own property and have employees in other countries or are part of international organisations with branches in several

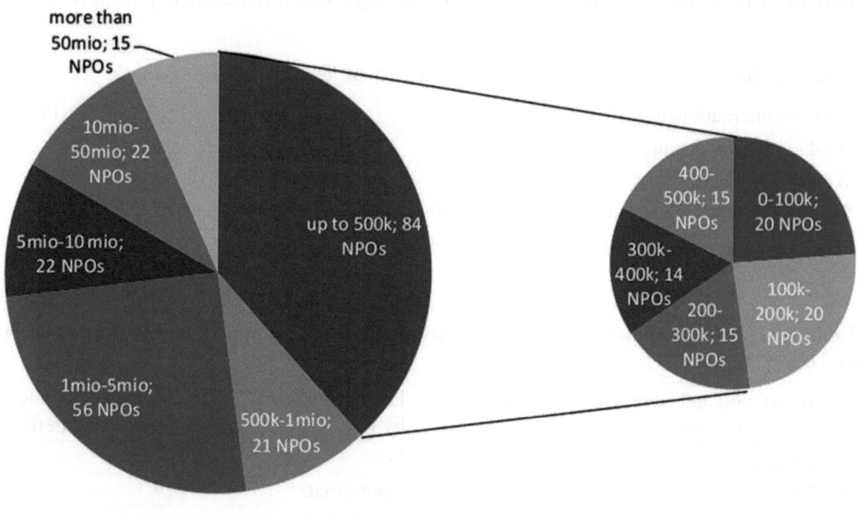

Fig. 6.4 Level of total revenue of German NPOs (Source: Author; based on Deutsches Zentralinstitut für soziale Fragen, n.d.)

countries. Looking at the number of countries NPOs work in or with, 79 German NPOs focus their work on one single country. On the other extreme, one NPO works in 122 specific countries and five NPOs state that they work worldwide. In sum, the level of internationality is divided in three groups: nationally working NPOs, internationally working NPOs, and supporting NPOs (see Table 6.2).

6.4.6 Fundraising Performance

Fundraising performance differentiates NPOs whose administration and advertising expenses are low, as accredited by the DZI, and whose majority of revenue is taken in through fundraising from those organisations fitting the opposite criteria. An assumption is that there is a connection between the fundraising performance of NPOs and their approach to the disclosure of IC. To establish the fundraising performance of NPOs, information provided by the DZI is utilised. The DZI labels the level of these expenses as low, appropriate, and acceptable. A low level is accredited if an organisation does not spend more than 10% of its total revenue in administration and advertising; an appropriate level is ascribed if the expenses remain between 10 to 20% compared to the total revenue; and an acceptable level is attributed in the case of administration and advertising expenses of 20 to 35% compared to the total revenue. For the current research, organisations are differentiated based on these expense levels (Table 6.3).

Ninety five NPOs are accredited a low level, 79 NPOs an appropriate level, and 46 NPOs an acceptable level of expenses. Within these groups, organisations are sorted by their ratio of administration and advertising expenses to the amount of their total revenue collected through fundraising. The most contrary organisations

Table 6.2 Segmentation of German NPOs based on their level of internationality

Level of internationality	Number of NPOs
Working internationally	95
Working nationally	53
Supporting other NPOs that work internationally	72

Source: Author; based on Deutsches Zentralinstitut für soziale Fragen (n.d.)

Table 6.3 Level of administration and advertising expenses of German NPOs as assigned by the DZI

Administration and advertising expenses versus total revenue (%)	Label as defined by DZI	Number of NPOs fitting the criteria
Less than 10	Low	95
10–20	Appropriate	79
20–35	Acceptable	46

Source: Author; based on Deutsches Zentralinstitut für soziale Fragen (n.d.)

are thus the three NPOs that attract all their revenue with a low level of administration and advertising expenses versus those NPOs that have an acceptable level of administration and advertising expenses but generate a small amount of revenue through fundraising. The organisation that fit the latter description generates one sixth of its revenue through fundraising at most.

However, since only one organisation in the sample fits the 'acceptable expenses and low fundraising' description, the significance of the findings of this segmentation is low. Further data generated as a side product of the initial comparison of the fundraising performance of German NPOs is their ranking based on the revenue generated and the amount of funds raised. Four NPOs generated more than 87% of their revenue via fundraising, while three organisations generated less than 16% via fundraising. This segmentation is thus utilised for the analysis.

6.4.7 Location

While laws and regulations for reporting are the same for every organisation in Germany, cultural differences can still bias the way IC is disclosed. Therefore, the location of the organisations needs to be taken into account during analysis. However, instead of comparing every county against all the others, the segmentation into North, South, East, and West (Fig. 6.5) suggested by Droß et al. (2013) is

Fig. 6.5 Division of the Bundesländer into four segments (Droß et al., 2013, p. 7)

adopted and utilized. North includes Schleswig-Holstein, Hamburg, Bremen, und Niedersachsen. South is comprised of Baden-Würtemberg and Bayern, while West includes Rheinland-Pfalz, Saarland, Hessen, and Nordrhein-Westfalen. Last but not least, East consists of Mecklenburg-Vorpommern, Brandenburg, Sachsen, Sachsen-Anhalt, Thüringen, and Berlin.

To gain a more detailed overview of the locations of the organisations, the NPOs were sorted according to their postcode, which reveals their location in Germany. Figure 6.6 visualises the distribution of the NPOs according to their postcode. It is noticeable that most NPOs are located in former West Germany. Of the 23 NPOs counted in postcode 1, 22 are located in Berlin, which is located in the east but partly belonged to West Germany before the unification. 18 of these NPOs located in Berlin campaign for their cause, which explains their choice of location close to the government. Interestingly, the district with the highest number of NPOs (postcode 5) is only the second largest in terms of population. The postcode with the least inhabitants (postcode 0) is the postcode with the least NPOs as well. For the sample, one organisation of each post code area was selected to ensure a fair representation of all areas.

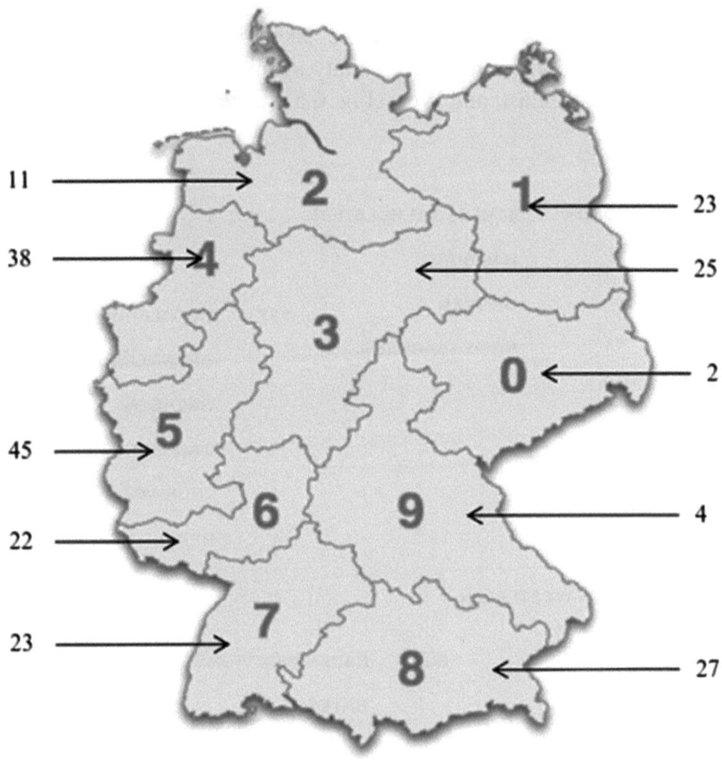

Fig. 6.6 Distribution of German NPOs with a Spenden-Siegel according to their Postcodes (Map with postcode areas available at: http://www.dhbv.de/images/postleitzahlen-deutschland.jpg)

6.4.8 Description of Sample

To determine a significant sample, the most contrary NPOs within the segments longevity, size, and level of expenses were identified first. Next, these NPOs were sorted according to their level of internationality and their post code. Since none of these organisations were located within Postcode 0, the original list was checked for NPOs fitting this criterion. Two organisations are located within the respective geographical area, one working locally in Germany and the other working internationally. Since fewer organisations identified were part of the segment "working in Germany", the corresponding NPO was selected for the sample. Unfortunately, none of the NPOs contacted in postcode sector 9 were willing to participate in the research. If more than one organisation fit the sample, the NPO that can be assigned to the most other segments as well was chosen to ensure the highest possible number within each segment for comparison. All NPOs of the sample fit more than one category at the same time and thus one organisation can represent more than one category for the analysis. Finally, the organisations identified for the individual segments were assigned to the other fitting segments as well. Consequently, a sample of nine NPOs was determined for the current research.

Table 6.4 lists the organisations in alphabetical order, the criteria the organisation fulfils, its post code and geographical area as well as the name of the representative available for an interview and the job title of this representative. For those participants who wish to stay anonymous, names and job titles are not provided but they are identified as 'representative of' their organisation.

With all segments covered, respective areas, i.e. north, east, south or west, were assigned. To ensure that the chosen NPOs represented the four areas realistically, the percentage of inhabitants living within each area versus the total population in Germany of 80,523,746 people in 2014 (Statistische Ämter des Bundes und der Länder, 2014) and the number of organisations selected per area versus the total of nine NPOs were compared (Table 6.5). The result showed an appropriate allocation of NPOs compared to the population density of the areas.

6.5 Data Collection

Empirical data was collected in the form of publicly available documents on the one hand and interviews on the other. Documents were collected via the websites of the organisations for three reasons: First, to check what documents are available this way and thus accessible for everyone. Second, the currentness of the documents available is high, and finally, to save paper as well as the time and costs for mailing. Since the content of websites can be changed rather easily (Striukova, Unerman, & Guthrie, 2008), information presented on websites that was not available as .pdf files was not included into the analysis. The documents of all NPOs in the sample were downloaded within a week, the first week of August 2014, to ensure

Table 6.4 The sample

Organisation (in alphabetical order)	Representative	Job title	Criteria fulfilled	Post code	Area
Albert-Schweitzer-Kinderdorf in Sachsen e.V.	Representative of Albert-Schweitzer-Kinderdorf in Sachsen e.V.	Representatives of Albert-Schweitzer-Kinderdorf in Sachsen e.V.	Working nationally	0	East
Caritasverband der Erzdiözese München und Freising e.V.	Adelheid Utters-Adam	Press Officer (Presse-sprecherin)	Long-standing, second biggest NPO (workforce and revenue), supports internationally, catholic	8	South
Christophorushilfe e.V.	Representative of Christophorushilfe e.V.	Board member	Smallest, working in Germany, protestant	7	South
Die Seenotretter—Deutsche Gesellschaft zur Rettung Schiffbrüchiger (DGzRS)	Christian Stipeldey	Press Officer & Public Relations Manager (Pressesprecher, Leiter der Presse- und Öffentlichkeits-arbeit)	Long-standing, working in Germany	2	North
Direkte Hilfe für Kinder in Not e.V.	Representative of Direkte Hilfe für Kinder in Not e.V.	Board member	Small, supporting internationally	6	West
Johanniter-Unfall-Hilfe e.V.	Therese Raatz	Press Officer (Presse-sprecherin)	Biggest NPO (workforce and revenue), working internationally	1	East
ProBrasil e.V.	Representative A of ProBrasil e.V. Representative B of ProBrasil e.V. Representative C of ProBrasil e.V.	Representatives of ProBrasil e.V.	Small, supporting internationally	4	West
Steinschleuder e.V.	Representative A of Steischleuder e.V. Representative B of Steinschleuder e.V.	Representatives of Steinschleuder e.V.	Small, working globally	5	North
TERRA TECH Förderverein e. V.	Christian Schmetz	Press Officer	Supports internationally, acceptable level of expenses and low level of fundraising	3	West

Source: Author

Table 6.5 Comparison of ratio of inhabitants per area and share of sample

Area	Number of inhabitants	% of overall population	Number of NPOs interviewed	% of sample
North	12,974,572	16.11	2	22.22
South	23,088,682	28.67	2	22.22
West	28,555,375	35.46	3	33.33
East	15,905,117	19.75	2	22.22

Source: Author

comparability at a single point in time. No particular documents were chosen for downloading, i.e. no document was rejected. Three documents had to be excluded from the analysis however, since several parts of each of these documents were not accessible due to technical problems.

Further empirical data was collected via semi-structured expert interviews, which were described in Sect. 6.2. These interviews were conducted face-to-face whenever possible to ensure more spontaneous answers of greater depth (Opdenakker, 2006). Some representatives of smaller organisations were only available for a telephone interview. Reasons indicated were that the NPO has no separate office but the work was done at their private homes or that representatives had only little time to spare and felt that a telephone conversation would take less time.

Following the recommendation by Bogner and Menz (2009a), introduced in Sect. 6.2, individuals whose expertise is of social relevance were chosen as experts for the interviews. In the context of the current research, the person who decides if (expert knowledge), how (technical knowledge), and where (process knowledge) IC is disclosed is considered the expert within an organisation for the topic in question. According to Bogner and Menz (2009a), experts also influence their area of work. A definition for influence is "the power to affect, change or control sb/sth" (Oxford Wordpower Dictionary, 2006, p. 382). While the individuals chosen for the current research might not actively influence the whole third sector, they all influence their respective organisations and their stakeholders, including other organisations, as a result their area of work and independent of the size of the NPO. Hence, possible participants were identified as those volunteers or employees who are in charge of external communication. For bigger NPOs, the responsibility for external communication lies mainly with the public relations department or media/press office. The smaller NPOs contacted do not have entire departments dedicated to external relations. External communication is one part of the work the (mostly) volunteers do for the respective organisations. As a result, the group of representatives interviewed consists of five press officers or public relations managers, four board members, and three representatives for whom external communication is one task of many. The attempt to gain access to accountants of NPOs for interviews was unfortunately unsuccessful.

Possible interviewees were contacted via a telephone call first. During this call the researcher introduced herself shortly and explained the main aim of the research project. Furthermore, anonymity was offered, the approximate investment of time stated, the topic of a possible interviews introduced without mentioning the term IC, and data protection arrangements illustrated. The term IC was not mentioned based on prior experience that IC was either not known or seen as negative. Avoiding the term thus facilitated better access, i.e. higher rate of agreements to participate and the chance to enquire about the awareness of IC during the interviews.

Only one representative contacted declined to take part right away due to lack of time. However, most representatives asked for further written information via e-mail and time to contemplate participation. Hence, they were sent an e-mail with an information sheet introducing the researcher, the project, and data protection arrangements previously introduced in Sect. 4.4.

The fear of being asked sensitive information about the organisation was detectable with several representatives during the initial contact. Therefore, possible interviewees received a list with some of the basic questions as guideline for the interview. Through the provision of these questions, a better idea of the information of interest was provided and consequently the reservations against participating were minimised. Contacts who did not ask for further written information were offered the same information via telephone. The time and place for face-to-face interviews were designated by the participants.

Since the questions in the interviews were open questions, the interviews were audio-recorded to ensure that no information was lost. Also, audio recording the interview meant that the interviewer was able to concentrate on the respondent, the answers given, and further questions to be asked without having to try to write down everything said at the same time. This procedure facilitated a more natural fluency of the discussion. Audio recording of interviews required the explicit consent of the participants which was obtained before the start of each interview by every interviewee present. All participants gave their explicit permission for audio recording. In addition to the audio recording, the interviewer took a few notes during the interviews for two main reasons. First, to help with further enquiries during the interviews, i.e. to remember topics mentioned that needed to be broached again. The second reason was to create a backup in case the audio recorder suddenly stopped working. When the audio recording was successful, the notes on the answers were no longer needed. Notes on disturbances and peculiarities were transferred to the contact summary (Miles & Huberman, 1994). This contact summary is based on the information sheet prepared for every NPO containing basic information on the organisation. The audio records were transcribed based on the transcription rules presented in Sect. 6.6.3 to facilitate their analysis via the analysis software introduced in the next Sect. 6.6.

6.6 Approaches to Analysis

6.6.1 Introduction of Software Utilised

The software used for the analysis is called MAXQDA (Version 11). It was first launched in 1989 and it enables the analysis of qualitative or mixed method data.

MAXQDA facilitates the organisation, categorisation, coding and retrieval of data among other features (Kuckartz, Dresing, Rädiker, & Stefer, 2008; VERBI Software. Consult. Sozialforschung GmbH, n.d.). In addition, it enables memos to be added to each code. For the current research, these memos are used to describe codes and thus help to ensure coherent coding. In case new codes emerge, they can be added at any time during the coding process or existing codes can be renamed or deleted easily if necessary. Another feature of MAXQDA is the possibility to add variables and use these for analysis. For example, the software is able to extract information with a specific code and those that fits a particular variable such as 'volunteers' and 'long-standing organisations'. It is thus a very efficient tool to find statements on specific topics or by organisations with similar characteristics. In sum, MAXQDA is a very helpful tool for systematically sorting and extracting relevant data and supporting the subsequent analysis.

6.6.2 Analysis of Documents

To ensure a systematic and comprehensive analysis of the data gathered, several consecutive steps of analysis were executed. First, all documents downloaded were transferred into MAXQDA and read to gain an impression of the content. Next each document was coded and subsequently all the codes were checked; both processes are described in Sect. 6.8 in more detail. The aim of coding is to discover "all items of relevance" (Fielding & Lee, 1998, p. 26). Based on the codes developed, themes (Creswell, 2009) or pattern codes (Miles & Huberman, 1994) can be distinguished as a basis for the analysis. Creswell (2009) suggests the development of no more than seven themes based on patterns emerging from the data. Thus, as a first step, the relevant text passages for each individual code were extracted and the main statement of each passage established. If a variety of statements emerged, they were checked for a possibility to merge them into fewer meta-level themes (Creswell, 2009) giving a summary of the content of the documents regarding IC. Additionally, recurring themes were identified. These themes offer a description of the content of the topic or capital represented by the particular code. This way, the information disclosed as part of a capital and the way information on IC was disclosed are established, answering three of the research questions at least partly: Are NPOs aware of the term IC and its concept? Is IC currently disclosed by German NPOs? How is IC disclosed by German NPOs?

To gain insight into the question regarding the reason for German NPOs to disclose their IC, the fourth research question, the documents were checked for interrelationships in the information offered. The importance of information or the relationship of information can be biased however. Bias can emerge during coding due to an unrecognized relation to a specific topic or organisation, or because information was delivered in a way easily remembered, thereby making the information seem more important than it actually was in comparison to other information. The tools offered by MAXQDA were thus utilised to establish the importance of single codes and to detect possible relations of codes while minimising the occurrence of bias. Tools provided by the software to this end are for instance Crosstabs and the Code Relation Browser. The latter visualises overlapping codes and thus points out possible relationships between them. The Code Relation Browser offers two ways of visualisation: in the form of dots with the size of the dots indicating the times the particular codes overlap in comparison to the other codes or as figures stating the number of times the codes overlap. MAXQDA facilitates finding the text passages in question by left clicking on the dot or figure indicating the respective combination. In a second step, these text passages can be extracted for further analysis.

The other tool, Crosstabs, is designed for mixed method approaches. However, it is a valuable starting point for a qualitative analysis as well. This tool enables the visual comparison of variables' code frequencies with one another (VERBI Software. Consult. Sozialforschung GmbH, n.d.). Again, MAXQDA enables the extraction of the text passages in question by left clicking on the figure indicating the respective combination of code and variable. For instance, if all text passages coded 'funding' of NPOs with the variable east are to be extracted, these can be selected via double clicking on the figure linking the row labelled 'funding' and the column labelled 'Location=East'. Thus these crosstabs are also a fast way to find and consequently extract text passages. A Crosstab was created for each variable in combination with the codes human capital, relational capital, structural capital, spiritual capital, and disclosure, including their sub-codes.

For the current research, the figures made available by MAXQDA were not used as numerical data but as signs as to where to look further. To this end, the highest and lowest combinations indicated in a Crosstab were checked more closely. Both tools, the Crosstabs and the Code Relations Browser, were also utilised to ensure that no important link was overlooked or valued unrealistically due to bias.

6.6.3 Analysis of Interviews

The interviews were analysed independently from the documents to facilitate a comparison and thus to establish the validity of the findings. Thus, the coding of the interview was not influenced by the coding of the documents but was based on the initial coding frame presented in Sect. 6.7. The presentation of the results in Chap. 7 was also kept apart to enable a comparison of the findings later on in the chapter.

Interviews were audio recorded during the actual interview and thus needed to be transcribed for the analysis. To this end, software called Express Scribe was used. It facilitated playing an audio recording slower or with breaks and can be operated via key assignments. These features allowed writing with minimal disturbance, for instance, through constant rewinding of the audio record. For the transcriptions of interviews, the following basic transcription rules presented by

Dresing and Prehl (2013) were chosen, since the nonverbal signals of an interviewee were not important for the current research (Dresing & Prehl, 2013):

- The interviews were transcribed word-by-word, i.e. no shorthand was used.
- Dialects were translated into standard German whenever possible. In case a precise translation was not possible, the dialect was kept.
- If words were slurred or abbreviated, e.g. "ne" instead of "eine", they were converted into standard German as well.
- Words that were not finished were transformed into whole words.
- Stutters were skipped and if words were doubled, the word was only transcribed once unless the doubling of words was used for emphasis.
- Punctuation was smoothed to ensure readability, i.e. if the voice was lowered, a comma or a full stop was added, depending on the meaning of the sentence.
- Sounds such as "ähm", "mhm", etc. were not transcribed.
- When the speaker changed, an empty line was inserted and a new paragraph begun.
- A time code was added at the end of each paragraph.

The transcripts were saved in .rtf format to enable the analysis via MAXQDA. After the interviews were transcribed, each transcription was checked carefully and mistakes were corrected (Saunders et al., 2009).

As a first step in the analysis, each interview was read carefully. While reading an interview, main arguments, interesting statements, and information seeming peculiar or telling were noted on the aforementioned contact summary. Information on the interviewee, such as his or her name and position within the organisation, and comments on the setting of the interview were recorded, as well as remarks on disruptions that occurred during the interview. Each contact summary was kept to a maximum length of one page.

Next, the interviews were coded and recurring themes identified as described for the analysis of the documents, providing information on the content of the codes. Then the interviews were also checked for interrelationships of the information offered via the Code Relations Browser. As for the documents, the variables were checked against the codes human capital, relational capital, structural capital, spiritual capital, and disclosure, including their sub-codes, using the Crosstabs function of MAXQDA. Finally, the interviews were checked for direct answers to the questions as to the awareness of the term and concept of IC which was posed directly during the interview.

6.6.4 Basic Consideration for Analysis

In Sect. 6.3, the approach used for the qualitative content analysis was introduced. This chapter is structured based on the approach and thus starts with basic considerations and a reminder of the aim and research questions. In the case of the current research, the aim was to develop a framework for German NPOs for the disclosure of IC. To this end, four questions were researched:

Q1: Are NPOs aware of the term intellectual capital and its concept?
Q2: Is IC currently disclosed by German NPOs?
Q3: How is IC disclosed by German NPOs?
Q4: What are the reasons for German NPOs to disclose their IC?

The literature review highlighted the challenges of the concept of IC and its disclosure as well as the heterogeneity of the third sector. Additionally, it showed that various approaches and motives for IC disclosure exist. Thus the following three assumptions are made:

- Not all German NPOs are aware of the term and concept of IC and thus do not disclose IC explicitly. Nevertheless, some organisations disclose IC unconsciously and implicitly.
- It is important for NPOs to signal trustworthiness, transparency, and to foster social acceptance.
- Since there are no profits to signal success, achievements are shown in other ways, for instance via highlighting the final aim the NPO works toward, the services it delivers, the steps necessary to deliver the process and the input necessary to finish the process (Drucker, 1990; Keehley & Abercrombie, 2008; Lichtsteiner, Gmür, Giroud, & Schauer, 2013).

For the current research, the relevant recoding units were the transcripts of the interviews conducted and the documents provided as .pdf on the web pages of the particular NPOs. As mentioned before, only documents available as .pdf were downloaded and analysed, since these types of documents do not change over time compared to websites (Striukova et al., 2008). The other group of documents to be coded and included into the analysis were the transcripts of the three telephone and six face-to-face interviews conducted. One of the telephone interviews was conducted spontaneously: When the contact of the NPO was called to arrange a date for an interview, he stated that he does not participate in research projects anymore since he received to many requests to take part in all of them, hence he declines them all. However, he offered to answer a couple of questions right away. Since the aim of the call was not to conduct the interview right away, an audio recording device was not available. Consequently, the interview was not recorded but notes were taken during the conversation. On the basis of these notes, memory minutes of the interview were written instead of a transcript. All other interviews were audio recorded and transcribed based on the rules presented in Sect. 6.6.3.

For narrative content often "words, terms, sentences, themes, paragraphs pages and whole texts" (Abhayawansa, 2011, p. 452) are employed as recoding units. Since IC is not expressed in a single word or even expressed implicitly, individual words were not defined as a coding unit (Abhayawansa, 2011). Thus, the minimum coding unit was a partial sentence, which is very common in the German language, and the maximum coding unit was a paragraph.

6.7 Development of the Coding Frame

A coding frame is a first measure to tell data that is relevant for the research question apart from data that is not relevant (Schreier, 2012). The coding frame consists of a few main categories and codes which are attributed to the categories. Codes are developed utilising a "combination of predetermined and emerging codes" (Creswell, 2009, p. 187). Hence, codes based on the literature review and prior knowledge were defined first (Fielding & Lee, 1998; Miles & Huberman, 1994) and codes that emerged during the analysis of the interviews and documents were added as they emerged.

To develop the basic codes and to ensure comprehensibility, the categories were determined first. Kuckartz (2012) identified six forms of possible categories. Factual categories relate to objective conditions, such as the name of a town or a profession. Topical categories include categories for a certain topic, argument, or stakeholder/protagonist. Categories based on the analysis of the researcher are analytical categories. "Natural" categories include expressions used by participants in their every-day life, ranging from professional terminology to linguistic code used by certain groups. Evaluative categories include different levels of distinctness, ranging from hardly noticeable to very distinct. Formal categories include data and information about the unit to be analysed, for instance the date and length of an interview or the name of the interviewer (Kuckartz, 2012). These categories are used as a guideline to develop predetermined codes and are neither included into the analysis nor pursued any further after the initial codes were developed.

The category 'factual' contained objective conditions, such as data on NPOs, data on interviews, data on interviewees, and data on documents. Since facts are also a type of disclosure, for addressing the research question on how IC is currently disclosed, a main code labelled 'disclosure' was established containing the sub-codes 'facts' and 'visual rhetoric' (Abhayawansa, 2011; Davison, 2014). The latter contained pictures, graphs, and other images that were used in the documents, and sub-codes for 'visual rhetoric' were thus 'pictures showing IC', 'graphs/tables', and 'tacit messages of IC'. Photos that conveyed a 'tacit message' imply IC, for example showing someone giving advice to another person, but cannot be linked to the NPO or its work unambiguously. Graphs and tables were coded in their entirety. They were assigned to both the code 'graph/table' and the code representing the content. In case various contents were represented by the graph, several codes were assigned.

Codes of the category 'topical' were the components of IC, i.e. human capital, relational capital, structural capital, and spiritual capital. The code was thus labelled 'capitals'. Human capital was coded via the codes 'volunteers' whenever volunteers were mentioned and 'employees' when paid staff was mentioned explicitly. The code 'staff' was used when no distinction was made between paid employees and unpaid volunteers. Further sub-codes were 'qualification of staff' and 'qualities of staff'. While the former code included reports on know-how, experience, education, etc. the latter contained information on motivation, commitment, and altruism, for instance.

As defined in Sect. 2.1, relational capital describes "the relations of the company to external stakeholders" (InCaS, 2008). Consequently, the sub-code 'relationship to external stakeholders' was defined as a sub-code to 'relational capital'. Descriptions of actions of the NPO aiming for public awareness were coded 'public relations' while the description of the image of an NPO was coded as such, i.e. 'image'. 'Cooperation' was another sub-code of 'relational capital', containing coding units that mentioned co-operations or partnerships.

The code 'structural capital' was split into the sub-codes 'structure', 'processes', 'organisational culture', and 'database/IT'. 'Structure' contained descriptions of how the NPO was structured, like which countries it worked in or who was responsible for what kind of task. The sub-code named 'processes' was created for information on how things were done within or by an NPO. 'Organisational culture' comprised descriptions of aims of the organisation and other statements giving the people involved a common perspective. Last but not least, the sub-code 'database/IT' enclosed information on available IT or databases as well as their benefits and challenges.

Expressions of spiritual capital, i.e. "the essence or positive spirit of the organization" (Hall, 1998, p. 78), were searched for as well, and coded accordingly. These expressions were abstract in contrast to statements coded 'organisational culture', and were articulated as a positive perspective.

Information on further capital was conducted to facilitate comparison if necessary. Natural capital is "the world's stock of natural assets" (Kenner, 2014, p. viii). A debate is currently ongoing on whether nature should be valued economically in the first place or if it has a purely intrinsic value and is thus priceless. Another issue discussed is whose responsibility nature, its preservation, and possibly its valuation is (Kenner, 2014). According to the IIRC, natural capital includes "water, land, minerals and forests, and biodiversity and eco-system health" (The IIRC, 2011, p. 11). Since every activity of an organisation has an effect on nature in a positive or negative way (The IIRC, 2011), information on these effects were coded as 'natural capital' for the current research.

Even though financial capital is not intangible and thus not part of intellectual capital, it is imperative for NPOs. Since possible relationships between financial capital and IC might exist, information on financials was coded as well. Sub-codes were 'financial capital' and 'fundraising'. The latter code was utilised to code information and data on fundraising and on fundraising activities. Another code for tangible assets was included, namely 'manufactured capital'. This code included descriptions of "physical objects [. . .] that are available to the organisation for the production of goods or the provision of services" (The IIRC, 2011, p. 11), including infrastructure, buildings, cars, etc.

According to Kuckartz (2012), the category 'analytical' consisted of codes that emerged from the literature review but were not components of IC and are thus not part of the category 'topical'. In the case of the current research, a code 'demands' was included containing information on demands put on the non-profit sector, namely trust, transparency, and social acceptance (Drucker, 1990; Glassman &

Spahn, 2012; Raynard, 1998; van Broekhoven, 2008). For the current research, no codes for the category 'evaluative' were defined.

These codes build the starting point for the analysis of the documents and interviews alike. Further codes are developed during the coding process, which is illustrated in the next Sect. 6.8. In summary, the following codes and sub-codes were defined:

1. Capitals
    - 1.1. Human capital
        - 1.1.1. Staff
        - 1.1.2. Volunteers
        - 1.1.3. Qualification of staff
        - 1.1.4. Qualities of staff (e.g. commitment, motivation, etc.)
    - 1.2. Relational capital
        - 1.2.1. Public relations
        - 1.2.2. Image
        - 1.2.3. Relationship to external stakeholders
        - 1.2.4. Co-operations
    - 1.3. Structural capital
        - 1.3.1. Structure
        - 1.3.2. Organisational culture
        - 1.3.3. Processes
        - 1.3.4. Databases
    - 1.4. Spiritual capital
    - 1.5. Natural capital
    - 1.6. Manufactured capital
    - 1.7. Financial capital
        - 1.7.1. Financial statements
        - 1.7.2. Fundraising
2. Disclosure
    - 2.1. Visual rhetoric
        - 2.1.1. Pictures showing IC
        - 2.1.2. Graphs/tables
        - 2.1.3. Tacit messages of IC
    - 2.2. Facts
        - 2.2.1. Data on NPOs
        - 2.2.2. Data on interviewees
        - 2.2.3. Data on interviews

3. Perspective on IC
    3.1. IC as liability
    3.2. IC expressed explicitly
4. Demands
    4.1. Trust
    4.2. Transparency
    4.3. Social acceptance

6.8 Coding of Selected Material

First, the documents in .pdf format downloaded from the web pages of the NPOs were imported into MAXQDA. In a separate project, both the audio records and the corresponding transcriptions of the interviews were transferred to MAXQDA. The software facilitates linking the audio records and the transcripts and thus, when a certain sentence needs to be listened to again, for instance, the exact part of the audio record can be played by activating it via the written transcript. Next, the coding frame was set up within the software for both projects alike. One coding unit should be matched with no more than one code of each category, if possible. If, for instance, a report on a project was included in an annual report, it is only coded once as "report on project" even though a chapter or paragraph might start with a report on a particular project, give information on the financial situation next, and go back to describing another facet of the same project. In this case, the description of the financial situation was coded accordingly, but the two parts reporting on the same project were coded only once. Whenever several codes were assigned, they could not be of the same category. Yet some coding units correlated with more than one code and could therefore not be split without losing their meaning. In such cases, the codes were examined first, as they might not be defined and separated distinctly enough or might make more sense when consolidated. If the codes were confirmed as appropriate, more than one code was ascribed to an individual coding unit since the number of times an expression was used was of inferior interest for the current research and used solely for guidance.

In sum, the following coding rules were developed during the coding process to ensure consistency:

- Only one code per category was assigned to one coding unit.
- The main codes were not assigned, only the sub-codes were used.
- If a document was available in more than one language, only the German document/parts of the document were coded.
- If particular information was given twice, it was only coded once. For instance, within the description of a project, the process of defining necessary action was illustrated as including discussions with the beneficiaries as well as the project partner XY. The project description ends with the statement: the project was

executed in cooperation with organisation XY and organisation YZ. Hence the cooperation with organisation XY was only coded once.

Additionally a list of codes, their definitions and examples was developed as an additional measure to ensure consistent coding (Miles & Huberman, 1994; Saunders et al., 2009). For the list of codes, please see the Appendix.

While coding, every sentence was read carefully to decide if it contained either data, information on IC, or included either directly or implied one of the following words: trust, transparency, social acceptance. When one of the codes was detected, the applicability of sub-codes was checked and the appropriate sub-code assigned. If none of the codes were detected, a decision on whether the sentence included important information was made, and if so, a new code was then defined. Alternatively, if the sentence did not include important information, it was not coded.

During the coding process, a few additional codes were defined which are described in Sect. 7.1.1 for the documents and Sect. 7.2.1 for the interviews. Whenever a new code was defined, all documents and interviews coded before were reviewed as to whether the code was detectable in them as well. For instance, based on the realisation that the sub-codes 'data on NPO' and 'staff' were regularly used for the same unit of coding, a new code labelled 'data on staff' was introduced, replacing the former two whenever both were assigned to the same unit of coding, for example, if the number of staff working for an organisation was mentioned.

Some documents of an individual NPO, for instance annual reports, were always structured the same way and some even used the same words over and over again. To ensure coherent coding in these cases, documents were compared through putting them side by side in MAXQDA whenever the particular phrases or parts of a document reappeared. As soon as such repeating phrases or parts of documents were discovered, these were coded in all documents immediately, i.e. the coding of one document after the other was interrupted. This approach made certain that these reappearing phrases and documents were recognised in every document. Since changes in the wording within these phrases or document sections were possible, all were thoroughly read and the coding of single units changed when necessary.

Two quality measures were taken during the coding. Check-coding is a quality measure proposed by Miles and Huberman (1994). First, a work group of three PhD-Students was established to spot check the coding that each group member carried out for her book. A confidentiality agreement was signed by all members of this group to ensure anonymity of the participants in the research projects. Differences in the way certain information was coded were discussed and either the definition of the code in question refined, sub-codes developed, or the coding changed if a mistake was discovered. As a second measure, all codes were checked independent of the document. If a code assigned did not fit to the coding unit as initially established, the code was changed accordingly or a new code or sub-code developed as described above.

References

Abeysekera, I. (2006). The project of intellectual capital disclosure: Researching the research. *Journal of Intellectual Capital, 7*(1), 61–77. doi:10.1108/14691930610639778.

Abhayawansa, S. (2011). A methodology for investigating intellectual capital information in analyst reports. *Journal of Intellectual Capital, 12*(3), 446–476. doi:10.1108/14691931111154733.

Beattie, V., & Jones, M. J. (1992). The use and abuse of graphs in annual reports: Theoretical framework and empirical study. *Accounting and Business Research, 22*(88), 291–303. doi:10.1080/00014788.1992.9729446.

Beattie, V., & Thomson, S. J. (2007). Lifting the lid on the use of content analysis to investigate intellectual capital disclosures. *Accounting Forum, 31*(2), 129–163. doi:10.1016/j.accfor.2007.02.001.

Bogner, A., & Menz, W. (2009a). Das theoriegenerierende Experteninterview – Erkenntnisinteresse, Wissensformen, Interaktion. In A. Bogner, B. Littig, & W. Menz (Eds.), *Experteninterviews* (pp. 61–98). Wiesbaden: VS Verlag für Sozialwissenschaften.

Bogner, A., & Menz, W. (2009b). Experteninterviews in der qualitativen Sozialforschung – Zur Einführung in eine sich intensivierende Methodendebatte. In A. Bogner, B. Littig, & W. Menz (Eds.), *Experteninterviews* (pp. 7–31). Wiesbaden: VS Verlag für Sozialwissenschaften.

Bonga, J., & Jegers, M. (2009). Graphical disclosures by charities: Clarification or distortion? The case of the Netherlands. *International Journal of Nonprofit and Voluntary Sector Marketing, 14*(3), 181–191. doi:10.1002/nvsm.

Brixius, H. (2011). *Gemeinnützige Körperschaften.* Koblenz. www.verhuelsdonk.de/pub/info/downloads/bro_koerperschaften.pdf

Brüggen, A., Vergauwen, P., & Dao, M. (2009). Determinants of intellectual capital disclosure: Evidence from Australia. *Management Decision, 47*(2), 233–245. doi:10.1108/00251740910938894.

Creswell, J. W. (2009). *Research design: Qualitative, quantitative, and mixed methods approaches* (3rd ed.). Thousand Oaks, CA: SAGE.

Davison, J. (2014). Visual rhetoric and the case of intellectual capital. In *BAFA Conference 2014*.

Denzin, N. K., & Lincoln, Y. S. (2011). The discipline and practice of qualitative research. In N. K. Denzin & Y. S. Lincoln (Eds.), *The Sage handbook of qualitative research* (pp. 1–17). Thousand Oaks, CA: SAGE.

Deutsches Zentralinstitut für soziale Fragen. (2011). *DZI Spenden-Siegel Leitlinien.* Accessed February 20, 2014, from http://www.dzi.de/spenderberatung/das-spenden-siegel/

Deutsches Zentralinstitut für soziale Fragen. (n.d.). *DZI Deutsches Zentralinstitut für soziale* Fragen. Accessed February 20, 2014, from http://www.dzi.de/dzi-institut/german-central-institute-for-social-issues/

Dresing, T., & Prehl, T. (2013). *Praxisbuch Interview, Transkription & Analyse. Anleitungen und Regelsysteme für qualitativ Forschende* (5th ed.). Marburg. Accessed September 09, 2014, from http://www.audiotranskription.de/download/praxisbuch _transkription.pdf?q=Praxisbuch-Transkription.pdf

Droß, P., Poldrack, C., Priller, E., Lysk, S., Blickenstorfer, M., Graf Strachwitz, R., et al. (2013). *6. Forschungsbericht: Statistiken zum deutschen Stiftungswesen 2013*. Berlin. Accessed July 25, 2014, from http://www.maecenata.eu/publikationen/reihe-opuscula/

Drucker, P. F. (1990). *Managing the non-profit organization.* Oxford: Butterworth-Heinemann.

Dumay, J., & Cai, L. (2014). A review and critique of content analysis as a methodology for inquiring into IC disclosure. *Journal of Intellectual Capital, 15*(2), 264–290. doi:10.1108/JIC-01-2014-0010.

Fielding, N. G., & Lee, R. M. (1998). *Computer analysis and qualitative research.* London: SAGE.

Gläser, J., & Laudel, G. (2010). *Experteninterviews und qualitative inhaltsanalyse* (4th ed.). Wiesbaden: VS Verlag für Sozialwissenschaften.

Glassman, D. M., & Spahn, K. (2012). Performance measurement for nonprofits. *Journal of Applied Corporate Finance, 24*(2), 72–77. doi:10.1111/j.1745-6622.2012.00381.x.

Guthrie, J., Petty, R., Yongvanich, K., & Ricceri, F. (2004). Using content analysis as a research method to inquire into intellectual capital reporting. *Journal of Intellectual Capital, 5*(2), 282–293. doi:10.1108/14691930410533704.

Hall, M. L. W. (1998). The confusion of the capitals: Surveying the cluttered landscape of intellectual 'capitals' and terminology. In P. H. Sullivan (Ed.), *Profiting from intellectual capital – Extracting value from innovation* (pp. 76–83). New York: Wiley.

InCaS. (2008). *Intellectual capital statement – Made in Europe*. Accessed January 31, 2010, from www.incas-europe.org

Keehley, P., & Abercrombie, N. N. (2008). *Benchmarking in the public and nonprofit sectors* (2nd ed.). San Francisco, CA: Wiley.

Kenner, D. (2014). *Who should value nature?* London. Accessed January 18, 2015, from http://whygreeneconomy.org/wp-content/uploads/2014/12/Who-should-value-nature.-Why-Green-Economy.pdf. ISBN: 978-0-85760-938-0.

Krippendorff, K. (2004). *Content analysis – An introduction to its methodology* (2nd ed.). Thousand Oaks, CA: SAGE.

Kuckartz, U. (2012). *Qualitative Inhaltsanalyse. Methoden, Praxis, Computerunterstützung*. Weinheim: Beltz Juventa.

Kuckartz, U., Dresing, T., Rädiker, S., & Stefer, C. (2008). *Qualitative evaluation* (2nd ed.). Wiesbaden: VS Verlag für Sozialwissenschaften.

Lichtsteiner, H., Gmür, M., Giroud, C., & Schauer, R. (2013). *Das Freiburger Management-Modell für Nonprofit Organisationen* (7th ed.). Bern: Haupt Verlag.

Mayring, P. (1996). *Einführung in die qualitative Sozialforschung* (3rd ed.). Weinheim: Psychologie Verlags Union.

Merkl-Davies, D., Brennan, N., & Vourvachis, P., (2014). Content analysis and discourse analysis in corporate narrative reporting research: A methodological guide. In *BAFA conference 2014*. Accessed May 08, 2014, from criticalperspectivesonaccounting.com/wp-content/uploads/2014/06/paper-cpa-021.pdf

Meuser, M., & Nagel, U. (2009). Experteninterview und der Wandel der Wissensproduktion. In A. Bogner, B. Littig, & W. Menz (Eds.), *Experteninterviews* (pp. 35–60). Wiesbaden: VS Verlag für Sozialwissenschaften.

Miles, M. B., & Huberman, A. M. (1994). *Qualitative data analysis* (2nd ed.). Thousand Oaks, CA: SAGE.

Neff, C. (2014, March 19). Telephone conversation with Christel Neff, DZI.

Opdenakker, R. (2006). Advantages and disadvantages of four interview techniques in qualitative research. *Forum Qualitative Sozialforschung, 7*(4). Accessed February 24, 2014, from http://www.qualitative-research.net/fqs/

Oxford Wordpower Dictionary. (2006). In J. Turnbull (Ed.), *Oxford wordpower dictionary* (3rd ed.). Oxford: Oxford University Press.

Raynard, P. (1998). Coming together. A review of contemporary approaches to social accounting, auditing and reporting in non-profit organisations. *Journal of Business Ethics, 17*, 1471–1479.

Rosenthal, G. (2008). *Interpretative Sozialforschung* (2nd ed.). Weinheim: Juventa Verlag.

Saunders, M., Lewis, P., & Thornhill, A. (2009). *Research methods for business students* (5th ed.). Harlow: Pearson Education.

Schreier, M. (2012). *Qualitative content analysis in practice*. London: SAGE.

Smith, M., & Taffler, R. J. (2000). The chairman's statement – A content analysis of discretionary narrative disclosure. *Accounting, Auditing and Accountability Journal, 13*(5), 624–646.

Statistische Ämter des Bundes und der Länder. (2014). Gebiet und Bevölkerung – Fläche und Bevölkerung. Accessed July 25, 2014, from http://www.statistik-portal.de/Statistik-Portal/de_jb01_jahrtab1.asp

Steenkamp, N., & Northcott, D. (2007). Content analysis in accounting research: The practical challenge. *Australian Accounting Review, 17*(43), 12–25. doi:10.1111/j.1835-2561.2007.tb00332.x.

Striukova, L., Unerman, J., & Guthrie, J. (2008). Corporate reporting of intellectual capital: Evidence from UK companies. *The British Accounting Review, 40*(4), 297–313. doi:10.1016/j.bar.2008.06.001.

Sveiby, K.-E. (1997). *The new organizational wealth* (1st ed.). San Francisco, CA: Berrett-Koehler.

The IIRC. (2011). *Towards integrated reporting – communicating value in the 21st century*. Accessed May 15, 2012, from http://www.theiirc.org/discussion-paper/

Trinczek, R. (2009). Wie befrage ich Manager? Methodische und methodologische Aspekte des Experteninterviews als qualitative Methode empirischer Sozialforschung. In A. Bogner, B. Littig, & W. Menz (Eds.), *Experteninterviews* (pp. 225–238). Wiesbaden: VS Verlag für Sozialwissenschaften.

van Broekhoven, R. A. (2008). *Engaging Donors' Trust*. Accessed February 20, 2014, from http://www.icfo.org/ICFO-Publications

VERBI Software. Consult. Sozialforschung GmbH. (n.d.). *MAXQDA Software für qualitative Datenanalyse*. Accessed November 25, 2014, from http://www.maxqda.de/about

Witzel, A. (2000). Das problemzentrierte interview. *Forum qualitative Sozialforschung, 1*(1). Accessed February 24, 2014, from http://www.qualitative-research.net/index.php/fqs/article/view/1132/2519

Witzel, A., & Reiter, H. (2012). *The problem-centred interview*. London: SAGE. Accessed February 25, 2014, from http://www.qualitative-research.net/index.php/fqs/article/view/1132/2519

Chapter 7
Presentation of Results

German donation-soliciting NPOs will profit from several findings presented in this chapter. For instance, demands imposed on German donation-soliciting NPOs and resources needed by them for survival and success are highlighted. For NPOs, the dependencies and interdependencies that exist between demands and resources are essential if they want to know what information to publish to what extent in order to satisfy their stakeholders. Additionally, the findings show a discrepancy between the awareness of IC, its concept, and its disclosure. On the one hand, the terms "intellectual capital" or any other capital were not used even once in the documents analysed and most representatives were unaware of IC and its concept according to interviews conducted. On the other hand, the document analysis showed that every NPO discloses IC. A conscious and purposeful handling and disclosure of IC could be beneficial for NPOs, however.

Based on the sample and the approach to analysis presented in the previous chapter, the empirical data collected was analysed. First the findings of the analysis of the documents are presented, starting with the illustration of the advancement of the coding frame. In other words, the codes and sub-codes that emerged during coding are described and supported by citations from documents to ensure transparency and replicability. With the coding frame completed, findings regarding the disclosure of capitals are reported in Sect. 7.1.2. The publications also offered insight into the way IC is currently disclosed. These findings are illustrated in Sect. 7.1.3. Additionally, the analysis of the documents based on the variables permitted to draw inferences about differences and similarities of IC disclosure by NPOs with different characteristics, presented in Sect. 7.1.4. After the findings from the analysis of the documents are highlighted, those from the analysis of the interviews are presented independently. The presentation follows the same chronology. First, the advancement of the coding frame is presented. Secondly, the findings regarding the disclosure of capitals are highlighted. Next, information on ways of disclosure is offered and finally, differences and similarities within the interviews are illustrated. Section 7.3 offers a comparison of the findings based on the documents and the interviews as a basis for the discussion and development of the framework presented in Chap. 8. The fourth section of this Chap. 7 addresses findings that

K. Blankenburg, *Intellectual Capital in German Non-profit Organisations*,
Contributions to Management Science, DOI 10.1007/978-3-319-62655-0_7

are independent of capital, disclosure, and variables, but which are nevertheless important for the disclosure of IC: the dependencies and interdependencies of necessary resources and demands imposed on German NPOs as perceived by themselves. Finally, in Sect. 7.5, a summary of the main findings is provided.

7.1 Documents

7.1.1 Advancement of Coding Frame

The sample documents included: 23 newsletters; 33 annual reports; 3 financial reports, 4 audit reports, 4 charter documents, 8 business reports, 5 information leaflets, 3 journals, 2 guidelines, 2 project reports, 3 brochures, 2 statistical documents. The documents analysed were of various lengths; the shortest document was one page long and the longest consists of 72 pages. In total, 92 documents with a total of 1803 pages were downloaded and coded for analysis. To ensure that this section is as comprehensive and transparent as possible, relevant text extracts from these documents are presented where appropriate. These statements are translated from documents originally written in German and, wherever necessary, are adapted to ensure the anonymity promised.

By analysing the documents, sub-codes were developed completing the coding frame presented in Sect. 6.7. For example, 'data on output' and 'data on staff' were added as sub-codes to the code 'facts'. 'Data on output' enclosed reports on the number of services offered, beneficiaries reached, and services executed as well as the number or names of the countries in which and/or with which the NPO works. 'Data on staff' was the code assigned to information on the number of staff working for the organisation and on the structure of the workforce, for instance volunteers versus employees, men vs. women, full time vs. part time staff.

Two codes were added to the category disclosure: 'stories or citations of individuals' and 'output–projects/services delivered'. The latter included mainly descriptions of services and activities and of the raison d'être of the organisation. All text units provided within the documents that are either written by individuals or tell stories of individuals, i.e., texts that are not objective reports by the particular NPO, were coded 'stories or citations of individuals'. The aim of coding these text units was to get an impression on how common this style of reporting is amongst the organisations within the sample.

Due to the massive amount of pictures presented within the documents analysed, the sub-code 'pictures showing IC' of the code visual rhetoric was segmented further into three sub-codes and coded accordingly. First, 'Pictures of staff' comprised photos of groups of employees and/or volunteers or individuals and thus indicating human capital. A second sub-code was 'pictures expressing IC and showing the work of a particular organisation'. This code was used for photos clearly showing the work or a member of staff of an NPO identified for instance via a logo on a jacket or equipment. Third, the code 'pictures with captions' was developed, since some pictures showed the work of the particular NPO but can only be identified as such through their caption and thus did not fit to any of the other codes. Finally, some pictures used in the documents did not show IC and could not be attributed to a specific NPO. For these pictures a new sub-code labelled 'random picture' was introduced.

The code 'relational capital' included the sub-code 'relationships to external stakeholders', which proved to be too broad, and the information included too heterogeneous. It was thus divided further. 'Relationship to beneficiaries' included reports on the individuals and groups the NPO reaches with their services and the opinions of beneficiaries. Furthermore, statements on the significance of and orientation towards the actual needs of beneficiaries were assigned to this sub-code, such as:

> Content and arrangement of the collaboration with biological parents depend on their ability and willingness has to be negotiated and coordinated with the responsible youth welfare service. (Albert-Schweitzer-Kinderdorf in Sachsen e.V., 2011, p.13)

> Since beginning of 2007 we offer educational counseling online, which is used by young people in the ages between 16 and 20 years of age. (Caritasverband der Erzdiözese München und Freising e.V., 2008, p.19)

Another sub-code that emerged from the division of 'relationship to external stakeholders' was 'relationship to public' comprising information on claims of support or official praise of the NPO, interaction with the public and provision of information or a point of contact. One NPO claimed that:

> A lot of people associate experiences, memories, special moments, and emotions with us. (DGzRS, 2014a, p.2)

Another organisation highlighted:

> In the course of last year we experienced a lot of support and goodwill for our work. (Caritasverband der Erzdiözese München und Freising e.V., 2013, p.3)

Regarding the interaction with the public, the following statement is an example:

> Public and society need to be sensitised for topics people usually only deal with reluctantly or in case they are affected themselves. (Caritasverband der Erzdiözese München und Freising e.V., 2002, p.26)

Acknowledgement of the significance of donations and illustrations of the integration of donors were coded 'relationship to donors', for instance:

> Within reasonable efforts, our donors are entitled to clear and comprehensible information on the organisation they support. (Johanniter-Unfall-Hilfe e.V., 2010, p.19)

> Therefore I am thankful for every contact with our donors. Praise and positive suggestions help us with our daily work as well as mistakes pointed out and critique. (Caritasverband der Erzdiözese München und Freising e.V., 2006, p.44)

Whenever cooperation or a partnership were mentioned but not characterised, the code 'co-operations' was utilised. However, if the cooperation or relationship was valued, the code 'relationship to partners/co-operations' was used instead. Additionally, this sub-code enclosed statements on the importance and impact of partners or co-operations, the contribution of tasks between the partners, and the quality of the partnership. If a NPO was a member of an association, the information was coded 'relationship to partners/co-operations' as well. Examples for statements assigned to this code are the following statements:

> We are still in close and very amicable contact with our project partners on-site. (Steinschleuder e.V., 2009, p.2)

> We face this challenge by building social networks—co-operations of agencies, communities, local authorities, associations etc., beyond all borders, to take advantage of synergistic effects, to contemplate challenges together and to develop solutions collaboratively. (Caritasverband der Erzdiözese München und Freising e.V., 2006, p.17)

A report on the number of times an NPO was mentioned in the press was coded 'relationship to press', as were awards to the press and those received, and the importance of the relationship to the press, as detectable in these declarations:

> Media exposure of the social field is no matter of course in Munich's „shark tank. (Caritasverband der Erzdiözese München und Freising e.V., 2004, p.30)

> Good contacts, upfront information and transparency are requirements to be mentioned in the media outside of scandals and bad news. (Caritasverband der Erzdiözese München und Freising e.V., 2004, p.30)

> During the reporting year we were mentioned around 22000 times in regional and national press, national radio, and TV-spots. That is around 60 times per day. (Johanniter-Unfall-Hilfe e.V., 2011, p.25)

Another important relationship according to the documents was of that to politics and officials, thus 'relationship to politics/officials' was another sub-code that emerged from 'relationships to external stakeholders'. It enclosed statements on the positive or negative impacts of such a relationship, its quality, reports on lobbying activities, and on meeting with politicians, for example:

> The start of the project, which had to be postponed over and over again due to administrative problems, is imminent. (TERRA TECH Förderverein e. V., 2009, p.2)

> We established good relationships to the community whilst working in the community over the last 12 years. (ProBrasil e.V., 2012, p.9)

Most new sub-codes were added to 'structural capital'. Based on the literature review, four sub-codes were defined initially, namely 'structure', 'processes', 'database/IT', and 'organisational culture'. When analysing the documents, however, another five sub-codes surfaced. While 'processes' enclosed information on processes affecting external parties, the code 'internal projects/processes' gave an insight into the internal processes or projects of an NPO like:

> During our last organisational meeting (September 08) it was agreed to put the focus of the next month on recruitment, i.e. to win interested young people for our new project in 2010. (Steinschleuder e.V., 2008, p.26)

> Within a short period of time since the start of the organisational development processes important internal changes were initiated. (Johanniter-Unfall-Hilfe e.V., 2013a, p.30)

'Work climate' and 'relationship to staff' were further sub-codes that emerged from the documents. 'Relationship to staff' comprised the recognition and praise for staff and volunteers as a group or for individuals. Additionally, the structures for a possible involvement of staff in general and of volunteers in particular as well as the recognition of their needs which NPOs recognised, such as family-orientation, safety, training needs, or psychological support, were assigned to this sub-code. The following statements are examples of information assigned to 'relationship to staff':

> With a strong involvement of employees a conceptual framework was developed. (Caritasverband der Erzdiözese München und Freising e.V., 2004, p.33)

> The "keep-in-touch and re-entry" programme for instance is a structured package of measures to facilitate employees to stay up to date during maternity leave and prepare them for their re-entry into the job. (Caritasverband der Erzdiözese München und Freising e.V., 2013, p.53)

'Work climate' included expressions of appreciation of the work delivered and of the necessary know-how, experience and expertise. Descriptions of events for employees and volunteers such as competitions, atmosphere of solidarity, and networking possibilities were assigned to this sub-code as well, for instance:

> Caritas is a community of employees and volunteers. (Caritasverband der Erzdiözese München und Freising e.V., 2002, p.3)

> I felt like I finally found people with the same mindset. Altogether I experienced the atmosphere as very pleasant, affectionate, and open-minded and there was lots of laughter. (Steinschleuder e.V., 2011, p.37)

Another sub-code of 'structural capital' developed was 'education/training', since the documents indicated a high importance of trainings and education offered to staff, volunteers, or interested public. Information within this sub-code was on trainings and education programmes offered, as well as how these were organised and accepted. Also, reports on further or newly developed trainings and training material and on the actual trainings conducted were available. Furthermore, the motivations for offering the trainings/education were presented within the documents analysed. These reasons for trainings and education can be summarized into retention of existing and attraction of new employees and volunteers, quality assurance through ensuring that all employees and volunteers have the appropriate know-how in order to fulfill their assigned roles efficiently and with the highest possible professionalism.

> Every volunteer who is currently working for us completed 40 teaching units according to § 86 Abs. 2 AVSG successfully. Through the support by employees and regularly held meetings, volunteers receive competent content related trainings, appropriate recognition and appreciation. (Caritasverband der Erzdiözese München und Freising e.V., 2012, p.22)

> To be able to exercise their responsibility, volunteers need a sound training and good support. (Johanniter-Unfall-Hilfe e.V., 2009, p.17)

'Professionalism' was added as a sub-code of human capital. It is defined as "a way of doing a job that shows great skill and experience" (Oxford Wordpower Dictionary, 2006, p.566). It thus expresses an "an occupational value" (Evetts, 2011, p.33). In other words, the term 'professional' refers to a job-related action performed at a high quality by an expert (Langer & Schröer, 2011; Evetts, 2011; Kleimann, 2011), i.e. a person "who can be trusted as a result of their competence and experience" (Evetts, 2011, p.35) independent of an organisation or market (Langer & Schröer, 2011, p.14). The code 'professionalism' includes statements such as the following on existing and/or offered professionalism, on its necessity, and on the development and furtherance of professionalism:

> The quality of the services offered originates from our professionality and subject-matter knowledge. (Caritasverband der Erzdiözese München und Freising e.V., 2012, p.35)

> Free from government support, independent, and professional. (DGzRS, 2012, p.50)

For the code 'demands', a further sub-code emerged: 'quality'. While the number of times the other demands social acceptance, trust, and transparency were mentioned is similar, quality was referred to more frequently. Influences on quality were stated, a validation of the level of quality given, and aims in regard to quality illustrated. Quality management activities were introduced, and the importance and impact of quality were reported on, as the following three statements illustrate.

> For our donors it comes down to the quality of our work, consistent impeccable behaviour, and humane and continuous communication—that is what we stand for. (Johanniter-Unfall-Hilfe e.V., 2010, p.18)

> When an organisation is successful for decades, this is due to the quality of products and services offered, its commitment, and the know-how of its staff and management. (Caritasverband der Erzdiözese München und Freising e.V., 2008, p.13)

> People in need have a justified right to quality, service, and benevolence. (Caritasverband der Erzdiözese München und Freising e.V., 2005, p.15)

'Necessary resources' was added as a code for statements on essential resources. Yet the code proved to be too heterogeneous. Thus, after all applicable text units were coded as 'necessary resources', these passages of texts were extracted and exported into an Excel sheet. Next, the main statements were filtered from each text passage. Similar statements were then combined into a theme, as suggested by Creswell (2009), leading to the following necessary resources: funds, human capital, support by external parties, reputation, practices, and further resources. The last theme is composed of statements that do not name explicit resources but the dependency on resources in general. 'Practices' was a combination of processes, approaches, and the underlying philosophy of how services were advertised, offered, and executed.

Table 7.1 Number of times main codes were allocated within all documents (Source: Author)

Code	Occurrences (including sub-codes)
Structural Capital	1441
Relational Capital	1132
Financial capital	729
Human Capital	244
Spiritual capital	128
Manufactured capital	97
Natural capital	27

7.1.2 Capitals

All NPOs disclosed information on their IC, but to various extents and without using the term "intellectual capital" or naming any of the capitals explicitly. To gain insight on which capitals the NPOs focused on in their disclosure, it was checked how often the codes were allocated in total, i.e. main codes including their sub-codes (Table 7.1). The actual numerical value of these numbers was of minor importance compared to the distribution they express.

Information on structural and relational capital was disclosed the most. Compared to structural capital, information on human capital was published far less often. Information on spiritual capital and manufactured capital was offered even less frequently. Information on natural capital is disclosed the least. In this case, it needs to be considered that no organisation focussing on environmental protection is part of the sample. For comparison, information on financial capital was presented less frequently than relational capital and structural capital, but more often than human capital, manufactured capital, natural capital, and spiritual capital.

To discover the main subject matter of each code, the approach used to establish the necessary resources was applied again. The text passages assigned to each individual code were extracted and the main statement of each text passage was identified. Next, similar statements were condensed into a few meta-level themes. In the end, only a few themes per code remained, expressing the main content matter (Creswell, 2009). The themes developed are summarised and illustrated in Table 7.2.

Information on structural capital was mainly expressed via reports on activities pursued, how activities were approached and why they were necessary. Activities pursued were illustrated by reports on trainings or education programs developed, offered, and conducted, and annual events for employees and volunteers. Descriptions on training and events such as the following statements were examples of reports on approaches to activities detectable within every sub-code of structural capital except 'structure':

> Before new employees take up their job, they receive extensive information on the tasks they are going to face and are permitted to sit in with existing work groups. (Albert-Schweitzer-Kinderdorf in Sachsen e.V., 2011, p.15)

Table 7.2 Themes of capitals disclosed in documents

Capitals	Themes identified
Structural capital	Approaches to activities
	Reasons for activities
	Reports on activities
Relational capital	Description of activities
	Valuations of relationships
	Impact and importance of these relationships
	Reports on public relation activities, aims and topics covered
	Description of image
	Public signals of good work
Human Capital	Structure of the workforce
	Description of activities
	Expression of demands on the workforce
	Recognition of the importance of the workforce
Spiritual capital	Workplace spirituality
	Description of self-understanding of the organisation and its work
	Addressed either existing supporters or possible future supporters
Financial capital	Fundraising
	Costs of human capital
	Financial statements
Manufactured capital	Reports on construction
	Information on financial implications
	Data about the manufactured capital
	Explanations of necessity

Source: Author

> With the close proximity of the learning venues (school and organisation) we succeed in sensitising future qualified nurses for the demands and needs of people with disabilities and in preparing them for practice with its changing concepts. (Caritasverband der Erzdiözese München und Freising e.V., 2007, p.50)

The necessity of activities was expressed via the effects created or demands met. For instance, activities affecting structural capital were internal and external processes employed for value creation or the use of databases and IT to provide information online. Further reported activities to influence the work climate of the NPO were the involvement of staff and volunteers alike in decision making, for example, or the provision of networking opportunities to foster an atmosphere of community. Another example is the introduction of new software which is believed to improve efficiency and reduced costs (Johanniter-Unfall-Hilfe e.V., 2005, p.14).

Certain objectives and approaches were derived from the self-awareness, views, and values of an organisation and coded as 'organisational culture', another sub-code of 'structural capital'. The following statements present these links:

> Our help is aimed at every human being independent of his religion, nationality, and culture. It is aimed at those in mental and emotional distress as well. (Johanniter-Unfall-Hilfe e.V., 2013a, p.39)

> Day and night, 365 days a year, 185 employees and more than 800 volunteers and our equipment are operational. (DGzRS, 2010, p.33)

> We try to open the minds and hearts of people by acting open, honest, and fair towards donors and beneficiaries alike. (Steinschleuder e.V., 2005, p.18)

Organisational culture has strong links to spiritual capital, workplace spirituality in particular. Statements by staff provided evidence of workplace spirituality as well as descriptions of the self-understanding of the organisation and its work:

> Nevertheless: The human being with his courage, expertise, and commitment takes the centre stage. (DGzRS, 2014b, p.5)

> For their whole life a lot of people carry about questions about the purpose of life, about one's own identity and about the world in general. It is thus a gift, when these questions are expressed and can be shared with people who have similar questions and dreams. (Steinschleuder e.V., 2010, p.2)

> Rather every person should be enabled to contribute to community in an optimal way, experience a full life, and participate in society with dignity. (Johanniter-Unfall-Hilfe e.V., 2012, p.11)

Further statements on spiritual capital were detectable in the documents. They differed depending on the target audience. On the one hand, statements appealed to those external stakeholders who supported the organisation in the past, and on the other hand, motivated the reader to either begin or continue supporting a good cause.

> Every Euro we receive via a donation, membership fee or inheritance symbolises a person who wants to do good, whose heart is open for the distress of others. (Caritasverband der Erzdiözese München und Freising e.V., 2013, p.42)

> We keep on counting on the willingness of people to open their hearts and hands and ensure that the centre for children endures, providing a place for children and parents to breathe easily since it offers them help and support. (Christophorushilfe e. V, 2014, p.2)

Compared to structural capital, there was only slightly less information on the relational capital of NPOs provided in the documents. Information on the activities of the NPOs addressing relational capital was presented. Distribution of tasks within co-operations illustrated some of these activities, as well as reports on lobbying activities and meetings with politicians, officials, or contact to the public. Further activities reported on were prizes awarded to members of the press or by the press. Reports on these were coded 'relational capital' since they demonstrated a good relationship to the press. Another theme detectable within the code 'relational capital' was the mentioning of the importance of relationships, for instance with partners for co-operations, the press, and donors. Also, the impact of these relationships and the importance of donations for the NPO were highlighted. Valuations of relationships with partners or officials and politicians were provided as well.

At the same time, NPOs reveal relational capital that has an influence on their work and the way they work. These influences were the opinions and needs of beneficiaries on the one hand and demands of donors on the other. According to the documents, a demand posed by the latter is transparency, impacting the means of disclosure of NPOs. Another source that influences NPOs is their relationship to officials and politicians. This relationship can impact the work of NPOs positively or negatively on various levels:

> Changes in the government of Eritrea lead to strong restriction for the work of non-native NPOs. We were among the last active NPOs that were forced to leave the country. (TERRA TECH Förderverein e. V., 2011, p.5)

> Thanks to the constructive cooperation with the responsible administrative district office, three women and on men are employed here. (Caritasverband der Erzdiözese München und Freising e.V., 2013, p.24)

Another theme in the statements assigned to 'relational capital' is reports on activities, aims, and topics covered by 'public relations'. For instance, activities such as exhibitions, lectures or events for external stakeholders were reported on, and the aims and the topics of such public relations were presented, such as:

> We conduct public relations work on every organisational level to report on activities to achieve the highest possible level of attention, transparency and support. (Johanniter-Unfall-Hilfe e.V., 2011, p.25)

'Relational capital' includes a further sub-code, namely 'image', which entails views and opinions of the NPO and its work by external parties as well as of the NPO itself. The themes belonging to this code are description of image, and public signals of good work. Statements counted to the former theme were expressed through citations of beneficiaries or statements of the respective NPO as the first of the following statements illustrates, while the latter statement illustrates public signals of good work:

> Our services are innovative, sustainable and of highest quality. (Johanniter-Unfall-Hilfe e.V., 2012, p.2)

> For our family-oriented human resource policy we were certified by „audit berufundfamilie" several times. (Caritasverband der Erzdiözese München und Freising e.V., 2013, p.52)

One theme of information on human capital disclosed was the structure of the workforce, including the tasks or areas of work in general and information on who was responsible for which of these tasks and areas of work in particular. Again, reports on activities of the NPO were provided, in this case addressing human capital, representing another theme. These activities targeted employees and volunteers, for instance trainings on or for the job, events, or staff development projects. NPOs also reported on recruitment activities and internal changes like the retirement of a member of staff or the election of a chair of a project group.

Another theme detectable was the recognition of the importance of the workforce, expressed through formula of thanks within the documents and the praise of the work of individual volunteers or employees, like:

> Without the commitment of our 550 volunteers such a tight event schedule would not be manageable. These men and women who donate their leisure time relentlessly, and their families who support such a commitment, we are indebted to! (DGzRS, 2014b, p.32)

Further demands on the workforce were expressed. Apart from the number of qualified staff required, qualities essential for the NPOs were mentioned, for example within the following statements:

> Crucial for the success were competent, motivated staff, who feel connected to the organisation and its objectives. (Caritasverband der Erzdiözese München und Freising e. V., 2004, p.22)

> Seemingly so easy in retrospect, it took a lot of skill, experience and cautiousness. (DGzRS, 2014b, p.13)

Financial capital was segmented into information on fundraising, costs of human capital, and financial statements. The latter were numerical data on expenditures, donations received, etc., as well as descriptions of these figures and explanation of changes compared to preceding years.

> Like in the preceding year the increase results from expansion of the services offered and from adjustment of remuneration due to increased personnel expenses and costs of material. (Johanniter-Unfall-Hilfe e.V., 2013b, p.30)

Costs of human capital were published as well, including information on the composition of these costs:

> Personnel expenditures include remuneration, social insurance contributions and expenditures for retirement benefits and expenses for volunteers. Main reasons for the increase compared to the preceding year are changes of the collective agreement, compliance with this agreement, and the engagement of personnel. (Johanniter-Unfall-Hilfe e.V., 2012, p.27)

The segment ‘fundraising’ included information on fundraising activities, the amount of funds raised (including comparison to the preceding year), explanations for a decrease or increase in the amount of funds collected, and how collected funds were provided:

> The additional services offered are financed through donations and sponsored working hours. (Albert-Schweitzer-Kinderdorf in Sachsen e.V., 2011, p.18)

> An agent for holiday homes forwards one Euro per booking to us. In the second half of 2013 we received 2000 Euro. (DGzRS, 2014a, p.20)

> Financially we are supported by ‘Aktion Deutschland Hilft’ and the ‘Benediktinerabtei Münsterschwarzach’. (TERRA TECH Förderverein e. V., 2009, p.2)

> All funds we use to support projects every year are exclusively financed via donations. (Steinschleuder e.V., 2005, p.17)

Information on manufactured capital was segmented into four themes: reports on construction, information on financial implications, data about the manufactured capital e.g. the size of a boat, and explanations of necessity were given, such as:

> These are real estate which are needed within the scope of the services provided according to our statutes. (Johanniter-Unfall-Hilfe e.V., 2008, p.22)

> The library is located in the head office of the organisation and has an inventory of approximately 1200 donated books, including children's books, comics, literature and educational books. (ProBrasil e.V., 2012, p.23)

Little information on natural capital was available in the documents. A few remarks on acting in an environmentally conscious manner and on environmental pollution and its effects were detectable. However, some projects aiming at raising environmental awareness or for the preservation of the environment were introduced.

> The environmental pollution caused by our long-distance flights and the extremely high costs for the participants are too high on a permanent basis. (Steinschleuder e.V., 2008, p.2)

> It is our responsibility that the children of tomorrow can play in fresh air and have a green Christmas tree in their living room. (Caritasverband der Erzdiözese München und Freising e.V., 2002, p.19)

7.1.3 Disclosure

There are three forms of disclosure detectable: numerical facts, visual rhetoric, and narratives. Information provided in form of numerical facts was data on output and data on staff e.g. the number of volunteers working for the organisation, the increase or decrease in the total number of staff, or the number of women working for the NPO compared to the number of men. Also, data on NPOs were provided consisting of names, bank account or address details as well as legal information, for instance:

> The organisation is registered as charitable and benevolent association in the register of associations of the district court. (Albert-Schweitzer-Kinderdorf in Sachsen e.V., 2011, p.4)

Data on output contained information on the number of times a service was performed, the number of beneficiaries reached, and the number of facilities provided:

> 2004 we operated ten hospices nationwide, five years later, in 2009, the number increased to 18 hospices. (Johanniter-Unfall-Hilfe e.V., 2009, p.10)

> Indirectly up to 60.000 people living in the region benefited from the project. (TERRA TECH Förderverein e. V., 2011, p.5)

Narrative disclosure was utilised to convey a descriptive type of information. Stories and citations of individuals describing their experience with the service offered by the NPOs were provided. Either stakeholders or beneficiaries wrote or told their stories and the NPO published their words, or the NPO presented a story about an individual. Some of these stories were written in a "storytelling style", for instance

> The way to the station is arduous this morning. Out of breath Sabrina enters the room. (Johanniter-Unfall-Hilfe e.V, 2009, p.5)

or

> There are people who fell out of the normal world at some point in time. People like Josef. (Caritasverband der Erzdiözese München und Freising e.V., 2007, p.32).

Apart from stories and citations, project outputs, aims, activities, processes, etc. were described in a narrative way as well. While reading the publications of NPOs, the focus on descriptions of projects and activities was apparent.

Visual rhetoric was used to introduce staff through their picture and to give an impression of the work of an NPO. Pictures illustrating the latter often showed staff doing their work or facilities being used or operated, e.g. a kindergarten or a refugee camp. A lot of pictures without an obvious link to the organisation or its work were included in the documents, for instance landscapes, animals, or people who were neither mentioned in a text nor could be identified through a caption. However, most of the times, a link could be drawn with a little imagination. If an NPO reports on a project in Africa, the chances are high that the picture of the landscape shown next to the text, was taken in proximity of the project site. Pictures showing people shaking hands, could be a sign for relationship or relational capital, but there is no way to verify this link for the reader of the documents.

7.1.4 Variables

Variables are features that differ for the contemplated object. They have at least two characteristics (Kuckartz, 2012). Variables defined for the current research were those used for sampling (Sect. 6.4), namely age, size and composition of staff, revenue, level of internationality, fundraising performance, and location.

Longevity

Two groups were defined to establish whether similarities and differences existed in the disclosure of capitals depending on the longevity of an organisation: NPOs founded after 2000 i.e. young NPOs, and long-standing NPOs founded before 1914. The segmentation of NPOs based on their longevity results from the assumption that longer-standing NPOs have different structures and different ways of working than younger NPOs. Looking at the codes assigned to documents published by the two groups, their similarities are remarkable. Both groups disclosed information on capitals mainly via reports on projects and services delivered, and focused on public relation activities first and descriptions of processes second. Both included pictures that can be clearly linked to the organisation, for instance through a logo or writing on the clothing. A few differences exist nevertheless. Young organisations more frequently reported on fundraising than they provided financial statements, while documents of long-standing NPOs showed the other precedence. Long-standing organisations put more emphasis on volunteers than staff, while young NPOs concentrated on staff over volunteers. In general, it is also noticeable that the amount of information offered by long-standing NPOs was far higher compared to the information published by young organisations.

Size and Composition of Workforce
NPOs with the lowest number of staff provided little information in general. The information they did provide focussed on fundraising, reports on services and projects delivered, and illustrations of their processes. Organisations with a high number of staff disclosed information concentrating on projects and services delivered, on their structure, and on reports of public relation activities. Additionally, financial statements were offered more frequently by organisations with a high number of staff. Comparing these two groups, i.e. NPOs with many employees and volunteers against organisations with a small workforce, only the focus on reports on projects and services delivered was similar. The aspect of structural capital focused on by the small NPOs was processes, while the big organisations focused on structure. Relationship to donors was the aspect of relational capital which the small organisations concentrated on. The big NPOs gave priority to reports on public relation activities as part of relational capital, to volunteers as an aspect of human capital, and to financial statements over fundraising. Small organisations did not provide any information on human capital at all and favoured fundraising over financial statements in their publications.

The assumption at the basis for the variable composition of staff was that paid employees were hired due to their abilities, which were needed by the NPO. Volunteers, on the other hand, were not necessarily chosen by an NPO based on demand, but rather chose the NPO they wished to work for. Both NPOs predominantly with employees and organisations consisting primarily of volunteers were intent on descriptions of processes, and on reports of public relation activities. NPOs working mainly with employees additionally disclosed a lot of financial statements. These organisations provided little information on natural capital and their relationships to the press, to the public, to unspecified further external stakeholders, and to partners. Organisations comprised only of volunteers did not report on costs for human capital, on education/training, image, and their relationships to the public, to the press, or to beneficiaries. They used stories and citations of individuals to disclose their capitals and focussed on reports of services and products delivered. While NPOs consisting of volunteers provided financial statements as well, they offered more information on fundraising. Another difference between these two groups of organisations was that the NPOs made up of volunteers generally focussed on staff in their documents. NPOs consisting of employees, on the other hand, reported more frequently on volunteers than on employees.

Revenue

Another assumption regarding the handling of IC by German NPOs was that the amount of revenue generated by the single organisation makes a difference in the way information on capitals was disclosed. According to the empirical data, NPOs with the highest revenue focused their disclosure of capitals on descriptions of projects and services delivered, public relation activities conducted, structure, and the provision of financial statements. Little information was offered on natural capital and the relationships of the NPOs to the press, the public, and further unspecified external stakeholders. Documents of NPOs with the lowest revenue within the sample contained no information on education/training, the costs of human capital, image, and relationships to the public, to the press, and to beneficiaries. The emphasis was on descriptions of projects and services delivered and public relation activities conducted. Additionally, processes were illustrated and stories and citation of individuals used for disclosure.

Level of Internationality

Based on the assumption that different demands and requirement exist for NPOs that work in Germany, compared to those that work internationally, or that support internationally operating NPOs, the sample was segmented accordingly (see Sect. 6.4.5). Organisations that work internationally predominantly provided data on output, i.e. how many beneficiaries were reached, how often people made use of their services and products, and the number of service stations or facilities provided. Financial statements and information on structures were offered as well. Little information was provided on their relationship to the press, costs for human capital, on their relationships to beneficiaries, or on qualities of their staff. Organisations working locally focused on reporting on public relations activities and processes. They also published financial statements. Less information was offered on natural capital and the relationships of the NPOs to the press, public, and unspecified further external stakeholders. Information on projects and services delivered, on co-operations, and on public relation activities were the topics NPOs supporting other organisations centred upon. NPOs assigned to this segment did not provide any information on costs for human capital, database/IT, education/training, relationship to staff, work climate, image, relationship to press, qualification of staff, or data on staff.

Four aspects were similar for NPOs of all three segments: a preference to report on capitals via descriptions of projects and services delivered. Also, all organisations focused on public relations activities and provided little information on costs of human capital and on their relationship to the press. In regard to human capital, NPOs working internationally and those supporting other NPOs provided more information on staff, i.e. employees and volunteers, than on volunteers explicitly, while organisations working locally put their focus on volunteers. The facet of structural capital reported on most by organisations working locally and those organisations supporting other NPOs was processes. Organisations working internationally provided more information on structure, internal processes, and organisational culture than on processes. A different composition emerged for the disclosure of financial capital. In this case NPOs working internationally and those organisations working locally both prioritised the provision of financial statements over reports on fundraising while NPOs supporting other organisations displayed the opposite prioritisation.

Fundraising Performance

High fundraising performance was ascribed to an organisation that raised funds with few expenses. Hence, the NPO that needed a rather high amount of money to raise the lowest ratio of collected funds of the total revenue was compared to organisations that needed similarly few expenses to achieve a high collected fund/total revenue ratio. A lot of similarities in the disclosure of capitals emerged. All NPOs focussed on the disclosure of information on processes, public relation activities, and fundraising. Additionally, all used narrative descriptions of the projects and services delivered to portray their respective organisations. However, the NPOs that invested little to collect a high amount of funds used mainly stories and citations of individuals to illustrate their capitals and added reports on services and products delivered. Also, while these organisations put a focus on the disclosure of information on public relation activities, the overall focus of the disclosure was on structural capital. The organisation on the other end of the fundraising performance continuum focussed on reports on co-operations while stories and citations of individuals were not provided at all. On the other hand, data on output was provided by the organisation that invested a higher amount into fundraising but not by the organisations that invested less.

Taking only the ratio of the total revenue collected via fundraising into account and disregarding the expenses for fundraising, a different picture presents itself. Organisations generating a low ratio of their total revenue via fundraising disclosed more information on their structural capital, specifically on their structure, processes, and organisational culture. NPOs that generated a high portion of the total revenue via fundraising put the spotlight in their publications on relational capital, particularly their public relation activities. Again, organisations on both ends of the fundraising performance continuum reported far less on human capital than on structural capital or relational capital.

Location

To establish whether cultural differences exist as to the handling of IC by German NPOs, the sample was compared accordingly. The variable location consisted of the characteristics north, south, west, east, as defined in Sect. 6.4.7 (see also Fig. 6.5). NPOs assigned the characteristic north disclosed their publicly available information mainly via stories or citations of individuals. The focus of their publications was on their public relation activities, followed by information on fundraising activities and their relationships to donors. The documents also revealed that information on the costs for human capital and on relationships to beneficiaries were provided the least.

For the most part, NPOs in southern Germany disclosed IC via reports on projects and services delivered. They reported mostly on their public relations activities and their processes. Financial statements were a significant part of the documents disclosed as well. The least information was offered on natural capital and relationships to the press, to the public and to partners.

NPOs located in western Germany disclosed information on capitals mainly via reports on projects and services delivered. Information on co-operations, public relations activities, fundraising activities, and financial statements was prevalent within their documents. In contrast, disclosure on costs for human capital, education/training, relationship to staff, work climate, image, and qualification of staff were not provided at all.

Comparable to the NPOs in southern and western Germany, NPOs located in the east disclosed information on capitals mainly via reports on projects and services delivered and financial statements can be found quite often within their published documents. The focus of NPOs in this region, however, was on structure, co-operations, and education/training. The fewest reports were available on their relationship to the press, on qualities of staff, on costs for human capital, and on natural capital.

To summarise, organisations from all regions put emphasis on reports on public relations activities and financial statements were provided. All NPOs included pictures in their documents, predominantly pictures with captions showing beneficiaries, project sites, staff at work, and photos of staff. Little information on the cost of human capital and on the work climate within the NPOs was available, independent of the organisations' locations. It is detectable that NPOs located in both northern and southern Germany focused their information first on public relation activities and on volunteers, with reports on co-operations and on staff coming second, while the focus of NPOs in eastern and western Germany was opposite, i.e. focusing on reports on co-operations and on staff first, and on public relation activities and volunteers second. A peculiarity of eastern NPOs was the focus on education; however, this could be due to a particular NPO within the sample that is considered a pioneer in this regard. A similarity of all NPOs was their preference towards narratives over numerical form to describe capitals.

7.2 Interviews

7.2.1 Advancement of Coding Frame

In addition to the analysis of the documents presented above, the interviews conducted were transcribed, coded, and analysed as described in Sect. 6.6.3. On average, each interview lasted 71 min, with the longest face-to-face interview lasting 95 min and the shortest telephone interview lasting 30 min. All interviews were held in German. In total, three interviews were conducted via telephone and six face-to-face. The interviews lasted a total of 9.5 h and resulted in 151 pages of transcript. Again, relevant text extracts were translated from German to English and are presented throughout this section where appropriate. For names of participants, their job titles, and the names and an overview of the characteristics of the NPOs which the interviewees represent, see Table 6.4.

As mentioned in Sect. 6.5 the interviewees belong to one of three different groups: board members, press officers and public relations managers, or staff. Looking at the statements made and information provided during the interviews, a distinct common perspective of members of a particular group is not detectable. This result is only partly surprising. On the one hand, board members are expected to have a comprehensive view on an organisation, and press officers and public relation manager to focus on external communication, while the focus of staff is likely to be restrained due to limited access to information. One the other hand, the interviews were designed as problem-centred and semi-structured. Therefore, all representatives were chosen as interview partners due to their responsibility for the external communication of their respective organisation. Major differences in the statements and perspectives expressed by members of each group were thus not anticipated when ask about external communication.

The training each member of the groups received, before they were assigned their task, is one differentiating factors. Press officers and public relations managers work for those NPOs that are professionalised to a higher level compared to the other NPOs in the sample. Members of this group are trained to see and communicate a comprehensive picture of their organisation. Members of staff, however, are not necessarily trained extensively in the task they are assigned. Board members are usually appointed due to their experience in a particular field or with a task important for the NPO. Hence, it was surprising to find that not one single interviewee was aware of the term intellectual capital and its concept in the context of NPOs.

The allocation of tasks is partly determined by the size of the workforce of an organisation. Board members are typically only responsible for the entire external communication of an NPO if there is no one else who the task can be assigned to, as it is the case in small NPOs with a small workforce. NPOs, for which not the board member but a member of staff is in charge of external reporting, are consequently neither very small nor very big. In organisations of this small to medium size, information is accessible to most members, strategies discussed, and decisions made as a group. A reliable comparison of statements attributed to the three different groups was therefore not achievable since it is not possible to establish whether the focus on one capital over another, for instance, is due to the size of the respective organisation or to the position of the interviewee held within that organisation. For the analysis of the data collected, the groups the interviewees belong to are thus not taken into account.

As for the documents, the coding frame presented in Sect. 6.7 was used as a basis, complemented by a few new codes that emerged during the coding process. To the code 'disclosure', five sub-codes were added: 'form of external communication', 'style of address', 'media used for external communication' and 'type of donors and target groups'. 'Form of external communication' included statements on how information was presented to external stakeholders, for instance as stories. The code 'style of address' described the language organisations used or explicitly did not use to convey a picture of themselves to their stakeholders. Two examples are the following statements:

> I don't want to compel people into donating, just because they think: they sent me something, now I feel guilty and have to donate some money in return. That is not a good motivation for donating money. (Representative of Albert-Schweitzer-Kinderdorf in Sachsen e.V.: 63)

> A donor should not get the impression that, if he or she does not donate any money, the organisation will have to close tomorrow and the poor children are on the streets. That would be a kind of advertising we do not want. (Representative of Christophorushilfe e.V.: 53)

As the label suggests, the sub-code 'type of donors and target groups' included information on donors on the one hand and target groups for external communication on the other, as in the following examples:

> But there are also donations of companies, hence we approach those too. We have diverse sources like anonymous donations, personal donations and donations of companies. However, I think the most intense ones are the personal ones. (Representative A of ProBrasil: 76)

> I would say that our regular donors are 50+ years of age on average, rather around 60. And those are the people we would approach to ask for donations. (Schmetz, TERRA TECH Förderverein e.V.: 24)

The code 'media used for external communication' is comprised of statements like the following on the media chosen or consciously not chosen by NPOs for disclosure, and the frequency of publications within a medium:

> Regarding the channels we use, there are limits. We could use Google+, we could tweet, and we could use Instagram. But at one point we have to set priorities due to our low staffing level. Therefore we focus on these priorities for the moment. We use Facebook, Youtube, and there is a small group on Xing. That is all at the moment. (Stipeldey, DGzRS - Die Seenotretter: 59)

Also, the DZI and its effects were discussed during the interviews and thus a code 'DZI' was introduced during the coding process. These statements centred on the benefits and problems due to the DZI Spenden-Siegel, as well as the DZI standards as guidelines for external disclosure, as these two statements illustrate:

> Yes, I think it is a fine line, and we try to adhere closely to the demands by the DZI, which are a very helpful corrective. They examine these documents and provide us feedback. (Representative of Christophorushilfe e.V.: 92)

> And we are restricted to a certain amount of administrative expenses due to the Spendensiegel. We cannot be incredibly generous with the use of our donations. There is only a specific percentage of the donations we receive we are allowed to use for administration and advertising expenses [. . .]. (Representative A of ProBrasil e.V.: 200)

'Expenditure' emerged as a sub-code for financial capital. This code accumulated statements regarding how donations were spent, as well as cost-effectiveness considerations, like:

> Because we pay everything ourselves on-site: the travel expenses, accommodation, food, etc., really everything flows into the project. (Representative B of Steinschleuder e.V.: 70)

> We would not be able to afford that, and would not want to either. The 15cent we spend on administration and advertising are kind of sacred to us, you could say. We hope to achieve them every year around. Sometimes it is 84cent, sometimes 86cent of every Euro that flow directly into our service—that is a lot compared to other organisations and institutions. (Stipeldey, DGzRS - Die Seenotretter: 78)

Within the statements ascribed to 'structural capital', some expressed similar content to statements found within the documents. Hence, the same labels for the codes were used, namely 'work climate' and 'professionalism', even though only little information was provided on the latter. The interviewees also offered descriptions of support, opportunities for participation, events for employees and volunteers, training opportunities, and a positive atmosphere, like the following statement which was coded 'work climate'.

> We are more open now in our structure, because we do not want to only do building projects. We noticed that our motivation lies elsewhere since most of us advanced professionally and why not supporting whatever is worth supporting. Now we respond more to the individual wishes of our members. (Representative A of Steinschleuder e.V.: 50)

Similar to the analysis of the documents, the sub-code 'relationships to external stakeholders' proved to be too broad and was split into further sub-codes referring to the parties the interviewees mentioned, namely 'donors', 'partners/co-operations', 'press', 'officials and politicians', and 'beneficiaries'. The last was rarely addressed explicitly, however. Statements on the relationships to these groups as well as descriptions of the challenges and benefits of these relationships were coded respectively. For example, the following quote was coded 'relationship to press':

> I work here since five years by now and I know whom to send what kind of information to and they know me as well. It differs. The papers are sometimes reluctant to report about donations if there are too many in a short period of time or if the amount donated is too small. Then they give me the feedback that someone presenting a cheque is not enough; that is not newsworthy. Especially before Christmas for example, they are not interested in reporting on donations of less than 500€. That is a dilemma for the public relations work for which these reports are important. It is also important for the donors to be recognised and it is important for other people to see: something is happening. That is always a bit of a fight at busy times. It is slightly easier in summer. (Representative of Christophorushilfe e.V.: 31)

Two sub-codes were added to the code 'human capital'. Stories of experiences of the individual interviewee with the organisation and its work were coded 'personal experience', for example:

> You can analyse things theoretically and think, that you find something important—real life has its own ways. One can only say, I have got to try. Previously I worried a lot about our reports etc. and it took me forever to polish them. Meanwhile I think, the best way is to just give it a try. There is no method that is perfect. (Representative of Albert-Schweitzer-Kinderdorf in Sachsen e.V.: 56)

Information on the recruitment process and recruiting activities was labelled 'recruitment', such as:

> We hope that our volunteers tell their families and friends about it and maybe they are interested as well. (Raatz, Johanniter-Unfall-Hilfe e.V.: 75)

> We keep on advertising. For instance the centres for volunteers offer "Engagement in einer Tour", a bus tour through their district or even further, where they visit very diverse social facilities to introduce them to these people interested in volunteering, offering a better basis for decision making as to where they want to volunteer. (Utters-Adam, Caritasverband der Erzdiözese München und Freising e.V.: 103)

Another topic addressed during the interviews was the differences and similarities with other organisations. Consequently, one code added was 'comparison to other NPOs'. Interviewees pointed out differences between NPOs mainly based on size and area of work. Interviewees stated that small organisations have the advantage of short distances for communication, both within the organisation as well as to external stakeholders (Representative B of ProBrasil e.V.: 76; Utters-Adam: 42). For instance, discussions including every active member of an organisation were possible (Representative C of Probrasil e.V.: 60). In contrast, bigger organisations have the advantage of using economies of scale, like reduced rates for a higher volume of printing material (Representative of Albert-Schweitzer-Kinderdorf in Sachsen e.V.: 44). Additionally, NPOs with a lot of staff have more know-how available to them compared to organisations with few staff members (Stipeldey, DGzRS - Die Seenotretter: 88; Representative B of Steinschleuder e.V.: 61). Missing know-how requires staff to become acquainted with the necessary rules and approaches, hindering them from working towards the social aim. For example, a volunteer who has to learn how to maintain a website from scratch requires a far longer time for this task than someone who already has the necessary know-how.

The main distinction regarding the area of work was highlighted as emergency relief organisation versus all other organisations. Emergency relief organisations raise a lot of their funds when a disaster has already happened (Stipeldey, DGzRS - Die Seenotretter: 93). Most of the time, a disaster like an earthquake, tsunami, or hurricane is all over the news and thus people are aware of the necessity of NPOs to help on site and their need for funding (Schmetz, TERRA TECH Förderverein e.V.: 19; Stipeldey, DGzRS - Die Seenotretter: 23). Organisations working for children in Germany, for example, or in countries where the need of the beneficiaries was not in the news, have to raise awareness for the situation themselves and thus have a harder time convincing people to donate to their cause. Additionally, it is easier to raise funds of those who either can identify with the cause or have an emotional connection to the organisation and/or its aim (Representative of Albert-Schweitzer-Kinderdorf in Sachsen e.V.: 91).

7.2.2 *Capitals*

Again, the main subject matter was identified for each capital. That is, the themes of the sub-codes were extracted and condensed into a few meta-level themes (Creswell, 2009). These themes are summarised in Table 7.3. As in the documents, the term intellectual capital or any of the capitals were not mentioned explicitly unless representatives were asked whether they knew the term intellectual capital.

Table 7.3 Themes of capitals disclosed in interviews

Capital	Themes identified
Structural capital	Approaches
	Principles
	Challenges
	Unique features
Relational capital	Approaches
	Challenges
	Aims
Human Capital	Approaches
	Challenges
	Importance of qualities and know-how
	Description of expertise
Spiritual capital	Description of emotional effects of getting involved
	Description of emotional effects of donating money
Financial capital	Fundraising
	Sources of funding
	Challenges
	Approaches and activities
	Explanations as to what donations are used for
	Reasons for expenses

It is observable that during the interviews information on relational capital and structural capital were provided most, followed by information on human capital and spiritual capital. None of the interviewees provided information on natural capital. Information on financial capital was again provided less frequently than on relational capital and structural capital but more often than on human capital and spiritual capital. Information on manufactured capital was only disclosed once (Table 7.4).

Structural capital included six sub-codes, namely 'structure', 'processes', 'database/IT', 'organisational culture', 'work climate' and 'professionalism'. Themes detectable across all sub-codes were descriptions of approaches, challenges, principles and unique features of the particular organisation the interviewee represented. The first theme, approaches, included descriptions of how NPOs distributed tasks and responsibilities within the organisations and of the processes in place for external communication, as the following examples illustrate:

> We are really a team and we distribute tasks as they arise and based on capacity. If there is something that needs to be translated, I cannot do that, obviously the request is forwarded to her. Or if anything else needs to be done everyone is asked 'Are you able to do this? Do you want to do this? Do you have the time to do this?' That is how tasks are distributed. (Representative A of ProBrasil: 214)

> Together with the responsible doctor we decide which child and which disorder we want to 'introduce'. Then I try, or the doctor tries, to get the permission of the family to have their photo taken, next we take the photos, and then the copywriter texts the corresponding letter which I then sign. Before that I have to approve the letter, I do have a bearing on it, for instance if I get the impression that something is not right or does not come across correctly,

Table 7.4 Number of times capitals were addressed during interviews

Code	Occurrences (including sub-codes)
Relational Capital	186
Structural Capital	150
Financial Capital	72
Human Capital	66
Spiritual Capital	3
Manufactured Capital	1
Natural Capital	0

then I dictate the text and approve the letter for printing and they mail it for us. (Representative of Christophorushilfe e.V.: 60)

Further, approaches to recruitment as described in Sect. 7.2.1, stakeholder management, and available structures to positively influence the work climate were described, such as recognition of work, events for staff, and the integration of staff into decision making. The following quote highlights the latter:

> Originally it was the idea of a volunteer, I have to stress. You see, we are partly driven by our own people and certainly embrace ideas like this gladly. It does not have to be someone in a managerial position who develops ideas. Not at all. (Stipeldey, DGzRS - Die Seenotretter: 59)

Several descriptions of principles of an organisation were evident in the interviews and represent the second theme. Principles are defined as a general idea of what good behaviour constitutes "based on what a person believes is right" (Oxford Wordpower Dictionary, 2006, p.563). These beliefs are rooted in the raison d'être of an organisation and manifest themselves in the way the NPO executes its work, like:

> It is very very important for us that we understand ourselves as supporters. We never introduce an idea for a project ourselves but support ideas that were developed on-site. (Representative A of Steinschleuder e.V.: 47)

Additionally, principles translate into how NPOs view their stakeholders, their view of and demands on staff, and who or what the orientation of their processes centres upon. For instance, the following sentence expresses the needs of its beneficiaries as the prime focus that the work of the particular organisation was based upon:

> As I mentioned before, youth welfare offices are often unable to imagine how important it is for us that the children find reliable people in the family that take them in, dependable people, and that they are really noticed as individuals and do not feel as if they are replaceable in any way. (Representative of Albert-Schweitzer-Kinderdorf in Sachsen e. V.: 130)

The first of the following statement shows how principles translate into views on internal relationships and resulting approaches to the distribution of tasks, while the second illustrates a principle for external communication:

> Characteristically for the way we work is that everyone can contribute to the area he or she has an aptitude for. (Representative B of ProBrasil: 209)

> Here we check very carefully what we issue, not because we want to hide anything but because we demand from ourselves that everything we issue has to be watertight, it has to bear any examination. (Stipeldey, DGzRS - Die Seenotretter: 57)

A third theme that emerged from the interviews was the description of challenges the NPO faced based on their internal structure, e.g. "the bigger problem is indeed again our internal decentralised structure" (Raatz, Johanniter-Unfall-Hilfe e.V.: 59), and on a perceived lack of professionalism. Professionalism was described during the interviews as advantageous and desirable, with a lack thereof creating a disadvantage, as this statement illustrates:

> And I think, to some extent they expected something different, more professional, and did not show any interest in participating further. (Representative B of Steinschleuder e.V.: 165)

According to the statements made during the interviews, available databases and IT are regarded as a double-edged sword. On the one hand, there were presented as a challenge, and on the other hand, databases were seen as helpful and utilised by NPOs as a foundation for fundraising and for relationship management, as the following statements highlight:

> The database enables us to capture a lot of information. If one is good at this—and we are not—it should not be a problem to screen and use the data in a more customised way. (Representative of Christophorushilfe e.V.: 90)

> And now we discovered via our own database, that there are particular donors who only donate once a year. You can establish that looking at the returns. Or there are people who write us "stop sending me that much paper, I want to support you, but do not to spend the money this way". It is great when people get in touch with us and let us know, then we can consider their wish, with the software that is possible. (Representative of Albert-Schweitzer-Kinderdorf in Sachsen e.V.: 50)

Unique features of the particular organisation, the fourth theme, were expressed in the course of descriptions of the organisational culture, like "family resembling form of care" (Representative of Albert-Schweitzer-Kinderdorf in Sachsen e.V.: 130) and of the work climate, for example:

> Friendships are formed within our organisation that possibly last a lifetime [...] there is a lot of friendship involved in our work. (Representative A of Steinschleuder e.V.: 108)

When analysing the statements assigned to the sub-codes of 'relational capital', three main themes emerged, namely approaches, challenges, and aims. The theme labelled approaches included statements like the following on how NPOs handle their relationship management with their external stakeholders, their co-operations, and their public relation activities:

> When I started working for this organisation, I made sure that I got in contact with the responsible editor. Additionally we moved into town two years ago which makes it easier for me to invite people to our office. I noticed that journalists like to quickly drop by. When you talk about something on the phone and you say 'I have got a bigger story for you', they drop by, have a look at our office and we can talk for half an hour. (Schmetz, TERRA TECH Förderverein e.V.: 13)

> We manage the small mailings ourselves, well not entirely: we print the letters but they are put into the envelopes by people working in a sheltered workshop who enjoy taking over this task, and finally we post the letters. (Representative of Albert-Schweitzer-Kinderdorf in Sachsen e.V.: 56)

> Yes and the volunteers on site wrote a blog which we partly linked to our Facebook profile. (Representative B of ProBrasil e.V.: 61)

Statements that described challenges occurring in relationships to external stakeholders or regarding public relations activities were another theme, e.g.:

> Interestingly, looking at supporting members, the number decreases continuously. I think that is a problem every donation-soliciting organisation is facing. Or at least every organisation constituted as an association. The willingness of younger people to commit to such a regular supporting membership is limited. (Raatz, Johanniter-Unfall-Hilfe e.V.: 90)

> Even if you sent them an article, you have to call and remind the newspapers of it. (Representative of Direkte Hilfe für Kinder in Not e.V.: 14)

> Apart from that, one of the challenges for our PR is that we are not an emergency relief organisation. We [...] work in long-range development projects, i.e. with duration of two to three years and usually in areas which do not get much attention from the public. That makes it difficult to promote a project, when it is not currently present in the media. (Schmetz, TERRA TECH Förderverein e.V.: 19)

> The construction of the clinic was finished in 2010 but it could not be opened due to various opponents, corrupt opponents from government circles and members of the local medical class. (Representative A of ProBrasil: 258)

The third theme that emerged from the statements assigned to the sub-codes of 'relational capital' was 'aim'. For instance, the aims of a relationship to the press, of partnerships, or the external presentation of an organisation were described, as the first of the following citations illustrates. The second statement highlights the aims of public relation activities:

> But the idea is to position ourselves as "Seniorenversteher" *[Annotation by the author: translates approximately into 'someone who understands the wants and needs of elderly people'],* as I would call it, but we are not there yet by a long shot. (Raatz, Johanniter-Unfall-Hilfe e.V.: 101)

> Our foremost task is to ensure that people have heard of us. If people even get to like us, that is the second step, they might consider donating eventually in the future. (Stipeldey, DGzRS - Die Seenotretter: 21)

In addition to the main themes, further topics unique to the individual sub-codes were addressed. For instance, the code partnerships/co-operations enveloped reports on reasons for co-operations as well as the division of tasks, i.e. who is responsible for what tasks relating to the project. Additionally, reasons for partnerships were offered, for instance sharing (Representative of Albert-Schweitzer-Kinderdorf in Sachsen e.V.: 122) and development of knowledge (Raatz, Johanniter-Unfall-Hilfe e.V.: 98).

For the sub-code 'image', a further theme labelled perception of NPO came into sight. The statements that were part of this theme can be segmented into two categories. First, the way the single interviewee believed the organisation was perceived by external parties, which may or may not have been learnt via actual discussion with external stakeholders, such as:

> I believe we are relatively transparent in our external presentation. (Raatz, Johanniter-Unfall-Hilfe e.V.: 13)

The second segment of statements counted to the theme perception of NPO were reports on differences in the perception of an organisation by the interviewees and how they believed it was generally perceived by external stakeholders. Also, reports on the difficulties to establish a common picture of the organisation internally and to convey a realistic picture to external stakeholders were offered. The next statements are examples of these difficulties.

> Sometimes it would be good to make ourselves conscious of what we actually have to offer. (Representative of Albert-Schweitz Kinderdorf: 114)

> Our organisation might be perceived as rather dry and formal—what makes our organisation special and what it actually means to us is hard to bring across. (Representative A of Steinschleuder e.V.: 118)

For the code 'human capital', approaches emerged again as a main theme. Interviewees described the approaches of their respective NPO to recognise the work of their staff and to recruit volunteers, donors and employees, such as:

> How we approach people? An event here and there: when Mr. X [*Annotation by author: the founder of the organisation*] is here from Brazil we use the abbey for events for instance. This year we went to a café and I gave a talk. Usually we do not make any money with those events. It is rather a mixture, I believe. And also, we appeal to our friends and relatives—some donors are part of our families and circles of friends. They donate because they know that someone is involved who they know. (Representative C of ProBrasil e.V.: 72)

A second main theme that came into sight was reports on challenges, comparable to the other two capitals already presented. Examples of challenges reported were difficulties with recruitment and the impact of the scarcity of staff, as expressed in the following statements:

> But we have to set priorities because of our very low staffing level. (Stipeldey, DGzRS - Die Seenotretter: 59)

> That is a problem we have had for many years and which we discuss on a constant basis: how do we recruit new participants and how can members be retained for the organisation. Unfortunately a lot of people join us for a year and leave when the year is over. But the organisation works only if some commit themselves for at least two or three years since our projects can only be accomplished if someone with experience takes part (...). If most people leave us after a short time only few remain among which necessary tasks can be divided. (Representative A of Steinschleuder e.V.: 64)

Another theme detectable within the interviews was statements highlighting the importance of qualities and know-how, like:

> We would love to have a couple more people who bring in their abilities and knowledge. We struggle a bit with these few people: very motivated and engaged but not enough. (Representative A of ProBrasil e.V.: 127)

> At the moment we don't have enough staff and thus do not put a focus on PR events since we don't have the energy to be creative. (Representative of Albert-Schweitzer-Kinderdorf in Sachsen e.V.: 85)

Description of expertise existing within the organisations was a further theme, such as:

> Experience shows that we, i.e. the responsible ones for media relations, need to try to bring our experts into the discussion. They are established experts in their fields and simply represent the entire know-how and expertise we have to offer, which is thus reflected outwardly through them. (Stipeldey, DGzRS - Die Seenotretter: 18)

Again statements of interviewees formed a theme within sub-codes that did not fit with the main codes. A sub-code specific theme was the different motivations for people to volunteer, such as the feeling of belonging and of being needed (Representative A of Steinschleuder e.V.: 35; Representative B of ProBrasil e.V.: 117; Representative A of ProBrasil e.V.: 208), identification with the aim of the respective organisation (Representative C of ProBrasil e.V.: 6; Utters-Adam, Caritasverband der Erzdiözese München und Freising e.V.: 109; Representative A of Steinschleuder e.V.: 104) or the desire to give something back to society in general and people in need in particular (Representative B of ProBrasil e.V.: 102; Representative A of ProBrasil e.V.: 208; Representative A of Steinschleuder e.V.: 164).

Spiritual capital was rarely described during the interviews, but whenever it was mentioned, it always addressed the emotional effects of getting involved or of donating money, like:

> That is, we 'sell' a good feeling at best, if you want to put is like that. There is no return service for a donation apart from the positive feeling that you did something good. (Stipeldey, DGzRS - Die Seenotretter: 74)

> Children open everyone's heart. (Representative of Albert-Schweitzer-Kinderdorf in Sachsen e.V.: 93)

Information provided on financial capital centred on fundraising on the one hand, stating sources of funds, challenges, approaches and activities in this regard as well as explanations as to what the donations were used for. On the other hand, reasons for expenses were offered. The following statement is an example of the description of an approach as well as a challenge:

> Our impression is that, if we make a comparison, that an appeal for donations that is very understandable for normal people is more successful—I had the impression, the appeal for donations for new windows, everyone in the area who built or is building a house can relate to the fact that you need proper windows. And they also have an idea how expensive a window is. At least that is an explanatory model I developed. [. . .] With other things, such as medical equipment, I think, people don't know what they are good for. (Representative of Christophorushilfe e.V.: 68)

> To replace the number of donors who die, move away, or who got into a situation where they now need help themselves—we do not manage that. At the moment we really do not succeed at that. (Representative of Albert-Schweitzer-Kinderdorf in Sachsen e.V.: 44)

7.2.3 Disclosure

As introduced in Sect. 7.2.1 the sub-code 'type of donors and target groups' emerged from the analysis of the interviews. Interviewees segmented their donors and target groups by age, geographical origin, or frequency/type of donation, as the following examples illustrate:

> Yes, we have approximately 700 members in our association who pay a small membership fee and that is their only donation and we have a high, high number of regular donors who are not members but who annually donate a fixed amount or who donate on demand. (Representative of Christophorushilfe e.V.: 19)

> The average donor [. . .] is about 70 years old, I think. (Raatz, Johanniter-Unfall-Hilfe e.V.: 90)

Principles that NPOs followed in their external communication were diverse. The statements assigned to the code 'style of address' show that the principles for external communication were based on negation most of the time, such as 'without pressure' and 'not exaggerated', for instance:

> I do not want letters that are pressing in any way or that make people feel guilty or anything of that sort. (Representative of Albert-Schweitzer-Kinderdorf in Sachsen e.V.: 63)

Most reports of interviewees about the 'form of external communication' showed that NPOs prefer to publish narratives over numbers to report on their work. One participant explains this preference:

> I think it is more fascinating for them [*Annotation by author: the donors*] to get information regarding our work and not the numbers. (Representative B of Steinschleuder e.V.: 94)

Analysing the statements on the media utilised for external communication, it was noticeable that traditional approaches like letters, booklets, information leaflets, etc. were still the media most commonly used. A lot of times, these documents were also available via the homepage of the respective NPO. None of the NPOs within the sample used e-mails or social media to appeal for donations, for instance. According to the interviewees, social media was used as "an information channel" (Schmetz, TERRA TECH Förderverein e.V.: 41) and to signal that the NPO was actively working on a project (Representative C of ProBrasil: 30) but not for recruitment or fundraising.

Very few numerical facts were offered during the interviews, such as the number of volunteers, employees and members, the longevity of an organisation, and the number of beneficiaries. The importance of pictures within publications was a topic addressed more frequently during the interviews, as illustrated by the following statements.

> Prime information is definitely the pictures. Most texts are not read completely anymore, we notice that on our Facebook page. Articles with pictures [...] are in higher demand. (Schmetz, TERRA TECH Förderverein e.V.: 39)

> Yes, I think and that is also my experience, people read less and less. They only read about topics they are interested in at that very moment. And I can only get their attention through a visual stimulus, a so called 'eye catcher', so that they pick up a booklet in the first place. (Representative of Christophorushilfe e.V.: 70)

Also, criterion for selecting photos were highlighted, such as "not too upsetting" (Schmetz, TERRA TECH Förderverein e.V.: 23), "respecting to the dignity of person shown" (Utters-Adam, Caritasverband der Erzdiözese München und Freising e.V.: 50) and "able to transport a message" (Utters-Adam, Caritasverband der Erzdiözese München und Freising e.V.: 54).

7.2.4 Variables

The variables used to analyse the interviews are the same as those used above for the analysis of the documents, namely longevity, size and composition of staff, revenue, level of internationality, fundraising performance, and location. These variables are not defined again in the following section since the definitions are offered in Sects. 6.4 and 7.1.4 already.

Longevity
Comparing the long-standing (founded before 1914) and the youngest (founded after 2000) organisations in the sample, the same high level of emphasis on information about public relations activities is noticeable. Another similarity is the importance put on organisational culture. However, young organisations provide even more information on their processes. Image is another topic about which the amount of information provided differs—long-standing NPOs put a much stronger focus on image than their younger counterparts. For instance, the following quote of the representative of the longstanding NPO shows that he is aware of the established reputation that needs to be fostered. Additionally, he mentions the reputation of the organisation eleven times during the interview.

> But we need to care for the reputation that we built over the last 150 years in everything we do every day. (Stipeldey, DGzRS - Die Seenotretter: 83)

The subsequent quote is one of two times a representative of one of the younger organisations mentioned reputation:

> I think Facebook is a good tool to show that we are active, in case someone looks us up in the internet. If someone reads our webpage he/she sees that we have 300 facebook followers, than he/she knows that we are not a big organisation but that we are not a 'nobody' either. (Representative C of ProBrasil e.V.: 30)

Comparing the level of attention that the capitals got, the distribution is similar: information coded as relational capital was provided the most, followed by reports on structural capital. Information on human capital was offered less frequently and expressions of spiritual capital were hardly ever mentioned by either the long-standing or the young NPOs.

Size and Composition of Staff
Representatives of NPOs with a lot of staff offered information on structural and relational capital with equal frequency, focussing mainly upon public relation activities and processes. A different picture presents itself looking at the information provided by small organisations. These NPOs put relational capital into the

spotlight, provided less information on structural capital, and hardly any information on human capital. Again, the main emphasis was on public relation activities, followed by information on the relationship to donors.

Information on relational capital was provided more frequently than information on other capitals by representatives of NPOs with a workforce consisting mainly of paid employees. The main focus was on public relation activities, followed by information on processes and on organisational culture. In comparison, NPOs composed of volunteers focused more on structural capital, specifically on processes, as expressed the following statement for instance:

> We have two types of meetings. On the one hand we have small weekend meetings and on the other organisational and strategy meetings. The latter are relatively big. That is where the really really important decisions are made. During those weekend meetings it is more about spending time together and talking about 'smaller' topics. (Representative A of Steinschleuder e.V.: 19)

Slightly less frequently, information on public relations activities and on organisational culture was provided. Regarding the comparison of these groups, it needs to be kept in mind that organisations consisting of volunteers do not necessarily have a public relations manager or press officer. However, the representative of employee-centred NPOs interviewed for the current research held exactly those positions within their organisations. A similarity is that interviewees of both segments gave little information on their relationship to beneficiaries and on volunteers.

Revenue

NPOs with the highest revenue were compared to those with the lowest revenue to check for differences and similarities. Representatives of the latter put processes and public relation activities into the spotlight, followed by information on the organisational culture of their NPOs. In other words, more information on structural capital than relational capital was provided. Interviewees of NPOs with high revenue gave the most information on public relation activities, processes, organisational culture and image. A similarity was that both groups offered little information on the relationship to beneficiaries and on human capital in general. The following statement is an example of a statement linking revenue to organisational culture, highlighting the importance for the respective organisation:

> We are asked over and over again why the state does not support us financially. It is the other way round! We decide against taking money from the state very consciously. (Stipeldey, DGzRS - Die Seenotretter: 15)

Level of Internationality

Representatives of NPOs working internationally emphasised processes and the organisational culture of their respective NPOs. More than half of all the information given was on structural capital. At the same time, NPOs working internationally did not offer any information on the relationship to the press and only little information on the relationship to partners. The focal point of interviewees of NPOs working locally was similar to that of representatives of NPOs that support other organisations. Both groups focused on relational capital in general, on public relations activities in particular, and gave little information on their volunteers. A difference was the importance put on the relationship to the press by the organisations working locally but not by organisations supporting other NPOs. Both groups provided only little information on their human capital and on the relationship to their beneficiaries. A representative of a supporting organisation gave the following example for the balance the organisation needs to keep between the geographical location they operate in, i.e. fundraise, and the project area they support.

> At the same time we live in an area with lots of students, which is not easy. Often we receive the feedback that people appreciate it that we don't use blatant pictures. Especially in this university context people are attentive that Africa is not only portrayed as a needy continent. (Schmetz, TERRA TECH Förderverein e.V.: 23)

Fundraising Performance

The information given by representatives of organisations that manage to raise a lot of funds in relation to the total revenue with low expenditure for fundraising was compared to those NPOs that spend an acceptable amount on fundraising in relation to the funds raised in proportion to total revenue. The latter focussed strongly on providing information on public relations activities and on their relationship to the press, i.e. relational capital. Human capital was talked about the least by both groups. Representatives of organisations that manage to raise a high amount of funds with little expenditures in comparison highlighted their processes and their organisational culture, i.e. structural capital, like:

> Yes, every one of us represents the organisation differently. For the one person the experiences gained while working abroad is central while to the other person the work we do here is more important. And I think, you represent to external people through what is closest to your heart because that is how you can bring across what we are all about and motivate others. (Representative A of Steinschleuder e.V.: 95)

Taking only the ratio of the total revenue collected via fundraising into account and disregarding the expenses for fundraising, a different picture presents itself as representatives of both groups spoke most frequently about their public relation activities, i.e. their relational capital, followed by information on structural capital. In other words, the focus of disclosure was the same independent of whether the ratio of funds raised via fundraising was high or small. Again, information on human capital was disclosed the least. Information on their relationship to beneficiaries and on their volunteers was hardly ever provided. Spiritual capital was not mentioned at all by either of the groups.

Location

There was not a big difference in the frequency in which information on relational capital and on structural capital were provided by representatives of NPOs from northern Germany. Most information was given on public relation activities, organisational culture, image, and processes. Human capital was discussed less often and mainly through descriptions of the necessary and available qualities of staff, for instance:

> [. . .] we are all volunteers, none of us receives any money for what we do and there is a whole lot of motivation and idealism behind it. (Representative B of Steinschleuder e.V.: 66)

Relationship to beneficiaries was not mentioned at all.

A third of the information provided by representatives of NPOs located in the south of Germany was on relational capital, with a focus on public relation activities and the relationship to the press. Far less information was provided on structural capital and human capital but was provided with similar frequency. Information on structural capital centred upon processes and organisational culture, and for human capital, information that focussed upon the qualification of staff was the facet reported on most. No information was provided on co-operations, staff, qualities of staff, or professionalism.

Representatives of NPOs located in the west of Germany put relational capital into the spotlight during the interviews. Public relation activities were at the centre of the information offered, followed by information on the relationship to the press. The link of public relation exposure and reports by the press are expressed by one respondent as follows:

> It is easier for the traditional emergency relief organisations, because if you see the effect of a typhoon in the news on TV, you are already sensitized for the topic. (Schmetz, TERRA TECH Förderverein e.V.: 19).

Structural capital was mainly expressed via information on processes or on the organisational culture of the organisation represented. Human capital was focussed on slightly less, with information provided mainly on staff. No information was offered on the relationship to donors or to beneficiaries, or on volunteers.

The analysis of the interviews conducted with representatives of NPOs located in the east of Germany revealed a focus on structural capital, followed by information on relational capital offered slightly less frequently. Information on structural capital centred upon processes and organisational culture, while information on relational capital concentrated on public relation activities. No information was given on the relationships to the press and to beneficiaries. Description of human capital consisted of information on recruitment and on qualities of staff for the most part. Volunteers were rarely mentioned at all.

7.3 Comparison

To establish the similarities and differences of the results presented, Table 7.5 lists the final coding frames to enable a comparison of the codes that emerged from the analysis of the documents and those that emerged from the interviews. Comparing the codes for the capitals, differences can mainly be found for structural capital, with new sub-codes 'education/training', 'relationship to staff' and internal processes'. These topics were not addressed during the interviews. Further codes unique to the coding framework for the documents were 'costs for human capital',

Table 7.5 Comparison of code frameworks documents versus interviews

Documents	Interviews
1. Capitals	**1. Capitals**
1.1 Human Capital	1.1 Human Capital
1.1.1 Staff	1.1.1 Staff
1.1.2 Volunteers	1.1.2 Volunteers
1.1.3 Qualification of staff	1.1.3 Qualification of staff
1.1.4 Qualities of staff	1.1.4 Qualities of staff
1.1.5 *Professionalism*	1.1.5 *Recruitment*
	1.1.6 *Experiences of the Interviewee*
	1.1.7 *Professionalism*
1.2 Relational Capital	1.2 Relational Capital
1.2.1 Public Relations	1.2.1 Public Relations
1.2.2 Image	1.2.2 Image
1.2.3 Relationship to external Stakeholders	1.2.3 Relationship to external Stakeholders
1.2.3.1 *Relationship to public*	1.2.3.1 *Relationship to donors*
1.2.3.2 *Relationship to donors*	1.2.3.2 *Relationship to press*
1.2.3.3 *Relationship to press*	1.2.3.3 *Relationship to partners*
1.2.3.4 *Relationship to partners*	1.2.3.4 *Relationship to beneficiaries*
1.2.3.5 *Relationship to beneficiaries*	1.2.3.5 *Relationship to politics and officials*
1.2.3.6 *Relationship to politics and officials*	
1.2.4 Co-operations	1.2.4 Co-operations
1.3 Structural Capital	1.3 Structural Capital
1.3.1 Structure	1.3.1 Structure
1.3.2 Organisational culture	1.3.2 Organisational culture
1.3.3 Processes	1.3.3 Processes
1.3.4 Databases/IT	1.3.4 Databases/IT
1.3.5 *Work climate*	1.3.5 *Work climate*
1.3.6 *Relationship to staff*	
1.3.7 *Internal processes*	
1.3.8 *Education/training*	
1.4 Spiritual Capital	1.4 Spiritual Capital
1.5 Natural Capital	1.5 Natural Capital
1.6 Manufactured Capital	1.6 Manufactured Capital
1.7 Financial Capital	1.7 Financial Capital
1.7.1 Financial statements	1.7.1 Financial statements
1.7.2 Fundraising	1.7.2 Fundraising
1.7.3 *Costs for human capital*	1.7.3 *Expenditure*
2. Disclosure	**2. Disclosure**
2.1 Visual rhetoric	2.1 Visual rhetoric

(continued)

Table 7.5 (continued)

Documents	Interviews
2.1.1 Random pictures	
2.1.2 Pictures of staff	
2.1.3 Pictures expressing IC and showing the work of the particular organisation	
2.1.4 Pictures expressing IC but not the work of the particular NPO	
2.1.5 Pictures with captions	
2.1.6 Graphs and tables	
2.1.7 Tacit messages	
2.2 Facts	2.2 Facts
2.2.1 Data on NPO	2.2.1 Data on NPO
2.2.2 *Data on output*	2.2.2 Data on interviewees
2.2.3 *Data on staff*	2.2.3 Data on interviews
	2.2.4 *History of NPO*
2.3 *Stories and citations of individuals*	2.3 *Type of donors and target groups*
2.4 *Output*	2.4 *Style of address*
2.4.1 *Projects/services delivered*	
2.4.2 *Aims and plans for projects*	
	2.5 *Medium used for external communication*
	2.6 *Form of external communication*
3. Perspective on IC	**3. Perspective on IC**
3.1 IC as liability	3.1 IC as liability
3.2 IC expressed explicitly	3.2 IC expressed explicitly
4. Demands	**4. Demands**
4.1 Trust	4.1 Trust
4.2 Transparency	4.2 Transparency
4.3 Social Acceptance	4.3 Social Acceptance
4.4 *Quality*	4.4 *Quality*
5. Necessary resources	***5. Necessary resources***
5.1 *Human resources*	5.1 *Human resources*
5.2 *Funding*	5.2 *Funding*
5.3 *Practices*	5.3 *Reputation*
5.4 *Reputation*	5.4 *Support by external parties*
5.5 *Support by external parties*	
	6. DZI
	7. Comparison to other NPOs

information on the NPO's 'relationship to the public', and 'practices' as a necessary resource. Also, two additional sub-codes were added describing possibilities to disclose IC: 'stories and citations of individuals' and 'output'. The latter code included reports on 'projects and services delivered' as well as on 'aims of and plans for projects'. The coding framework for the interviews was complemented with further sub-codes for disclosure as well, namely the 'type of donors and target groups', 'style of address', 'mediums used for external communication' and 'forms of external communication'.

A reason for these different sub-codes for disclosure is the target groups of the data collected. The documents were prepared for external stakeholders of the NPO, hence certain information regarding preliminary decisions, such as the target groups for a publication and the style of disclosure, were not disclosed. At the same time, information on the actual conversion into publications, such as the usage of stories or citations of individuals, were not discussed during the interviews. This consideration of the target group addressed by the data collected was also valid and responsible for two further codes that did not emerge from the documents: 'DZI' and 'comparison to other NPOs'.

Apart from the inductive codes that were part of either the coding frame of the documents or of the interviews, several codes emerged from the documents and from the interviews alike, for instance 'professionalism' as a sub-code of human capital. The perception of professionalism conveyed through the documents as well as via the interviews was as positive and desirable trait which, if lacking, can put organisations at a disadvantage. Furthermore, work climate as a sub-code of structural capital emerged from the documents and the interviews alike. Statements assigned to this code, independent of the source, described approaches and activities of the respective NPO to influence the work climate of the organisation in a positive way.

For the analysis of the documents and the interviews alike, the sub-code 'relationship to external stakeholders' was segmented according to the stakeholder mentioned in the coding units. The preliminary purpose of this segmentation was to transform a code that included a lot of statements into smaller and clearer groups of information. All in all, the statements described how relationships were approached and managed, and why these relationships needed to be addressed e.g. because of their importance for the NPO or the influence of the particular group on the work of the organisation. Additionally, statements ascribed to this code described activities and approaches, illustrating how NPOs work with or for stakeholders. While challenges of relationships were addressed during the interviews, these were hardly ever mentioned in the documents.

A demand on NPOs that was not identifiable from the literature but expressed within both the documents and the interviews was quality of the services offered. While transparency was the demand most frequently mentioned during the interviews and quality was mentioned far less often, quality was the demand highlighted most frequently in the documents.

A further code that emerged from both the documents and the interviews was necessary resources as well as its sub-codes human resources, funding, support by external parties, and reputation. These resources were described as essential for the survival of the NPO, or at the very least that a lack of these resources would have a negative impact on the organisation.

Three similarities across all variables and sources of data attracted attention. One similarity was the low frequency of information provided on human capital compared to structural capital and relational capital despite the importance of human capital stated during the interviews. Also, information on spiritual capital was hardly ever provided within any of the variables. Another similarity was the predominance of information on public relation activities, most possibly due to the way the data was collected. Interviewees were chosen based on their responsibility for external communication for their respective NPO and it was thus to be expected that public relation activities would be a focus of their statements. Documents were prepared for and targeted external stakeholders. However, such a strong focus on the description of public relation activities themselves was surprising.

A clear focus on one of the capitals across both the interviews and documents was evident in a few cases: organisations assigned to the variable west focussed on relational capital, as did organisations which utilized an acceptable amount of expenses to raise a rather low amount of funds. Also, organisations supporting other NPOs centred their disclosure upon relational capital. In contrast, NPOs mainly run by volunteers did not put emphasis on any one capital. They disclosed roughly the same amount of information on structural capital as on relational capital. A focus on human capital was not detectable in any of the interviews or documents.

Table 7.6 shows the focus on one of the capitals during the interviews and in the documents of NPOs assigned to certain variables. Similar challenge that all NPOs face emerged: the relatively high average age of existing members and donors (Representative of Albert-Schweitzer-Kinderdorf in Sachsen e.V.: 63; Representative of Christophorushilfe e.V.: 78; Raatz, Johanniter-Unfall-Hilfe e.V.: 90), the difficulty to recruit new donors (Raatz, Johanniter-Unfall-Hilfe e.V.: 75; Representative of Albert-Schweitzer-Kinderdorf in Sachsen e.V.: 44; Representative B of Steinschleuder e.V.: 162; Representative A of ProBrasil: 78) and the retention of donors and supporters (Stipeldey, DGzRS - Die Seenotretter: 74; Representative A of Steinschleuder e.V.: 144).

Long-standing and young NPOs displayed a similar focus on relational capital over structural capital in the interviews. In the documents, the young organisations showed the same focus, while the focus of the long-standing organisations shifted towards structural capital over relational capital. The emphasis of both long-standing and young organisations alike on a particular capital was less distinct in the documents compared to the interviews.

NPOs with a big workforce put their structural capital into the spotlight during the interviews as well as in the documents. Organisations with a small number of staff provided more information on structural capital within their documents and focused on relational capital during the interviews. Analysing the documents, it was

Table 7.6 Focus of variables during interviews versus focus in documents

Focus on relational capital		Focus on structural capital	
Documents	Interviews	Documents	Interviews
	South	South	
West	West	East	East
North	North		
	Long-standing	Long-standing	
Young	Young		
Supporting	Supporting	International	International
	Local	Local	
Low funds/acceptable expenses	Low funds/acceptable expenses	High funds/low expenses	High funds/low expenses
		Big workforce	Big workforce
	Small workforce	Small workforce	
Low revenue			Low revenue
	High revenue	High revenue	
	Employees	Employees	
Volunteers			Volunteers

noteworthy that the distribution of attention to the capitals was very similar for both groups.

The analysis of the variable 'composition of staff' showed that, during the interviews, the focus was on other capitals than in the documents. NPOs primarily comprised of employees provided more information on relational capital over structural capital during the interviews but offered more information on structural capital compared to relational capital in the documents. NPOs comprised mainly of volunteers disclosed more information on structural capital during the interviews and slightly more on relational capital in the documents.

A slightly stronger focus on relational capital was detectable in the documents published by organisations with the lowest revenue of the sample. During the interviews, structural capital was mentioned with a higher frequency. Organisations with high revenue put the emphasis the other way around, i.e. on structural capital in the documents and on relational capital during the interviews.

Organisations that work internationally put structural capital into the spotlight in their documents and during the interviews. NPO supporting the work of other organisations focused on relational capital according to both sources of data. Information of NPOs working locally centred upon structural capital in their documents and upon relational capital during the interviews.

The analysis of possible dependencies of the fundraising performance and the disclosure of intellectual capital illustrated that NPOs which generate a low portion of funds with an acceptable amount of expenses put a strong emphasis on relational capital in both the documents and during the interviews alike. Organisations at the other end of the continuum disclosed more information on structural capital than relational capital, again in the documents and during the interviews.

For the variable south, representatives of NPOs put a clear emphasis on relational capital during interviews, while their documents exhibited a focus on structural capital. Organisations located in the north and west focused on relational capital across interviews and documents. During the interviews, NPOs located in the east disclosed more information on structural capital than on relational capital, a tendency even more distinct in the documents.

7.4 Dependencies and Interdependencies of Necessary Resources and Demands

According to literature, demands imposed upon all organisations and NPOs in particular are trust, transparency, and social acceptance (Glassman & Spahn, 2012; Raynard, 1998; Drucker, 1990; van Broekhoven, 2008). These three demands emerged from the analysis of the documents and interviews as well, but complemented by quality. While the demands developed from the empirical data solely reflect the perception of the NPOs, their congruency with the demands stated in literature and those detectable in the interviews indicate their validity. To establish how German NPOs handle these demands, the Code Relations Browser provided by MAXQDA (introduced in Sect. 6.6.1) was used to establish overlapping codes and thus possible relationships between them. These links are visualised in Fig. 7.1.

Words in boxes are the demands established. From the data produced by the Code Relations Browser, it is not possible to determine the direction of influence unambiguously. However, examples from the documents and interviews point out the directions that NPOs believe dependencies exist, in Fig. 7.1 indicated via arrows.

The available data indicated that public relations affects image, and both affect social acceptance. Public relations activities aim to build and strengthen the image of an organisation and use signs of social acceptance for this purpose. The award of a certificate for the efforts to create work conditions that meet the needs of families, for instance, is used to create a positive image (Caritasverband der Erzdiözese München und Freising e.V., 2004: p.17). Image affects social acceptance and is affected by it as well. Signs of social acceptance strengthen the image of an organisation and a positive image increases social acceptance. Image is also linked to quality and trust. The combination of image and trust is essential, for instance, for fundraising (Caritasverband der Erzdiözese München und Freising e.V., 2007: p.30) and quality is a part of, and at the same time affects, the image of an organisation. Interdependency exists between quality and internal and external processes, since quality is affected by the way these processes are designed and executed while quality standards influence these processes simultaneously (Caritasverband der Erzdiözese München und Freising e.V., 2010: p.33; Johanniter-

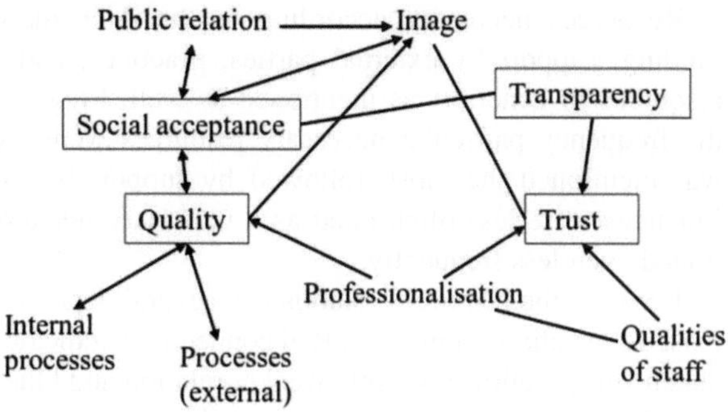

Fig. 7.1 Most significant links of demands

Unfall-Hilfe e.V., 2008, p.7). Quality is also influenced by professionalisation. As one German NPO stated in its business report:

> The quality of our services offered is based on our professionalism and our subject-matter knowledge. (Caritasverband der Erzdiözese München und Freising e.V. 2012: p.35)

Professionalisation also increases trust and is mentioned within the documents analysed alongside other qualities of staff, like quick thinking (DGzRS, 2014a, p.7) or engagement (Caritasverband der Erzdiözese München und Freising e.V., 2009: p.42). Qualities of staff such as engagement and expertise in turn affect trust.

Three direct links between the demands exit, namely between transparency and trust, social acceptance and quality, as well as between social acceptance and transparency. According to the data available, an increase in transparency leads to an increase in trust, as the following statement indicates:

> Transparency and openness shape the co-operation and contribute to donors trusting us and supporting us not only with words and deeds, but also with donation of commodities and financial donations. (Caritasverband der Erzdiözese München und Freising e.V., 2011; p.38)

Regarding quality and social acceptance, the relationship goes both ways. If quality increases, social acceptance increases as well, because the organisation shows that it is capable of delivering services as expected, if not better.

> Crucial for this development was the high quality of the services provided on the one hand and the resulting high approval by the public on the other. (Caritasverband der Erzdiözese München und Freising e.V., 2005; p.17)

In the other direction, signs of social acceptance are considered signals for transparency, like an award for transparency or for quality:

> In November the national association was certified and awarded the TÜV-Siegel "audited according to DIN EN ISO 9001". This signals: quality and customer focus are indeed offered here. (Johanniter-Unfall-Hilfe, 2005, p.21)

Also, an increase in social acceptance affects quality due to higher support in the form of funding and human resources. This link emerged when looking at the resources.

Resources necessary according to the data analysed are human resources, funding, support by external parties, practices, and reputation. Dependency on resources in general was mentioned as well. Figure 7.2 offers a visualisation of the frequency particular necessary resources were mentioned. Human resources was mentioned the most, followed by support by external parties and funding. Practices were less often cited as a necessary resource and reputation was mentioned even less frequently.

Between the resources established, several dependencies and interdependencies exist as visualised in Fig. 7.3. Red connections indicate a strong interdependency or dependency, yellow a slightly weaker relation and blue an even weaker connection. The strongest interdependency emerged between human resources and funding and is thus highlighted via a bold red arrow. Without funding, training of workforce is not possible, knowledge cannot be developed further and employees with expertise cannot be paid. The other way around applies as well; know-how and social skills are necessary for fundraising.

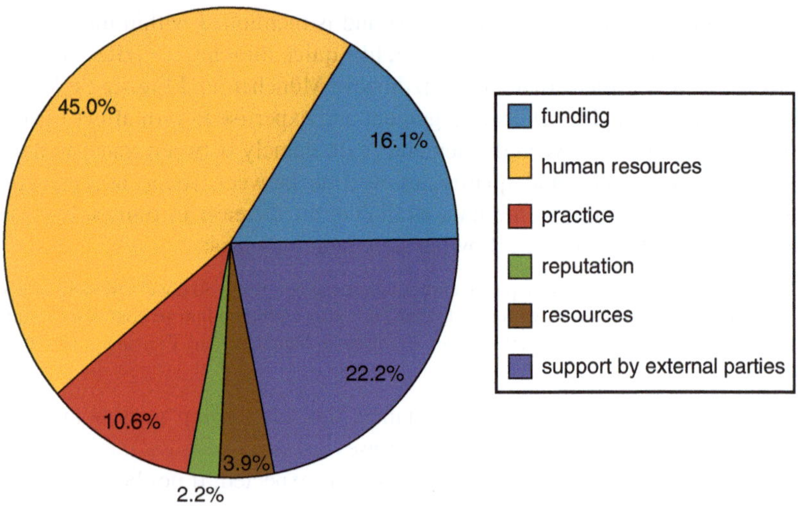

Fig. 7.2 Distribution of times particular necessary resources were mentioned

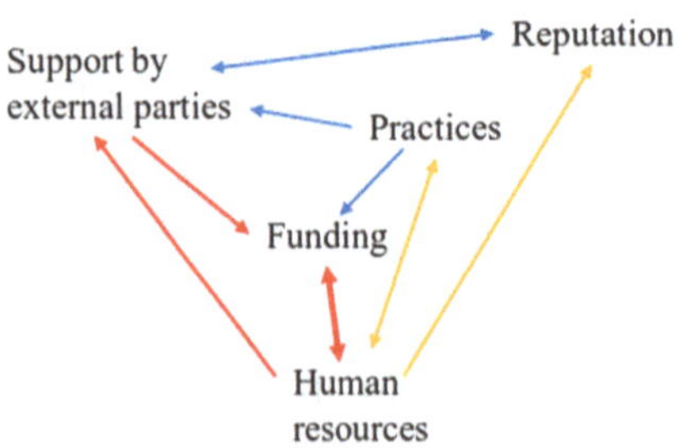

Fig. 7.3 Dependencies and interdependencies of resources

Funding is also dependent on support by external parties. This link is not surprising since the NPOs within the sample are all donation-soliciting organisations and thus dependent on donations of time and money. Another strong link exists between support by external parties and human resources which are both mentioned together 20 times as reasons for success, for example:

> We would like to thank all our donors, volunteers and the local newspaper. Without them this project would not have been realisable. (TERRA TECH Förderverein e. V., 2013, p.1)

Also, human resources affect support by external parties in the form of the ability of individuals of the workforce to build relationships with decision makers in governments and administrations.

A weaker relationship exists between human resources and practices, which include processes, structures, management approaches, and best practices. Human resources are necessary to execute the practices, and practices such as trainings are needed for the development of human resources. Practices in form of consistent strategies influence fundraising and support by external parties. The latter is also affected by the reputation of the organisation since support declines if the reputation of an organisation suffers. The other way round, support by a respectable person or questionable group, for example, affects the reputation of an organisation. Last but not least, influences between human resources and reputation were detectable, as one organisation states:

> These measures were supported by highly motivated employees, who are crucial for the reputation of social institutions. (Caritasverband der Erzdiözese München und Freising e.V., 2006: p.19)

Apart from dependencies of resources among each other and demands among each other, several dependencies and interdependencies of demands and resources emerged from the analysis of the data. These are of great importance since they show the effect NPOs have to take into account when developing their strategies in general and make communication decisions in particular.

Figure 7.4 illustrates the relationships whereby demands are on the right side of the figure (with the grey background) and written in italic, and the resources are on the left side of the figure (with the blue background). The brown lines highlight relationships that emerged from the documents as well as the interviews, the blue line show links detectable in the documents and the green lines those relationships that emerge only from the interviews. In the following paragraph, only the links between resources and demands are discussed, since these were not highlighted yet.

A strong relationship was evident between human resources and quality. On the one hand, human resources are essential for the provision of services in high quality. On the other hand, an increase in the demand for high quality puts pressure on staff to stay on top of developments within the sector in which the organisation works, and pushes NPOs to offer trainings for their workforce to ensure the availability of know-how and even expertise, if possible (Utters-Adam, Caritasverband der Erzdiözese München und Freising e.V.: 127). Only during the analysis of the interviews did a link between quality and trust come into sight. In the

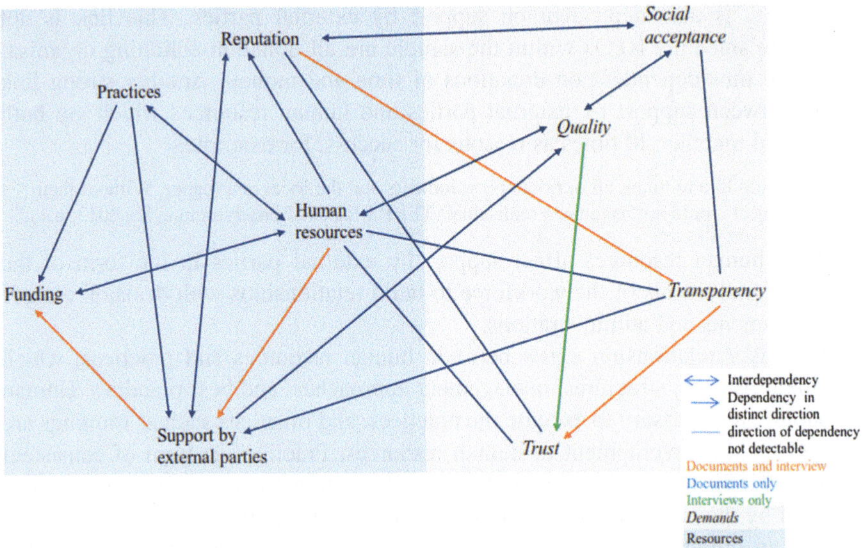

Fig. 7.4 Interdependencies of necessary resources and demands

example given by two NPOs, the quality of prior services led stakeholders to trust in the quality of the services provided currently (Utters-Adam, Caritasverband der Erzdiözese München und Freising e.V.: 17; Stipeldey, DGzRS - Die Seenotretter: 57). Quality is also linked to support by external parties. One interviewee offered an example of this link when he reported that cooperation with another organisation increased the quality of the work of both participants due to lessons learnt during the project (Representative of Albert-Schweitzer-Kinderdorf in Sachsen e.V.: 122).

In the interviews, organisations stated that trustworthiness is a desirable characteristic of reputation. In the documents, the importance of a positive reputation and the trust of stakeholders, as well as the availability of human resources, were mentioned as essential for the success of an organisation. Furthermore, a weak link of human resources to transparency emerged through statements of their importance for success and as an effect of internal transparency between departments on the know-how available to each member of staff (Caritasverband der Erzdiözese München und Freising e.V., 2007: p.26). Transparency and reputation again are both important for the success of an organisation and thus share a weak link.

7.5 Summary of the Main Findings

In light of the research questions, the following findings are the most important ones:

- The terms "intellectual capital", "human capital", "relational capital", "structural capital", "spiritual capital", or any other capital were not used even once in the documents. During interviews they were only used when representatives were asked about these terms explicitly.
- Narratives are mainly used for the disclosure of IC, supported by numbers and visual rhetoric.
- In the documents and during the interviews alike, a lower frequency of information on human capital is noticeable compared to information on relational capital and on structural capital. Also, hardly any information on spiritual capital is provided via either source of data.

  Organisations located in the west and north, young organisations, NPOs supporting other organisations, and NPOs that generate little funding with the use of an acceptable amount of expenses displayed a focus on relational capital. On the other side, NPOs located in eastern German, organisations that work internationally, NPOs that raise a high level of funding using a small amount of expenses, as well as organisations with a high number of employees and volunteers put their structural capital into the spotlight.
- According to the documents and interviews, German donation-soliciting NPOs regard trust, transparency, social acceptance, and quality as demands imposed on them by their stakeholders. The documents and interviews imply that trust does not affect any other demand while transparency is not affected by any other demand. Additionally, the data provided by the NPOs indicate a strong link between quality and social acceptance.
- Professionalism is perceived as positive and desirable by the organisations and the analysis implies that it influences the demands of trust and quality.
- German donation-soliciting NPOs regard five resources as necessary for survival: human resources, funding, practices, reputation, and support by external parties. Strong links between funding and human resources, human resources and support by external parties, and support by external parties and funding are detectable.
- Dependencies and interdependencies between demands and resources exist. However, only the links between reputation and transparency, between human resources and support by external parties, and between the support by external parties and funding are detectable in both the documents and the interviews. The strongest interdependency according to the documents exists between human resources and quality.

References

Albert-Schweitzer-Kinderdorf in Sachsen e.V. (2011). *Pädagogisches Konzept*. Accessed August 06, 2014, from http://www.kinderdorf-online.de/

Caritasverband der Erzdiözese München und Freising e.V. (2002). *Jahresbericht 2002*. Accessed September 23, 2014, from https://www.caritas-nah-am-naechsten.de/media/Media0253820.PDF

Caritasverband der Erzdiözese München und Freising e.V. (2004). *Jahresbericht 2003/2004*. Accessed September 23, 2014, from https://www.caritas-nah-am-naechsten.de/media/Media0253720.PDF

Caritasverband der Erzdiözese München und Freising e.V. (2005). *Jahresbericht 2004/2005*. Accessed September 23, 2014, from https://www.caritas-nah-am-naechsten.de/media/Media0253620.PDF

Caritasverband der Erzdiözese München und Freising e.V. (2006). *Jahresbericht 2005/2006*. Accessed September 23, 2014, from https://www.caritas-nah-am-naechsten.de/media/Media0253520.PDF

Caritasverband der Erzdiözese München und Freising e.V. (2007). *Jahresbericht 2006/2007*. Accessed September 23, 2014, from https://www.caritas-nah-am-naechsten.de/media/Media0253420.PDF

Caritasverband der Erzdiözese München und Freising e.V. (2008). *Geschäftsbericht 2007/2008*. Accessed September 23, 2014, from https://www.caritas-nah-am-naechsten.de/media/Media0253220.PDF

Caritasverband der Erzdiözese München und Freising e.V. (2009). *Geschäftsbericht 2008/2009*. Accessed September 23, 2014, from https://www.caritas-nah-am-naechsten.de/media/Media0253120.PDF

Caritasverband der Erzdiözese München und Freising e.V. (2010). *Geschäftsbericht 2009/2010*. Accessed September 23, 2014, from https://www.caritas-nah-am-naechsten.de/media/Media0253020.PDF

Caritasverband der Erzdiözese München und Freising e.V. (2011). *Geschäftsbericht 2010/2011*. Accessed September 23, 2014, from https://www.caritas-nah-am-naechsten.de/media/Media0252920.PDF

Caritasverband der Erzdiözese München und Freising e.V. (2012). *Geschäftsbericht 2011/2012*. Accessed September 23, 2014, from https://www.caritas-nah-am-naechsten.de/media/Media0524820.PDF

Caritasverband der Erzdiözese München und Freising e.V. (2013). *Geschäftsbericht 2012/2013*. Accessed September 23, 2014, from https://www.caritas-nah-am-naechsten.de/media/Media1049520.PDF

Christophorushilfe e.V. (2014). *Rundbrief Ausgabe 12*. Accessed August 01, 2014, from www.christophorushilfe.de/fileadmin/mediapool/gemeinden/D_christophorushilfe/downloads/5265_rundbrief_0514_Homepage.pdf

Creswell, J. W. (2009). *Research design: Qualitative, quantitative, and mixed methods approaches* (3rd ed.). Thousand Oaks, CA: SAGE.

DGzRS. (2010). *Sicher auf See*. Accessed August 01, 2014, from https://www.seenotretter.de/mediathek/

DGzRS. (2012). *Technik Broschüre*. Accessed August 01, 2014, from https://www.seenotretter.de/mediathek/index.php?eID=tx_nawsecuredl&u=0&g=0&t=1495611797&hash=73820c2b5c046e4cb451255e6361d9f306b535e3&file=/fileadmin/Subnavi/Mediathek/Information/Technikbroschuere_2012.pdf

DGzRS. (2014a). *Laengsseits 2014-02*. Accessed August 01, 2014, from https://www.seenotretter.de/mediathek/index.php?eID=tx_nawsecuredl&u=0&g=0&t=1495611797&hash=4df05ef4c3bce5c6bef98348496f74908281cada&file=/fileadmin/Subnavi/Mediathek/Längsseits/Laengsseits-02-2014.pdf

DGzRS. (2014b). *Jahrbuch*. Accessed August 11, 2014, from https://www.seenotretter.de/mediathek/index.php?eID=tx_nawsecuredl&u=0&g=0&t=1495611797&hash=a3cbf1fbe0cf033c318bf38f4e5e093d1a77607d&file=/fileadmin/Subnavi/Mediathek/Information/Jahrbuch-2014.pdf

Drucker, P. F. (1990). *Managing the non-profit organization*. Oxford: Butterworth-Heinemann.

Evetts, J. (2011). Professionalism and management in public sector (Not-for-profit organizations): Challenges and opportunities. In A. Langer & A. Schröer (Eds.), *Professionalisierung in nonprofit management* (pp. 33–44). Wiesbaden: VS Verlag für Sozialwissenschaften.

Glassman, D. M., & Spahn, K. (2012). Performance measurement for nonprofits. *Journal of Applied Corporate Finance, 24*(2), 72–77. doi:10.1111/j.1745-6622.2012.00381.x.

Johanniter-Unfall-Hilfe e.V. (2005). *Jahresbericht 2005*. Berlin. Accessed August 07, 2014, from http://www.johanniter.de/die-johanniter/johanniter-unfall-hilfe/ueber-uns/bundesgeschaeftsstelle/publikationen/jahresberichte/

Johanniter-Unfall-Hilfe e.V. (2008). *Jahresbericht 2008*. Berlin. Accessed August 07, 2014, from http://www.johanniter.de/die-johanniter/johanniter-unfall-hilfe/ueber-uns/bundesgeschaeftsstelle/publikationen/jahresberichte/

Johanniter-Unfall-Hilfe e.V. (2009). *Jahresbericht 2009*. Berlin. Accessed August 07, 2014, from http://www.johanniter.de/die-johanniter/johanniter-unfall-hilfe/ueber-uns/bundesgeschaeftsstelle/publikationen/jahresberichte/

Johanniter-Unfall-Hilfe e.V. (2010). *Jahresbericht 2010*. Berlin. Accessed August 07, 2014, from http://www.johanniter.de/die-johanniter/johanniter-unfall-hilfe/ueber-uns/bundesgeschaeftsstelle/publikationen/jahresberichte/

Johanniter-Unfall-Hilfe e.V. (2011). *Jahresbericht 2011*. Berlin. Accessed August 07, 2014, from http://www.johanniter.de/die-johanniter/johanniter-unfall-hilfe/ueber-uns/bundesgeschaeftsstelle/publikationen/jahresberichte/

Johanniter-Unfall-Hilfe e.V. (2012). *Jahresbericht 2012*. Berlin. Accessed August 07, 2014, from http://www.johanniter.de/die-johanniter/johanniter-unfall-hilfe/ueber-uns/bundesgeschaeftsstelle/publikationen/jahresberichte/

Johanniter-Unfall-Hilfe e.V. (2013a). *Jahresbericht 2013*. Berlin. Accessed August 06, 2014, from http://www.johanniter.de/die-johanniter/johanniter-unfall-hilfe/ueber-uns/bundesgeschaeftsstelle/publikationen/jahresberichte/

Johanniter-Unfall-Hilfe e.V. (2013b). *Projektbericht 2013*. Berlin. Accessed August 06, 2014, from http://www.johanniter.de/fileadmin/user_upload/Dokumente/JUH/BG/Publikationen/Jahresbericht/Auslandsarbeitprojektbericht2013.pdf

Kleimann, B. (2011). Professionalisierung der Hochschulleitung? In A. Langer & A. Schröer (Eds.), *Professionalisierung in nonprofit management* (pp. 201–226). Wiesbaden: VS Verlag für Sozialwissenschaften.

Kuckartz, U. (2012). *Qualitative Inhaltsanalyse. Methoden, Praxis, Computerunterstützung*. Weinheim: Beltz Juventa.

Langer, A., & Schröer, A. (2011). Professionalisierung in nonprofit management. In A. Langer & A. Schröer (Eds.), *Professionalisierung in nonprofit management* (pp. 9–31). Wiesbaden: VS Verlag für Sozialwissenschaften.

Oxford Wordpower Dictionary. (2006). In J. Turnbull (Ed.), *Oxford wordpower dictionary* (3rd ed.). Oxford: Oxford University Press.

ProBrasil. (2012). *Bericht aus Brasilien*. Accessed August 06, 2014, from http://www.probrasil.de/wp-content/uploads/2013/02/Bericht-aus-Brasilien-2012.pdf

Raynard, P. (1998). Coming together. A review of contemporary approaches to social accounting, auditing and reporting in non-profit organisations. *Journal of Business Ethics, 17*, 1471–1479.

Raatz, T. (2014, March 28). Conversation with Theresa Raatz of Johanniter-Unfall-Hilfe e.V.

Representative of Albert-Schweitzer-Kinderdorf in Sachsen e.V. (2014, August 08). Conversation with "Representative of Albert-Schweitzer-Kinderdorf in Sachsen e.V.".

Representative of Chirstophorushilfe e.V. (2014, August 05). Telephone conversation with "Representative of Chirstophorushilfe e.V.".

Representative A of ProBrasil e.V. (2014, August 27). Conversation with "Representative A of ProBrasil e.V.".

Representative B of ProBrasil e.V. (2014, August 27). Conversation with "Representative B of ProBrasil e.V.".

Representative C of ProBrasil e.V. (2014, August 27). Conversation with "Representative C of ProBrasil e.V.".
Representative A of Steinschleuder e.V. (2014, September 10). Conversation with "Representative A of Steinschleuder e.V.".
Representative B of Steinschleuder e.V. (2014, September 10). Conversation with "Representative B of Steinschleuder e.V.".
Schmetz. (2014, March 18). Telephone conversation with Christian Schmetz of TERRA TECH Förderverein e.V.
Steinschleuder e.V. (2005). *Infoheft Nr. 24*. Accessed August 07, 2014, from https://steinschleuder-ev.jimdo.com/fileadmin/user_upload/PDF/Infohefte/Infoheft_Nr._24.pdf
Steinschleuder e.V. (2008). *Rundbrief Nr4_Oktober*. Accessed August 07, 2014, from https://steinschleuder-ev.jimdo.com/fileadmin/user_upload/Datenarchiv/Inlandsarbeit/Mitgliederwartung/Rundbriefe/Nr.4_Rundbrief_2008.pdf
Steinschleuder e.V. (2009). *Rundbrief Nr5_Oktober*. Accessed August 07, 2014, from https://steinschleuder-ev.jimdo.com/fileadmin/user_upload/Datenarchiv/Inlandsarbeit/Mitgliederwartung/Rundbriefe/Nr.5_Rundbrief_2009.pdf
Steinschleuder e.V. (2010). *Infoheft Nr. 29*. Accessed August 07, 2014, from https://steinschleuder-ev.jimdo.com/fileadmin/user_upload/PDF/Infohefte/Infoheft_Nr._29.pdf
Steinschleuder e.V. (2011). *Infoheft Nr. 30*. Accessed August 07, 2014, from https://steinschleuder-ev.jimdo.com/fileadmin/user_upload/PDF/Infohefte/Infoheft_Nr._30.pdf
Stipeldey. (2014, August 12). Conversation with Christian Stipeldey of DGzRS – Die Seenotretter.
TERRA TECH Förderverein e. V. (2009). *Rundbrief 2-09*. Accessed August 07, 2014, from http://www.terratech-ngo.de/images/mediathek/rundbriefe/terra-tech-rundbrief_02-2009.pdf
TERRA TECH Förderverein e. V. (2011). *Annual report 2011*. Accessed August 07, 2014, from http://www.terratech-ngo.de/images/mediathek/jahresberichte/terra-tech-jahresbericht2011.pdf
TERRA TECH Förderverein e. V. (2013). *Rundbrief 2-13*. Accessed August 07, 2014, from http://www.terratech-ngo.de/images/mediathek/rundbriefe/terra-tech-rundbrief_02-2013.pdf
Utters-Adam. (2014, October 28). Conversation with Adelheid Utters-Adam of Caritasverband der Erzdiözese München und Freising e.V.
van Broekhoven, R. A. (2008). *Engaging Donors' Trust*. Accessed February 20, 2014, from http://www.icfo.org/ICFO-Publications

Chapter 8
Discussion

After the findings from the empirical research were presented in the previous chapter, this chapter aims to establish the link between these findings, and the prior literature, and addresses the research questions posed for the current research:

1. Are German NPOs aware of the term IC and its concept?
2. Is IC currently disclosed by German NPOs?
3. How is IC currently disclosed by German NPOs?
4. What are the reasons for NPOs to disclose information on their IC?

Hence, the current state of the disclosure of IC by German NPOs is illustrated first and research questions one, two, and three are answered. These answers developed offer comprehensive insight into the current state of the disclosure of information on IC by German NPOs. Reasons for NPOs for the disclosure of IC are discussed in Sect. 8.2 and thus the fourth research question is answered. Assumptions made for sampling and the consequent variables used are checked for their validity and impact on the development of recommendations in Sect. 8.3. Since the aim of the current research was to develop a framework for German NPOs for the disclosure of their IC, Sect. 8.3 also highlights the implications for IC disclosure resulting from the preceding discussions. The actual framework for German NPOs for the disclosure of their IC is presented in Sect. 8.4.

K. Blankenburg, *Intellectual Capital in German Non-profit Organisations*,
Contributions to Management Science, DOI 10.1007/978-3-319-62655-0_8

8.1 Current State of Disclosure of Intellectual Capital by German NPOs

8.1.1 Research Question 1: Are NPOs Aware of the Term Intellectual Capital and Its Concept?

There is no information available in literature on the matter of awareness. Thus the answer is deduced from empirical data. Reading the documents published by NPOs, it was noticeable that the term intellectual capital was not used once, nor were the terms human capital, relational capital, structural capital, or spiritual capital ever mentioned. Only one organisation used the term immaterial assets in their annual report, which were describes as 'mostly purchased software and database licenses for accounting, payroll accounting, electronic filing, quality management, and standard software' (Johanniter-Unfall-Hilfe e.V., 2013, p.30).

To ensure a comprehensive perspective on the question, representatives of the NPOs were asked during the interviews whether they knew the term intellectual capital and its concept. Nine of the twelve interviewees replied that they recognized neither the term nor the concept.

> "So far I haven't encountered intellectual capital as a term. Also, it is not an issue for us; I think" (Raatz, Johanniter-Unfall-Hilfe e.V.: 129)

Two respondents had heard of IC before, one at a former job and the other one during studies, but not in the context of the organisation they represented. Thus the answer to the first research question is that German NPOs are not aware of the term intellectual capital and its concept. This finding and the importance of IC for NPOs stated in literature (Kong & Prior, 2008; Kong, 2010b; Lichtsteiner et al., 2013) reveal that the theory has not yet reached practitioners and is thus neither implemented nor applied. In other words, the theory-practice gap that step three of IC research attempts to close (Dumay, 2009; Bontis, 2003) still exists. Further, in the case of German NPOs, it might be necessary for researchers to go back to step one, i.e. to create awareness of the importance of IC as a value driver (Marr & Chatzkel, 2004; Tan et al., 2008; Petty & Guthrie, 2000).

8.1.2 Research Question 2: Is Intellectual Capital Currently Disclosed by German NPOs?

Since German NPOs are not aware of the term and concept of IC, it suggests that the second research question 'Is IC currently disclosed by German NPOs?', is obsolete, since organisations unaware of intellectual capital are unlikely to disclose information on IC. Again, literature does not provide information on the current state of IC reporting by German NPOs or on actual reporting practice for IC disclosure of German NPOs. Surprisingly, the qualitative content analysis of the 92 documents

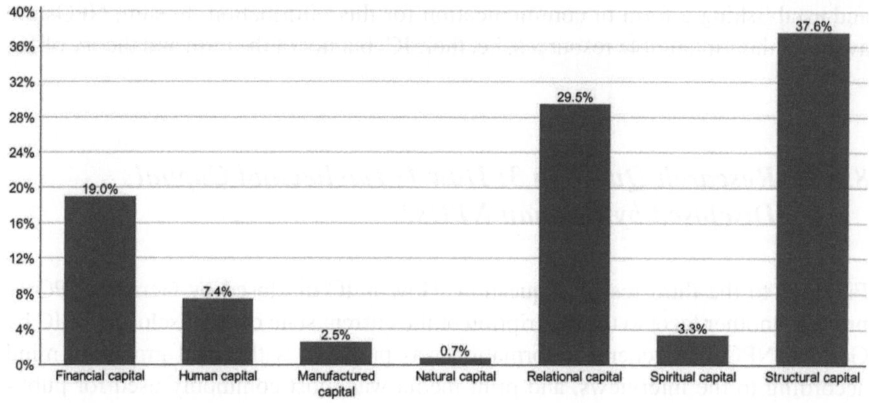

Fig. 8.1 Comparison of the frequency of disclosure of information on capitals in the documents analysed

proved this assumption to be wrong. All NPOs of the sample remarked on their IC within their documents, however to varying extents. Within the sample, relational capital and structural capital were the intangible capitals disclosed most frequently in the documents, followed by human capital and spiritual capital, as illustrated in Fig. 8.1.

Apart from the intangible capitals, financial capital, manufactured capital, and natural capital were included in the comparison to gain a comprehensive picture about the information German NPOs disclosed. A question that needs to be considered regarding the interpretation of the frequency of IC disclosure, as presented in Fig. 8.1, is whether limited disclosure of certain capitals illustrates that these are either not regarded as important by NPOs, or are not known to NPOs.

Yet if organisations are not aware that they disclose information on IC, is the information they disclose actually IC? While it would be possible to write a complex philosophical essay on this question, critical realism, the philosophical perspective adopted for the current research, assumes that reality is rather independent from the human mind. Consequently, if we see or sense something that we cannot process, it exists nevertheless, even if we cannot label it. In other words, information that fits the description of intellectual capital is regarded and labelled as intellectual capital for this project.

While professionalisation of NPOs gains momentum and importance, currently, most of the time volunteers spend running an NPO for various reasons and do not necessarily have a background in management, economics, accounting, or the like. As a result, they do not necessarily know of the theory of IC, as proven by this research. However, another assumption in this regard is that the information disclosed in documents was chosen deliberately by the organisations. If they did not consider the information important, independent of whether a label was ascribed, NPOs would not spend time and money on collecting the information and establishing a form of communication for this information. In sum, NPOs are aware of their intangible resources, i.e. their IC, but not of the term and theory of IC.

8.1.3 Research Question 3: How Is Intellectual Capital Disclosed by German NPOs?

Findings to the third research question 'How is IC disclosed by German NPOs?' provide another facet to the description of the current state of the disclosure of IC by German NPOs. In general, information was prepared with target groups in mind according to the interviews, and print media was most commonly used for publication. Within these publications, three forms of disclosure were detectable: numerical, narrative, and visual. These forms of expressing IC can be tied to the discussion presented in Sect. 2.1 on the accounting versus the management perspective taken on for IC and to the challenges of IC reporting introduced in Sect. 2.6. For accounting, the intangible nature is a major challenge since it prohibits expressing the value of IC in numerical units and a common means to interpret IC disclosure does not exist yet (Bjurström et al., 2003; Zambon, 2004). As a result, the realisation that the traditional financial accounting is deficient and cannot account for IC (Mouritsen, 2003) and the absence of a common language speak for a disclosure via narration. Additionally, according to German law, IC developed internally and for internal use cannot be capitalised in the balance sheet (Schruff & Haaker, 2009). Consequently, IC cannot be disclosed via traditional financial accounting. This is also visible in the findings of the analysis of the documents, which reveals that numerical values were used far less frequently than narrative or visual forms. The analysis of the empirical data confirmed that numerical presentation was used for countable information only, such as the number of volunteers, of beneficiaries reached, or of services provided, and that lots of information on intellectual capital was provided in a descriptive way instead. Several approaches to narrative disclosure can be differentiated:

- reports from NPOs that were kept objective and factual like descriptions of structures or processes;
- subjective and emotional reports from NPOs, for instance illustrating the story of a particular beneficiary;
- reports by other parties than the NPO, like beneficiaries, volunteers, employees, or members, whose reports were subjective as well.

Pictures were used to introduce staff and provide an impression of project sites and, most importantly, to get people to read the narratives provided in the first place, as highlighted in Sect. 7.2.3. As a result, photos used in reports need to be chosen carefully, since they convey a first impression and impact the number of people reached through a publication. In the best case, photos convey the message of the accompanying text (Utters-Adam, Caritasverband der Erzdiözese München und Freising e.V.: 54) or signal values of the organisation. A photo that upsets a reader too much would cause him or her to refrain from engaging with the content and the topic addressed, and would thus be counterproductive. In sum, NPOs try to find a balance between photos that attract attention on the one hand but not act as a deterrent on the other.

8.2 Reasons for Disclosure of Information on Intellectual Capital

While the findings to the first three research questions answered if, where (via which medium), and how IC is disclosed by German NPOs, the fourth research question 'What are the reasons for NPOs to disclose information on their IC?' aims to establish the motivation for IC disclosure.

From an accounting perspective, NPOs need to generate enough revenue to cover their expenses if they want to survive in the long run, just like businesses, even if the sources of this revenue differ from those of for-profit organisations. German NPOs are not obliged by law to generate an annual report but every organisation needs to provide a report on income and expenditure. A report on IC is not required. Nevertheless, signalling proper handling of resources is imperative for NPOs. Not only is the tax shelter status of NPOs dependent on the information on the allocation of resources (KPMG, 2012), but donors and volunteers want to be sure that the money and time they donate is used in a considerate way towards the social aim, as the quote highlights:

> "Generally we have more and more donors who want to know exactly what their donations are used for." (Representative of Christophorushilfe: 68)

A report on income and expenses does not address these demands in full, and neither does balancing assets versus liabilities and equity, i.e. a balance sheet. Adding intangibles, however, offers a more comprehensive perspective on an organisation (Kong & Prior, 2008; Kong, 2010a). A reasonable cause for the decision to disclose information on intangibles is thus that by solely reporting on financial capital, NPOs would not be able to address the issue of transparency and the demands of their donors (Kong & Prior, 2008). Consequently, many NPOs choose to prepare and publish an annual report. They are liable to the same rules and standards for the preparation of a report as for-profit business, including DRS 20, introduced in Sect. 2.4, which recommends the disclosure of information on IC in the management report.

Further basic reasons according to literature, apart from legal requirements (KPMG, 2012), are to convey the raison d'être, to demonstrate trustworthiness (van Broekhoven, 2008), to illustrate the ability to handle competition (van Broekhoven, 2008; Lichtsteiner et al., 2013), and to communicate results and successes achieved (Drucker, 1990). Social acceptances and support by stakeholder is of great importance for German NPOs. The former is achieved through conformity and legitimacy. By signalling trustworthiness as well as effective and efficient use of resources, stakeholder support is gained and retained, which impacts the availability of crucial resources, another reason for the disclosure of IC.

As described in Sect. 2.5, competition is regarded as a disincentive for IC disclosure in the sense that competitors might gain information that they could use to harm the competitive advantage of the organisation. At the same time, Petrash (1996) regarded competitiveness as a reason for IC reporting. Neither the interviews nor the documents analysed provided insight into the perception of German NPOs regarding these contrasting views. However, according to the interviews, eight of the nine NPOs actively solicit for donations of time and funds and compete with other organisations for these resources. Competition is consequently an issue German NPOs are confronted with in practice.

NPOs cannot present themselves and their successes exactly like private companies (see also Sect. 3.1). Nevertheless, both NPOs and businesses need to define for themselves what success entails for them based on their aim. The approach to define NPOs by their success in achieving their aim, as suggested by Crossan and van Til (2008), is challenging due to the intangibility of most projects. Organisations and their stakeholders can only measure their success and their results when the aim is clearly defined and communicated. An NPO can have various aims at the same time if they are not mutually exclusive. The aims can put the organisation itself, its stakeholder or the third sector into the spotlight (see also Table 8). Measures of success can be financially driven (Representative A of ProBrasil e. V.: 123; Utters-Adam, Caritasverband der Erzdiözese München und Freising e.V.: 138), concentrate on the social mission (Utters-Adam, Caritasverband der Erzdiözese München und Freising e.V.: 140), focus on the market (Raatz, Johanniter-Unfall-Hilfe e.V.: 52) or centre upon the relationship to stakeholders (Raatz, Johanniter-Unfall-Hilfe e.V.: 101) (Helmig & Boenigk, 2012). By having to formulate the information on their capitals, NPOs are reminded of their vision and aims. Consequently, the risk of NPOs losing sight of their social goal over management orientation and efficiency (Alexander, 1999; Ryan, 1999; van Broekhoven, 2008) decreases, providing another motivation for IC disclosure.

An interesting question in this regard is how NPOs define success, and some of the interviewees provided insight into the approaches of their respective organisations to this question. Analysing the insights offered, the importance of funding is noticeable. However, all organisations were well aware that sufficient funding is essential for the accomplishment of their social projects but that it is a means to an end and not their final aim, as the following quote illustrates:

> We are successful if we can do everything we consider necessary in the current situation from a financial point of view as well. [...] That is, if we can manage and provide everything that is needed by society at the moment, and if it really reaches people, I think, that is good and successful. (Utters-Adam, Caritasverband der Erzdiözese München und Freising e.V.: 138–140)

Even for organisations with the mission to support other organisations, which in turn work in foreign countries, funding was not the initial aim. Their raison d'être is aligned with the organisations they support. They do not execute projects themselves but see themselves as facilitators of an essential resource for the value creation process towards a social goal (Representative A of Steinschleuder e.V.: 131; TERRA TECH Förderverein e. V., 2012b, p.3).

Another reason for the disclosure of IC is the increasing professionalism and the demand for quality and efficiency. Professionalism in the sense of an "occupational value" (Evetts, 2011, p.33) is linked to the trust a client has that a person or organisation has the appropriate knowledge and experience to manage and finish a task successfully and to a certain quality. This trust in turn leads to support and legitimacy (Evetts, 2011). Expectations regarding quality can give rise to a certain amount of standardisation, which can be helpful or "can be a disincentive to the creative, innovative, and inspirational professional" (Evetts, 2011, p.40). One organisation defined its raison d'être as a professional organisation offering professional help for people in distress and representatives of further NPOs regarded professionalism as a characteristic to aim for and work towards. With the professionalisation of tasks within the third sector the demands on the work of NPOs and their relation to stakeholders change. Instead of focussing on their social mission, NPOs have to deal with relationship management, public relation activities, and quality management (Evetts, 2011) to be able to stay competitive. These areas identified by Evett (2011) are comparable to those developed by Lichtsteiner et al. (2013) described in Sect. 3.4. Implications for NPOs are expressed by one NPO within the sample as follows:

> Private suppliers entices "customers" away from NPOs and where we "merely" helped in the past, suddenly a strategy has to "sell" the quality of the same work to the public. (Caritasverband der Erzdiözese München und Freising e.V., 2007, p.18)

Increasing professionalism within the third sector can be regarded as one reaction to intensifying competition. As demands on communication and transparency are rising, especially regarding the use of funds, NPOs are thus taking on a standardised business approach. Consequently, organisations are pushed to employ a person with the fitting skill set, accountants for instance, who are aware of IC and are trained in reporting and thereby the disclosure of IC. The reason for the disclosure of IC due to increasing professionalism is thus the increasing know-how due to the employment of 'professionals' and to signal professionalism, i.e. the quality and efficiency of the services provided.

Analysing the documents pointed towards another motivation for the disclosure of IC. The analysis illustrated that information on human capital is disclosed less frequently compared to information on relational capital and on structural capital. This low frequency of information on human capital can be credited to the fact that the documents analysed target an external audience. External stakeholders demand transparency to be able to ensure that "their donations are used for the purposes for which they were donated" (van Broekhoven, 2008, p.20). Accordingly, information on the projects executed, the services delivered, and the successes achieved are important for them. A lot of projects are not concluded within one reporting period, though. Hence, NPOs signal the transparency demanded by reporting on how projects are approached, i.e. via information on structural capital. On the one hand, these reports illustrate that the organisation is still pursuing the project, and explain why the project is not yet concluded on the other. Relational capital expresses the external view of the organisation and reports on support by other organisations, communities and governments, or beneficiaries, for instance. Such positive perspectives by other parties reassure donors that they chose a trustworthy organisation. Information on human capital is thus less important for external stakeholders, apart from learning that the employees and/or volunteers have the necessary experience and know-how for the project in question. The example of the low frequency of disclosure of information on human capital illustrated the interdependency between the resources the NPO depended on most and the focus on one capital in publications. If support by external parties was expressed as the prime resource to the organisation within the documents, information on relational capital was provided most. In cases where human resources were identified as most important, information on structural capital was presented predominantly. A motivation visible within these links is to ensure the availability of necessary resources and to signal success, or at least illustrate the means utilised for success in order to satisfy stakeholders.

One aim that is not explicitly stated in literature or mentioned in the data analysed is the most important and, at the same time, the most basic: survival. Since organisations depend on their environment for the acquisition of resources essential for survival (Pfeffer & Salancik, 2003), they need to satisfy two sets of requirements. On the one side, the demands of stakeholders need to be answered, and on the other side, the availability of the resources necessary needs to be ensured (Horak & Speckbacher, 2013). As established, the demands and essential resources are mainly intangible, with funding being an exception. NPOs need to be aware that addressing one demand or one of the necessary resources individually also affects the other demands and resources, as discussed in more detail in Sect. 7.4.

The theoretical framework for the motivation of NPOs to disclose information on their IC developed in Sect. 5.7 offers further reasons for the disclosure of IC. The link between agency theory and stakeholder theory was built upon the notion that financial stakeholders are one group of stakeholders of any organisation. For NPOs, financial stakeholders are private and commercial donors, members, and the state (if the organisation receives government grants). Disclosure of information on quality standards, for instance, offers stakeholders the means to assess the services delivered in a more accurate way which was a positive effect of IC disclosure pointed out in literature (Bukh et al., 2005) and sought after by representatives of German NPOs interviewed (Raatz, Johanniter-Unfall-Hilfe e.V.: 170; Representative A of Steinschleuder e.V.: 118). Also, as indicated by the quote at the beginning of this section, a demand of these financial stakeholders is a decrease in information asymmetry regarding the use of their donations (Representative of Christophorushilfe e.V.: 68). Three further interviewees confirmed the demand for comprehensive reporting on the use of donations (Stipeldey, DGzRS - Die Seenotretter: 125; Representative A of Steinschleuder e.V.: 134, Representative of Direkte Hilfe für Kinder in Not: 15). The representatives of these two organisations and two interviewees of other NPOs stated that people are more easily convinced to donate money if they know exactly what they are donating for, and three approaches to make the value of donations more transparent are detectable within the examples provided by the interviewees already: to denote how much a particular amount donated can finance e.g. one euro for one brick of a new school

(Representative A of ProBrasil e.V.: 37), to state the total amount that needs to be collected to fund a particular item e.g. a powerful lamp (Stipeldey, DGzRS - Die Seenotretter: 59), or to collect for an item which people are already familiar with or which they can easily research the funding required e.g. a window (Representative of Christophorushilfe: 66). A link between the decrease in information asymmetries (agency theory) as a demand of stakeholder (stakeholder theory) and an increase in donations and support is thus empirically verified.

According to stakeholder theory, the demands of stakeholders are heterogeneous and sometimes even conflicting. Hence, organisations have to identify which demands they need to attend to and which they can or must ignore (Pfeffer & Salancik, 2003) while still maintaining legitimacy. Legitimacy in turn depends on a positive perspective of society on the work of an organisation. The example of Unicef, illustrated in Sect. 5.3, highlights the importance of legitimacy (legitimacy theory) based on transparency and trust of stakeholders (stakeholder theory) to obtain necessary resources such as funding (resource dependency theory). Interviewees confirmed these relationships of conformity with rules and moral values (institutional theory) and legitimacy, as well as effects on support of stakeholders (stakeholder theory) (Stipeldey, DGzRS - Die Seenotretter: 125; Representative of Direkte Hilfe für Kinder in Not: 20).

> If we would embezzle money for instance, we would not be able to go out on the street here anymore (Representative of Direkte Hilfe für Kinder in Not: 20)

A perspective noticeable in the aforementioned approaches to disclose IC is that organisations regard themselves as interacting with their environment, which they attempt to display in their publications. Resource dependency theory is based on the same perspective of interaction as stakeholder theory. Both theories offer explanations for the integration of stakeholders into reporting of IC, for instance through own reports. Stakeholder theory concludes that organisations need to take the interests and demands of their stakeholders into account. By giving stakeholders a voice in the publications, the NPO signals attention to their interests and encourages their continued support. A positive effect on continuous support, and consequently on the provision of resources the NPO depends upon, is an approach to survival, according to resource dependency theory. The influence of stakeholders on resources is expressed within the documents and by interviewees alike. Resource dependency theory argues that organisations need to interpret their environment and act accordingly to ensure availability of resources (Pfeffer & Salancik, 2003). One interviewee gave the following example showing this link of environment, impacts and availability of resources for her organisation (Raatz, Johanniter-Unfall-Hilfe e.V.: 103): The "aging of the population" and "the erosion of social structures" lead to people attributing a new meaning to rescue services "offering a lot of possibilities in the future. Funding is an obvious question though." (Raatz, Johanniter-Unfall-Hilfe e.V.: 103). An example of this new meaning of rescue services is that, due to the shift towards the majority of elderly people living alone in their homes, rescue services have introduced emergency buttons that these individuals can carry with them as they move around in their home and press in case they need help. This help can range from severe health problems like a stroke, to the person needing help with getting back up after falling down, even if they are not hurt. The latter is only necessary because no family is around to help, as was the case in most households a couple of decades ago.

Further statements indicated the importance of stakeholder support for the availability of resources such as know-how (Representative A of ProBrasil e.V.: 127), funding (Representative B of Steinschleuder e.V.: 65; Representative of Albert-Schweitzer-Kinderdorf in Sachsen e.V.: 74; TERRA TECH Förderverein e. V., 2012a, p.2; Johanniter-Unfall-Hilfe, 2005:17), working power (Caritasverband der Erzdiözese München und Freising e.V., 2004, p.3; TERRA TECH Förderverein e. V., 2011, p.2), and the reduction of administrative challenges (TERRA TECH Förderverein e. V., 2006, p.5; Representative B of ProBrasil e.V.: 263). These verifications of links between theories via empirical findings show that the conclusion of the theoretical framework described in Sect. 5.7 is applicable for the current research. Consequently, the framework for German NPOs for the disclosure of information on their IC, developed in Sect. 8.4, is based on stakeholder theory and resource dependency theory.

Another motivation for NPOs to disclose information on their IC is to evoke a positive effect on the willingness of people to donate time, material, or funds, as aforementioned in Sect. 3.1. A basic necessity to get people to donate for a particular organisation is that people are aware of the NPO, its aims, and its work (Bekkers and Wiepking, 2010, cited by Helmig & Boenigk, 2012). This need was confirmed explicitly by interviewees:

> First, people need to get to know us, then they have to get to like us and only then people are willing to donate to us. (Stipeldey, DGzRS - Die Seenotretter: 84).

> We provide information boards and hope that people who have noticed us somehow and maybe receive a mailing are going to react to it. (Representative of Albert-Schweitzer-Kinderdorf in Sachsen e.V.: 87)

> Only someone who is informed sufficiently about what we offer will decide in favour of us. (Caritasverband der Erzdiözese München und Freising e.V., 2004, p.29)

Further influences on donation decisions are the perceived benefits for the individual donor and his or her level of altruism (Bekkers und Wiepking, 2010, cited by Helmig & Boenigk, 2012). As described in Sect. 3.4, the motivation for individuals to volunteer, i.e. donate time and human capital, changed from traditional and collective behaviour to individualistic reflexive behaviour (Hustinx & Lammertyn, 2003). In other words, today, an increasing number of volunteers are motivated by personal interests rather than the identification with the aim and values of an NPO. The consequences of this development are described by interviewees for the current research as well. Organisations started to promote volunteering via benefits such as trainings, (Johanniter-Unfall-Hilfe, Caritasverband der Erzdiözese München und Freising e.V.) or via a feeling of community (ProBrasil e.V., Steinschleuder e.V.). As a result, external and internal communication need to consider these developments if NPOs want to win and retain volunteers.

Yet not only volunteers, but also qualified employees, need to be recruited. The three biggest NPOs in the sample explicitly confirmed that they execute initiatives against the scarcity of qualified staff. Since the other NPOs do not necessarily have the funds for comparable initiatives, the fact that five NPOs do not react likewise does not mean that they do not notice and try to counteract the effect as best as possible. Prior research found that IC disclosure impacts this fight against the scarcity of qualified staff (Alwert et al., 2005; Zerfaß, 2009), and on existing human resources as well by winning and keeping the trust of staff (Beattie & Thomson, 2010). The importance of qualified staff implicated by these incentives was also valid for interviewees of seven of the nine NPOs within the sample; only two did not mention the quality of staff explicitly. A reason for NPOs to disclose information on their IC is thus to find new and retain existing qualified staff and volunteers.

In sum, the analysis of the data found seven reasons for German NPOs to disclose information on their IC apart from legal requirements:

i. to ensure the availability of essential resources;
ii. to answer the demand for quality and efficiency;
iii. to signal trustworthiness and success or at least the processes in place to finish a project successfully;
iv. to increase and signal competitiveness;
v. to win new and retain existing qualified staff;
vi. to influence the willingness of people to donate;
vii. to facilitate accurate assessment of the organisation and the resources it needs.

Overall, NPOs need to address the demands of their stakeholder and ensure the availability of resources.

8.3 Implications for the Disclosure of Intellectual Capital

One aim of the current research is to help organisations to provide the information demanded and necessary to stay competitive and survive through the development of a framework for the disclosure of IC. Before this framework can be developed, implications resulting from the finding for the disclosure of IC need to be illustrated, since these shall be the foundation of the framework presented in the following Sect. 8.4.

However, before implications for the disclosure of IC are presented, reasons for the development and against the use of existing frameworks are pointed out. Several challenges are detectable for the use by NPOs in all ICS alike. First, none of these frameworks included spiritual capital, which is of interest for NPOs and their stakeholders. Also, none of the frameworks were developed specifically for NPOs, and therefore most of the frameworks would need to be adapted to the requirements of NPOs since they are based on the aim of profit maximisation. A major challenge of the existing statements is their complexity, which leads to high

Table 8.1 Comparison of features of ICS that applicable and not applicable/missing

	Applicable features	Features not applicable/ missing
Intangible Asset Monitor	– Output based on human action – Applicable for monitoring – Matrix as basis for reporting	– No interdependencies illustrated – No comparison to other NPOs possible – Based on idea of profit equals success
Skandia Navigator	Time frame	– Financial focus needs to be adapted – No comparison to other NPOs possible – No interdependencies illustrated – Based on idea of profit equals success
MERITUM model	– Link vision to value creation – Objectives and critical intangibles	– No interdependencies illustrated – No comparison to other NPOs possible
ICS by the Danish Agency for Trade and Industry	Requirement: write understandably, convincing and trustworthy; explain methods	– Very focussed on knowledge – what about the other capitals? – No comparison to other NPOs possible
Wissensbilanz/InCaS	Show interdependencies	– Complex and time consuming – No comparison to other NPOs possible
<IR>	– Illustrate aim – Clear, concise, connected, comparable – Holistic approach	– Complex and time consuming

investments for NPOs of time, funds, or both. Small organisations are not able to absorb these investments without severe effects on their services offered (van Broekhoven, 2008).

Three of the ICS were developed as management tools rather than for reporting and are thus less applicable as frameworks for IC disclosure, namely the Intangible Asset Monitor, Skandia Navigator, and the Intellectual Capital Statement by the Danish Agency for Trade and Industry. The aim of the framework developed for the current research is therefore to provide a concise and straightforward guideline for the disclosure of IC for German donation-soliciting NPOs. A number of main features of ICS that are applicable along with those that are not applicable or missing are presented in Table 8.1.

8.3.1 *Implications on the Way Intellectual Capital Is Disclosed*

The analysis showed that, currently, German NPOs use mostly narratives, supported by some numbers and pictures, to provide information on IC. Numbers, like income and expenses, are part of the demands posed upon NPOs by law. Whenever possible, numbers are also used to give the exact number of a resource needed, for instance: four new windows, two new life jackets, at least three volunteers per project. While numeric information offers a higher comparability if it was generated in the same way, narratives offer organisations the means to describe what cannot be measured, to convey stories a reader can identify with, and to introduce beneficiaries the reader of a publication can feel sympathetic to (van Broekhoven, 2008) and thus build a link to the organisation. Additionally, narrative disclosure facilitates illustrating the link of IC to value creation as recommended in literature (Bukh, 2003; Arvidsson, 2011; Beattie & Smith, 2013). However, as German NPOs are not aware of IC and thus do not know the literature on IC, a link to this theoretical rational can neither be validated nor invalidated. Also no empirically established reasons for the preference towards words and pictures over numbers can be presented, since this would require a conscious approach to IC disclosure. The approaches currently adopted are not strategic but originate from practical circumstances, like demands of stakeholders. Interviewees from different organisations provided the following statements regarding their preferred form for disclosure:

> I think most of the young people we recruit as members at the moment don't care if we need €10.000 or €12.000 for a project. I think it is far more fascinating for them to get content related information and not figures and the like (Representative B of Steinschleuder e.V.: 94)

> Every time when we illustrate something, even the services we offer, it is always about [...] people, their stories, how they were aided, the fortunes behind all of it, we have to provide these information usually. That is not always easy. (Utters-Adam, Caritasverband der Erzdiözese München und Freising e.V.: 18)

These statements also show that different, more emotional and subjective information was provided via a narrative form than a numerical or visual form. The aims of conveying information the narrative way are similar: to facilitate a comprehensible picture of the organisation, to invoke sympathy, and to build a relationship between the reader and the context. Additionally, while numbers are regarded as comparable and thus facilitate benchmarking, they are also backward-looking. Narrative reporting enables NPOs to provide information on the present situation and predictions about the future development (Bontis, 2003; Möller & Gamerschlag, 2009), i.e. a comprehensive picture of the organisation's situation. For the disclosure of IC, the use of a combination of numbers for countable data and narratives for uncountable information is thus recommendable. Since this mixture of forms of disclosure is established in the reporting practice of German NPOs already, it is taken on for the framework developed in Sect. 8.4.

8.3.2 Implications on IC Disclosure Based on Variables

Five assumptions on the handling of IC and the resulting influences on IC disclosure were the basis for the sample used for the current research. Similarities and differences illustrate which variables need to be taken into account for the framework to facilitate applicability for the majority of organisations. Further factors described in the following paragraphs need to be considered for the framework: organisational culture, workplace spirituality, spiritual capital, measurement challenges, demands and resources, and possible complexity of IC disclosure.

Longevity

Longevity does not emerge as a major differentiating factor in the way German NPOs handle their IC. Long-standing organisations included in the sample turned out to also be those NPOs with high revenue and those that work domestically. An explanation for the focus of long-standing organisations on national issues is that when these long-standing organisations were founded, international engagement was hardly imaginable and much more difficult to undertake. Reliable information on foreign countries was probably hard to come by before 1900 and travelling was hazardous and tedious. Young NPOs of the sample, founded after 2000, generate low revenue and support other organisations. As a lot of NPOs exist today already, the support of a worthy cause executed by another organisation is easier to accomplish and more rational than establishing oneself as competitor working for the same cause but lacking the experience that the other organisation already has. The assumption that long-standing organisations have strong structures and that small NPOs are likely to be less professionalised was confirmed when representatives were contacted and are reflected in the existing or not existing job titles of the interviewees: press officers or public relations manager and board members versus members of staff for whom external communication is just one task of many. However, the data did not confirm that longer-standing organisations are less able to react to change.

Size and Composition of Workforce

A further implication can be derived from the composition of the workforce. NPOs consisting primarily of volunteers tend to focus slightly more on relational capital than structural capital in their document. At the same time, all organisations with a focus on relational capital were those consisting of volunteers. While reports on public relation activities were provided most frequently, information on the relationship to donors were given surprisingly often when compared with the number of times information on the topic was provided by organisations consisting mainly of employees. A reason is not explicitly mentioned by any of the organisations, but resource dependency theory offers a reasonable explanation. Looking at the NPOs fitting the description, NPOs consisting of volunteers generate the least amount of revenue compared to the other organisations in the sample. It is therefore imperative for them to manage and expand the relationship to their donors to ensure that resources are obtained successfully in the future. A link between NPOs consisting of volunteers to other variables, like the fundraising performance, is not clearly given.

Interdependence emerged between a focus on either relational or structural capital and the composition of the workforce. NPOs composed of employees put an emphasis on the reporting of information on structural capital in the documents. This interdependence holds true the other way around as well, i.e. organisations with a preference for reporting on structural capital are those consisting of employees. These organisations reported most frequently on processes, structure and organisational culture. In other words, they report on who is responsible for what task, how things are approached, and why they are approached that way. Noticeable is that NPOs included in the sample consisting solely of employees are those organisations that operate nationally. A link in the other direction is not possible, i.e. NPOs working nationally are not necessarily the NPOs consisting solely of employees, and neither is a link to any other variable. Drawing on the stakeholder theory and resource dependency theory, reasons for the focus on structural capital emerge. Employees are stakeholders and own resources the NPOs need, for example experience, know-how, and networks. Effective acquisition and maintaining of resources as well as a certain amount of control over these resources is essential for organisations according to the resource dependency theory (Pfeffer & Salancik, 2003). As mentioned in Sect. 5.6, an organisation has several possibilities to increase its control over resources. In the case of employees, NPOs cannot possess the resources but they can influence their access to the resources through the implementation of structures and the promotion of a positive organisational culture. Structures and processes serve organisations as tools to control the use of resources available to a certain extent. In sum, the assumption that the composition of the workforce impacts on the disclosure of IC is confirmed. The different foci need to be taken into account for the development of recommendations.

Another theme that emerged for small organisations is the importance of personal relationships or, in other words, of a face to the name or organisation (Representative of Christophorushilfe e.V.: 29, Representative C of ProBrasil: 72, Elbert, Direkte Hilfe für Kinder in Not: 12, Representative A of Steinschleuder e.V.: 116). An implication of this finding is that NPOs should include pictures of their workforce in their publications. While a photo does not substitute direct contact to a person, it has the power to create a link and to encourage the reader to continue reading.

Revenue

The comparison of the smallest and largest organisations based on their revenue did not allow an unambiguous finding. While organisations with high revenue show a preference for the disclosure of structural capital in their documents, information on their relational capital was disclosed most during the interviews. Organisations with a low revenue concentrated on their structural capital during the interviews and on relational capital in their documents. Size according to revenue is thus not an appropriate differentiating factor.

	Social acceptance	Trust	Transparency	Quality
A	0	0	0	1
J	8	37	25	52
H	0	0	1	0
C	1	5	0	0
total:	9	42	26	53

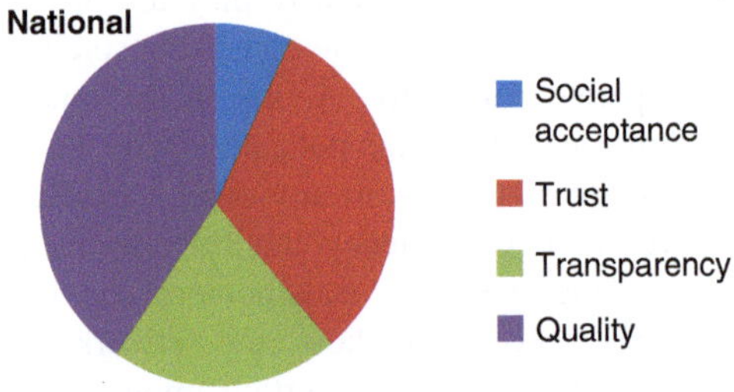

Fig. 8.2 Demands put on NPOs operating nationally as perceived by the NPOs themselves documents analysed

Demands Due to Level of Internationality

Another assumption was that NPOs with international branches face different demands than those based and working solely in Germany. According to the data revealing the demands NPOs perceived as imposed upon themselves, differences in these perceived demands exist. Figures 8.2, 8.3, 8.4, 8.5, 8.6, and 8.7 illustrate these demands perceived as put on NPOs of the three levels of internationality. Each figure is composed of a table and a graph, representing the data from the documents on the left (Fig. 8.2, 8.4, 8.6), and the data from the interviews on the right (Figs. 8.3, 8.5, 8.7).

A demand for quality was solely mentioned by NPOs working nationally, which was surprising, considering that quality was mentioned most frequently as a demand within the documents of NPOs working nationally and those operating internationally. At the same time, organisations supporting other NPOs did not mention quality at all i.e. neither within the documents available nor during the interviews. A possible reason is that, as these NPOs do not provide any products or services themselves but focus on the support of other NPOs, they do not consider their own quality as highly important. In general, supporting NPOs did not provide a lot of information on demands put on them and the little information given is not consistent, apart from the indifference to quality. Since social acceptance is mentioned in the documents by two of the three supporting NPOs, and the one that did not mention social acceptance did not provide any information on demands at all, it can be assumed that this demand is of importance to this group of German NPOs. Social acceptance was also mentioned frequently within the documents of NPOs working internationally. Documents of NPOs operating nationally also point out the

	Social acceptance	Trust	Transparency	Quality
A	0	0	0	0
J	0	3	2	1
H	0	2	2	0
C	0	2	5	1
total:	0	7	9	2

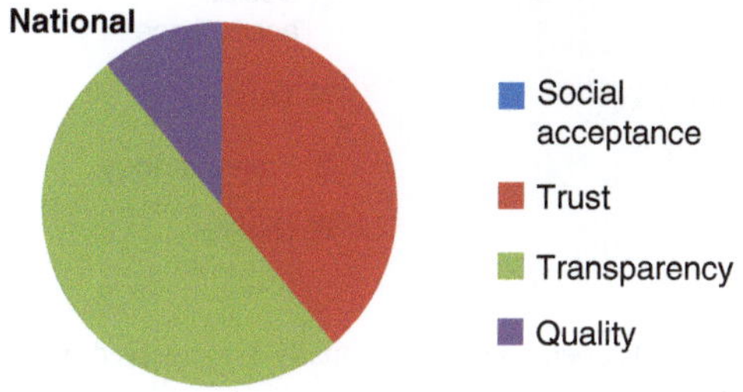

Fig. 8.3 Demands put on NPOs operating nationally as perceived by the NPOs according to themselves according to interviews analysed

	Social acceptance	Trust	Transparency	Quality
B	44	12	22	65
F	0	3	4	0
total:	44	15	26	65

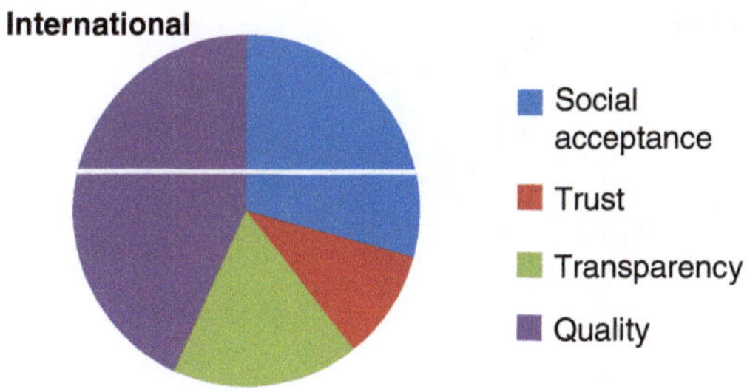

Fig. 8.4 Demands put on NPOs operating internationally as perceived by the NPOs themselves according to documents analysed

importance of social acceptance, but not as frequently compared to the documents of the other groups of NPOs. However, during the interviews, social acceptance was not mentioned by any of the representatives.

Trust and transparency were both mentioned in the documents and interviews, independent of the level of internationality of the NPO. In sum, transparency was

	Social acceptance	Trust	Transparency	Quality
B	0	0	1	0
F	0	1	4	0
total:	0	1	5	0

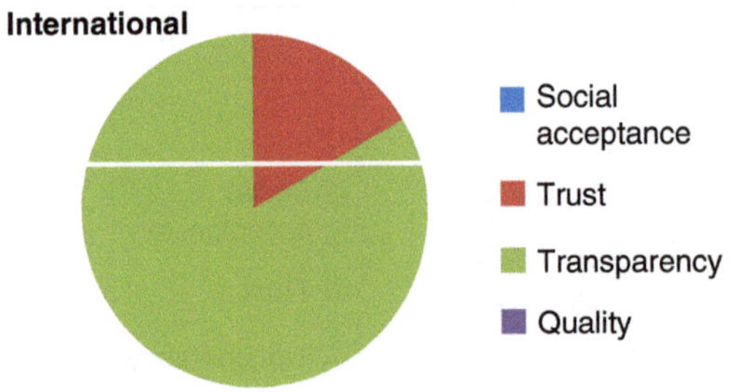

Fig. 8.5 Demands put on NPOs operating internationally as perceived by the NPOs themselves according to interviews analysed

	Social acceptance	Trust	Transparency	Quality
G	1	4	2	0
E	2	0	0	0
D	0	0	0	0
total:	3	4	2	0

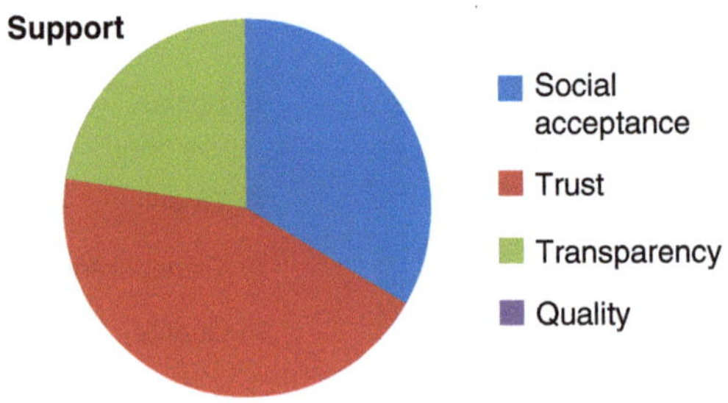

Fig. 8.6 Demands put on NPOs supporting other organisations as perceived by the NPOs themselves according to documents analysed

mentioned more often than trust. Nevertheless, it cannot be deduced that transparency is more important than trust, since this is not the case looking at the individual organisations within the levels. The two NPOs that mentioned neither trust nor transparency provided hardly any information on these demands at all.

	Social acceptance	Trust	Transparency	Quality
G	0	1	1	0
E	0	0	1	0
D	0	0	0	0
total:	0	1	2	0

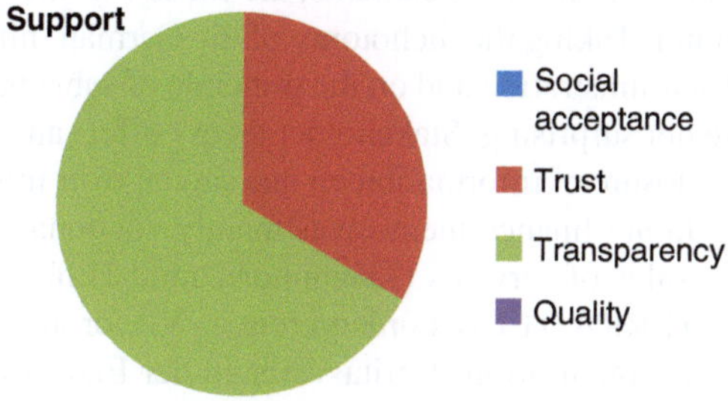

Fig. 8.7 Demands put on NPOs supporting other organisations as perceived by the NPOs themselves according to interviews analysed

In the documents, demands were mentioned more frequently than during interviews but to varying extents and with diverse foci, which holds true for interviews as well. Considering that the number of times a demand was mentioned does not offer any indication of the importance of this demand, the findings presented are to be treated with caution. Since there was no specific question during the interviews regarding demands, it is not to be overrated or overanalysed. Nevertheless, the findings indicate that the combination of the level of internationality and the demands put on them is not an approach recommendable to differentiate German NPOs by. Demands, however, need to be considered by all NPOs.

For the development of the framework, further findings provided by segmentation based on the level of internationality are to be considered. As mentioned in Sect. 6.3, NPOs supporting other organisations focus on the disclosure of information on their relational capital. The supporting NPO is the liaison between the donor and supported NPO which works on-site toward the common social aim. As a result, supporting NPOs need to provide their stakeholders mainly with information on the organisation they support, i.e. relational capital. Nationally and internationally operating NPOs, on the other hand, need to provide information on their strategies and processes in order to reach their social aim, i.e. structural capital.

Fundraising Performance

A further assumption was that a connection between the fundraising performance of NPOs and their approach to the disclosure of IC exists. Empirical data from the interviews as well as the documents confirm the assumption. NPOs with acceptable expenses and a low ratio of revenue generated via fundraising exhibit a strong focus on the disclosure of information on relational capital. Organisations with low expenses but a high ratio of the revenue generated via fundraising focus on structural capital instead, mainly providing information on processes.

Based on the interviews, the comparison of organisations that generated a high amount of the total revenue via fundraising and those at the other end of the continuum indicated a contrasting picture. NPOs raising a low ratio of the revenue generated via fundraising disclosed more information on relational capital than structural capital during the interviews, which can be ascribed to the tasks and responsibilities of the representatives of these NPOs which were mainly in the field of external communication. In the documents, the focus was the other way around, i.e. on structural capital. Taking the dichotomy of the German third sector based on the principle of self-administration and on the principle of subsidiarity into account, these differences are not surprising. Stakeholder theory offers an explanation for the preference of the disclosure of information on one capital over information on other capitals. NPOs that do not finance themselves mainly via donations generate their revenue through the sales of services (Johanniter-Unfall-Hilfe e.V.), for instance, government grants (TERRA TECH Förderverein e. V.), or are funded or at least supported by a parent organisation (Caritasverband der Erzdiözese München und Freising e.V.). Stakeholders who are the sources of funding in these cases demand a different set of information than individual donors. Beneficiaries who make use of services offered and who either pay for these services directly or via their health insurance require information on the ways these services are executed. Government grants are awarded for particular projects, for instance, and therefore the progress of these projects needs to be described to satisfy this stakeholder. If organisations are supported by parent organisations, the information demanded is again on the way the funds are used.

Organisations raising a high ratio of revenue via fundraising reported mainly on relational capital during the interviews and in the documents alike. In order for NPOs to be successful in fundraising, they are dependent on the continuous support of existing donors as well as the recruitment of new donors. A focus on relational capital, like the initiation and management of relationships to stakeholders, is thus essential. An important issue that needs to be taken into account in this regard is that the essential part is not necessarily the disclosure of information on relational capital, but the actual building and maintenance of relational capital. In other words, the reports on public relation activities the NPO executed are important to show stakeholders the efforts undertaken to raise funds on the one hand and, on the other hand, to justify the expenses for these activities by highlighting their success and implications for the work towards the social aim of the NPOs. However, these activities are the actual crucial factor for fundraising and the reports play a supporting role. NPOs need to be acutely aware of this connection. An implication for the development of recommendations is thus that NPOs need to be conscious of the target group of their reports and disclose the information demanded accordingly.

Location
Major differences of the way IC was disclosed based on the location of the NPOs were not detectable. Therefore, the location of organisations does not need to be taken into account for the development of a framework.

Organisational Capital and Workplace Spirituality
The information on organisational culture provided in the documents is linked to the levels of workplace spirituality presented in Sect. 3.4. On the individual level, the awareness of the importance of the work a person does for the achievement of the social aims increases the satisfaction of the individual with his or her work. To achieve such awareness, every employee or volunteer needs to know the processes and structure of an organisation and how he or she fits therein. A common aim and a positive organisational culture foster a sense of belonging and of community, i.e. workplace spirituality on the group level. NPOs cannot necessarily influence the alignment with organisational values as such, but they can ensure that every employee and volunteer is conscious of these values and consequently offer an honest basis for positive workplace spirituality on the organisational level. For the recommendations, it is thus important to consider the significance of introducing these values and report on organisational culture. Structures and process need to be communicated as well, but it would be sufficient if these are disclosed internally by the NPOs.

Spiritual Capital
Information on spiritual capital in general addressed self-understanding of the organisation and its work, emotional effects of getting involved or of donating money, and appealed to stakeholders to either begin or continue supporting a good cause. Implications for the content of the framework cannot be derived from the little information available. The underrepresentation of spiritual capital in the documents and interviews can also be due to the challenge of expressing spiritual capital and not due to a lack of interest or importance. Thus, suggestions for the disclosure of spiritual capital should be included in the framework to support German NPOs in their endeavour to provide a comprehensive picture of their organisations.

Measurement
In literature, the challenge of the valuation and measurement of IC (Zambon, 2004; Dumay & Rooney, 2011) was pointed out and met by calls for more holistic approaches (Roslender, 2004) and more cross-disciplinary thinking (Edvinsson, 2013). Since IC itself is not of any value and organisations need to use it to create value (Beattie & Smith, 2013), it is not possible to draw meaningful inferences from the amount of capitals available about the sustainability and the success of an organisation. As a result, reporting of measurements of available IC is not meaningful enough. The challenges of the American non-profit sector in this regard, pointed out by Salamon et al. (2012), are partly applicable for the organisations analysed for the current research. Stakeholders demand that the contributions of the particular NPO are communicated. During the interviews, representatives of

German NPOs confirmed that stakeholders do not have a full grasp of the value of the organisation and its work (Raatz, Johanniter-Unfall-Hilfe e.V.: 170; Schmetz, TERRA TECH Förderverein e.V.: 65), leading to NPOs having to remind them of their raison d'être and the value of their work constantly. Another challenge, the difficulty to communicate these values, was confirmed as well (Representative A of Steinschleuder e.V.: 121; Representative B of Steinschleuder e.V.: 125). Consequently, NPOs need to illustrate how they use IC for value creation and their dependencies and interdependencies. As pointed out in Sect. 2.6, several researchers called upon organisations to link IC disclosure to their value creation process. The disclosure of German NPOs should thus reflect on and illustrate the mission of the organisation, highlight the services it delivers, describe the processes necessary to deliver these services, and reveal the resources necessary (Keehley & Abercrombie, 2008).

Demands and Resources

With all the dependencies and interdependencies between demands and necessary resources, as introduced in Sect. 7.4, NPOs would have a tough time to consider and address all the links in their corporate communication. Publications would be too complex and too voluminous. However, the dependencies and interdependencies established help German NPOs to decide which resources to focus on and which demands to express, depending on their aim. Looking at the links, three findings need to be emphasised in this regard. First, only trust does not affect any of the other demands or resources; the others affect at least one. Secondly, if an organisation wants to ensure that all demands and resources are affected, a few of these are central to address. Human resources have a direct effect on five of the eight resources and demands established, namely on funding, support by external parties, reputation, practices, and quality. Additionally, they have an indirect effect on two of the remaining three, i.e. on trust via quality and on social acceptance via quality and via reputation. The third finding to emphasise is that the only demand affected neither directly nor indirectly is transparency. Consequently, NPOs that wish to affect all resources and demands need to make sure that they address and manage human resources and transparency explicitly. This certainly does not imply that the other demands and resources should be disregarded. However, if those two, i.e. human resources and transparency, are not addressed, the other resources and demands will not flourish either.

While the dependencies and interdependencies provide helpful information, several links expected prior the analysis did not emerge. A dependency of support by external parties on quality was not detectable during the analysis. Also, the data did not show a relationship between trust and support by external stakeholders. In this regard, it needs to be considered that the documents and interviews focused on the perspectives of the NPOs and did not include views of stakeholders.

Complexity

Based on the critique of the growing complexity and increasing quantity of information stakeholders are confronted with (Bukh & Johanson, 2003; Nielsen & Madsen, 2009; Gowthorpe, 2009; Beattie & Smith, 2013), addressed in Sect. 2.5, a question emerged for the disclosure of information on IC: Is it necessary for NPOs to provide comprehensive information on its IC? The aim of any report addressed at external stakeholders is to signal the capability of the organisation to survive and consequently convince these stakeholders to support the organisation through various measures, from granting legitimisation and social acceptance to the provision of tangible resources and the donation of their time. Thus, the signals stakeholders need to receive are that the organisation is competitive, trustworthy, and capable and that it is able to remain this way in the future. A comprehensive list of available IC does not provide these signals. Information on the way IC is integrated into the value creation process as called for by several researchers (Bukh, 2003; Arvidsson, 2011; Beattie & Smith, 2013) does the job much better. Going one step further, it should be discussed whether the whole value chain and every way IC is integrated need to be described in external reports. Is it not sufficient to focus on the unique features of the IC of an organisation and thus show why it makes sense to support this particular NPO over its competitors? Taking the available resources of NPOs for the creation of reports into account, as well as the aforementioned aim of these reports, such an approach appears to be recommendable. In other words, NPOs should focus on the disclosure of unique characteristics of the link between their IC and their value creation, instead of attempting to disclose as much information on IC as possible.

8.3.3 Summary of Implications on Intellectual Capital Disclosure

In sum, the following recommendations based on findings need to be taken into account for the development a framework for the IC disclosure by NPOs:

- NPOs should illustrate how they proceed to achieve the social change they aim for (link to value-chain)
- NPOs should maintain a mix of forms of disclosure:
  - narratives to create an emotional link between the reader and the organisation, to describe what cannot be measured, to link IC to the value creation of the organisation
  - numbers for countable data
  - pictures of the workforce and work sites to facilitate building a relation to the organisation and its projects
- NPOs need to be conscious of the target groups of their reports and disclose the information demanded accordingly
- Supporting NPOs should provide their stakeholders mainly with information on the organisation they support, i.e. relational capital. Nationally and internationally operating NPOs on the other hand should provide information on their strategies to reach their social aim, i.e. structural capital

- NPOs that wish to attract volunteers should attend to the various types and reasons for people to volunteer, considering that a decreasing number of people are looking for long-time engagement
- NPOs in general but particularly those composed of employees should present their aim, principles, and organisational culture
- Disclosure should highlight the mission of the organisation, the services it delivers, describe the processes necessary to deliver these services, and reveal the resources necessary (Keehley & Abercrombie, 2008).
- NPOs should ensure that information on human resources and transparency is provided
- NPOs should focus on the disclosure of unique characteristics of the link between their IC and their value creation

8.4 Framework for the Disclosure of Information on Intellectual Capital by German NPOs

The following framework is based on the recommendations presented at the end of Sect. 8.3. It is to be understood as a supplement to the financial reports required by law, which is why financial data is not considered. NPOs that choose to prepare a balance sheet and an income statement can integrate the information recommended by the following framework into their reporting. Associations and foundations that instead decide to provide a report on income and expenditures and an inventory can use the framework to create an additional report or to supplement further publications like newsletters, brochures, etc. The framework does not suggest a particular amount of information to be disclosed or a certain length of the report generated. It does not claim to ensure comparability with other NPOs or to be all-encompassing. The framework aims to offer German donation-soliciting NPOs some ideas and guidance to point out their uniqueness via the disclosure of their IC in order to increase their competitiveness with a minimum amount of investment of resources. Before any publication, NPOs need to reflect on the target group of their reports. Flyer or brochures for the recruitment of new donors should include different information than newsletters for regular donors or annual reports which are read by institutional donors and government officials as well. Flyer and brochures can only address a fraction of the issues that an annual report can attend to. Any disclosure helps to varying extents to ensure that stakeholders receive the future-oriented information they need, encouraging them to facilitate necessary resources. Also, the disclosure and resulting support by stakeholders supports organisations in remaining competitive and in achieving their social aims. NPOs that wish to disclose more extensive information on their IC are very much invited to do so. For them, adapting one of the existing frameworks introduced in Sect. 2.9 of this chapter is possible and recommendable.

The structure of the framework is inspired by the parts through which NPOs connect their purpose to their everyday operation as defined by Keehley and Abercrombie (2008, p.28). For the following framework the recommended description of services and of the processes necessary (Keehley & Abercrombie, 2008) are combined into one part which is thus segmented into three parts. The first part of the following framework covers five basic considerations which lead to information that organisations are recommended to disclose. Descriptions of the services delivered and the processes established to deliver these services are the focus of the second part. To ensure that all capitals are considered, this part is segmented by capitals and offers questions for NPOs to establish their uniqueness via their IC. Finally, in the third part, necessary resources to deliver these services and to achieve the initial aim are pointed out. These parts are consecutive and create a comprehensive picture of the intangible side of the organisation, including the role of IC and the necessary resources for value creation. Thus the framework responds to the call by Bukh (2003), Arvidsson (2011) and Beattie and Smith (2013). Questions developed for the individual sections are informed by the Wissensbilanz (Alwert et al., 2006). As for the question of measurement of IC, the framework follows the aforementioned recommendation of Dumay and Rooney (2011) to present narrative reports on the use of IC. For orientation, the capitals addressed by the individual questions are stated in brackets after each question.

8.4.1 Part 1: Five Basic Considerations of the Framework

i) What is the mission of the organisation? (Structural Capital)
The mission of an organisation is its signpost and shows internal as well as external stakeholders the raison d'être of the organisation and its self-understanding. This information is important for stakeholders to know since it is one of the few indications they can use to assess whether the work of the organisation develops in the right direction. Also, the long-term strategy and short-term aims are based on the mission. Consequently, without a clearly defined mission, an organisation has no references for its aims, decisions, and work.

ii) What are the key principles or core values of the organisation? (Structural Capital)
As mentioned in Sect. 6.2.2, principles are founded on the believes of a person or entity that help define what constitutes "good behaviour" (Oxford Wordpower Dictionary, 2006, p.563). Examples for key principles stated by NPO's insight in the sample are: dependability, independence from government funding, reliability, or approachability for all stakeholders. These principles influence the mission of the organisation and all activities deduced from it, including everyday activities.

iii) What are the aims of the organisation? (Structural Capital)
While an NPO only has one mission, it can have several aims if these are not mutually exclusive as pointed out in Sect. 3.2. These aims can centre upon the

organisation itself, its stakeholders, or the third sector in general. Further, aims can have an internal or external focus. Aims for internal projects or processes do not need to be disclosed in documents for external stakeholders unless these are affected by these aims. Another way to segment aims is according to their timeframe, i.e. long-term versus short-term, or their scope. Aims can be defined for the whole organisation, individual departments or project, or parts of projects. All of these aims are important for the definition of success and consequently for the assessment of activities, processes, and strategies of the organisation.

iv) How is success defined for the organisation in general and for single projects in particular? (Structural Capital and influences Relational Capital)
Internal and external stakeholders should be introduced to how success is defined for the organisation. Milestones set for a projects can help to define successes leading towards the completion of the project. Examples of success are: the completion of a project, securing financial resources for a defined period of time or a particular project, meeting a pre-set reaction time in case of emergencies, recruiting a certain number of new members or volunteers, reaching a certain group of beneficiaries, etc. A mix of narratives and numbers proved to be most appealing to describe success. Numbers provide comparability with those numbers reported in previous years and achievements that cannot be measured are described in a narrative way and can thus be included into the assessment of the organisation. To facilitate a comprehensive picture of the organisation, NPOs should also include information on risks, challenges, or liabilities regarding IC (Caddy, 2000). In sum, the definitions of success and the mixture of forms of disclosure help stakeholders to assess the work of the organisation in a fair and true way and, as a result, prevent unrealistic expectations and resulting disappointment.

v) What makes the organisation unique?(all IC)
The unique features of an organisation are what make it competitive. NPOs should thus state clearly what differentiates them from other organisations in their area of work. Uniqueness of NPOs can mostly be found in their IC or combination of various capitals. The following questions and remarks on structural capital, relational capital, human capital, and spiritual capital are meant to help NPOs identify available IC, which organisations can then use to describe their unique features. These questions are not exhaustive, but cover basic features of the individual capitals.

Structural Capital

- How are people connected within the organisation? Does a strong/positive organisational culture exist, like a familiar atmosphere or a strong team spirit, or do friendships or participation play a dominant role in the way the organisation works?
- Does the organisation use processes or approaches that are not the norm? If it does, why? What are the benefits of these approaches?
- What types of volunteering does the organisation support and offer? How are volunteers integrated into the workforce?

- Do approaches exist to keep know-how in the organisation if employees or volunteers leave?
- How are tasks assigned? Who is responsible for what tasks? Pictures of the workforce and work sites facilitate building a relation to the organisation and its projects and should thus be included if possible.

Relational Capital
- Do relationships or links exist to other organisations, officials, foreign governments, members of the press, etc.? Why are these relationships important?
- Who does the organisation receive new knowledge from? Who does the organisation share knowledge with? Information on these relationships signals willingness for further development and hint at the direction this development might take.
- Does the organisation have any influential supporters?
- Supporting NPOs should further provide information on the organisation(s) they support.

Human Capital
- Is particular know-how essential for the execution of the tasks necessary to provide the services offered? How is this know-how developed? What measures of trainings and education are offered?
- How do the key principles or core values affect the behaviour of the workforce?
- Does the organisation provide any special offers for its workforce, like internal competitions or emergency child care? Offers like these have a positive influence on the loyalty of the workforce, prevent staff turnover, and consequently offer stability.
- How are the knowledge and the social skills of the workforce used for value creation?

Spiritual Capital
- What are the emotional benefits for getting involved or donating money or material to the organisation?

Workplace spirituality is addressed implicitly when the mission, principles, and aims are defined, since these allow employees and volunteers to identify with the organisation and to appraise the value of their own work and contribution to these aims.

If expertise, professionalism, specialised structures, or deeply rooted relationships are stated as unique characteristics, organisations should make sure to provide detailed descriptions of these features. Stakeholders can only value, for instance, professionalism correctly if their understanding of professionalism matches that of the organisation. Also, NPOs need to consider that stakeholders have various expectations and thus perceive the value of characteristics differently. Independence from government funding might be perceived as very positive since it also signals that government cannot interfere with the work of the organisation. On the other hand, stakeholders might perceive government funding as a sign of trustworthiness, since the government will not invest in organisations that do not use donations properly. Nevertheless, NPOs should be aware of and promote their uniqueness if they want to stay competitive.

8.4.2 Part 2: Services Delivered

What services are offered? (Structural Capital)
Services offered are deduced from the mission and aims of the organisation. A short description of this dependency creates a sense of rationality behind the activities of the organisation. Descriptions of what the services entail should be at the heart of this part of the report.

What key steps are necessary to deliver the services offered? (all IC)
It is neither necessary nor advisable to describe every step of the process of service delivery. Offering insight on all steps could give away information detrimental to competitive advantage. Rather, steps dependent of the support of stakeholders should be illustrated and the resources necessary for particular steps highlighted in order to show the reader the importance of his or her donation of time, money, or material. Keeping the strong link between human resources, funding, and support by external parties in mind, internal stakeholders and their impact need to be considered when the steps to be explained are chosen. It is not possible to recommend an exact number of steps that should be explained. Providing information on this question, NPOs need to find a balance between highest possible transparency and limited complexity that fits best to their aim and the demands of their stakeholders.

Who is able to take advantage of these services? (Relational Capital)
Even though it seems as if the target group of the services offered is clearly detectable within the descriptions of the services offered, organisations should be sure to name beneficiaries explicitly. Not everyone reads the whole report and thus an extra sentence on who is able to take advantage of the service is recommendable. Also, the obvious beneficiaries are not the only possible beneficiaries. For example, 'meals on wheels' is associated with older people as the target group, but it can also be a very helpful service for younger people who are temporarily not able to cook their own meal due to illness. For NPOs whose beneficiaries do not read their publications, for instance children or people in foreign countries who do not have access to reports, this is not necessary. However, these organisations should consider whether there is a way for them to reach these target groups nevertheless.

8.4.3 Part 3: Resources Necessary

This question has two objectives: first, that the organisation becomes aware of the resources upon which it depends, and second, if stakeholders are unaware of the resources required by the organisation, they are not going to provide these unasked. Hence, organisations need to consider and communicate what resources they require to provide the services they offer. The current research established five resources German NPOs consider necessary: human resources, funding, support by external parties, practices, and reputation. Every organisation has to individually establish which resources it needs for value creation and who it needs to address in order to obtain these resources. To define these resources, a question NPOs should consider is: Are there one or several resources that, if lacking, would seriously harm or even stop the value creation process? The answer to this question does not need to be included in any external report, but has to be discussed internally on a regular basis. However, based on the current research, it is crucial that every NPO provides information on human resources and transparency. The following questions are again not exhaustive but meant as inspiration:

- What knowledge and social skills are essential to provide the services offered at the quality intended?
- How is the availability of knowledge and necessary social skills ensured?
- What differentiates the workforce of the organisation from that of another NPO?
- What is the role of the human resources in the value creation process?
- What measures does the organisation take to ensure transparency? Are these measures audited?

References

Alexander, J. (1999). The impact of devolution on nonprofits. *Nonprofit Management and Leadership, 10*(1), 57–70. doi:10.1002/nml.10105.

Alwert, K., Bornemann, M., & Will, M. (2006). *Wissensbilanz – made in Germany*. Berlin: Bundesministerium für Wirtschaft und Technologie.

Alwert, K., Heisig, P., & Mertins, K. (2005). Wissensbilanzen – Intellektuelles Kapital erfolgreich nutzen und entwickeln. In K. Mertins, K. Alwert, & P. Heisig (Eds.), *Wissensbilanzen – Intellektuelles Kapital erfolgreich nutzen und entwickeln* (pp. 1–18). Heidelberg: Springer.

Arvidsson, S. (2011). Disclosure of non-financial information in the annual report: A management-team perspective. *Journal of Intellectual Capital, 12*(2), 277–300. doi:10.1108/14691931111123421.

Beattie, V., & Smith, S. J. (2013). Value creation and business models: Refocusing the intellectual capital debate. *The British Accounting Review, 45*(4), 234–254. doi:10.1016/j.bar.2013.06.001.

Beattie, V., & Thomson, S. J. (2010). *Intellectual capital reporting: Academic utopia or corporate reality in a brave new world?* Edinburgh: The Institure of Chartered Accountants of Scotland.

Bjurström, E., Catasus, B., & Johanson, U. (2003). *A European research arena on intangibles (E*KNOW-NET)*. Accessed April 2, 2012, from http://www.pnbukh.com/site/files/pdf_filer/Final_report_WP2.pdf

Bontis, N. (2003). Intellectual capital disclosure in Canadian corporations. *Journal of Human Resource Costing and Accounting, 7*(1), 9–20. doi:10.1108/eb029076.

Bukh, P. N. (2003). The relevance of intellectual capital disclosure: A paradox? *Accounting, Auditing and Accountability Journal, 16*(1), 49–56. doi:10.1108/09513570310464273.

Bukh, P. N., & Johanson, U. (2003). Research and knowledge interaction: Guidelines for intellectual capital reporting. *Journal of Intellectual Capital, 4*(4), 576–587. doi:10.1108/14691930310504572.

Bukh, P. N., Nielsen, C., Gormsen, P., & Mouritsen, J. (2005). Disclosure of information on intellectual capital in Danish IPO prospectuses. *Accounting, Auditing and Accountability Journal, 18*(6), 713–732. doi:10.1108/09513570510627685.

Caddy, I. (2000). Intellectual capital: Recognizing both assets and liabilities. *Journal of Intellectual Capital, 1*(2), 129–146. doi:10.1108/14691930010377469.

Caritasverband der Erzdiözese München und Freising e.V. (2004). *Jahresbericht 2003/2004*. Accessed September 23, 2014, from https://www.caritas-nah-am-naechsten.de/media/Media0253720.PDF

Caritasverband der Erzdiözese München und Freising e.V. (2007). *Jahresbericht 2006/2007*. Accessed September 23, 2014, from https://www.caritas-nah-am-naechsten.de/media/Media0253420.PDF

Crossan, D., & Van Til, J. (2008). Towards a classification framework for not-for-profit organisation – The importance of measurement indicators. In *EMED conference: The third sector and sustainable social change: New frontiers for research* (pp. 1–25). Barcelona.

Drucker, P. F. (1990). *Managing the non-profit organization*. Oxford: Butterworth-Heinemann.

Dumay, J. (2009). Reflective discourse about intellectual capital: Research and practice. *Journal of Intellectual Capital, 10*(s), 489–503. doi:10.1108/14691930910996607.

Dumay, J., & Rooney, J. (2011). 'Measuring for managing?' An IC practice case study. *Journal of Intellectual Capital, 12*(3), 344–355. doi:10.1108/14691931111154670.

Edvinsson, L. (2013). IC 21: Reflections from 21 years of IC practice and theory. *Journal of Intellectual Capital, 14*(1), 163–172. doi:10.1108/14691931311289075.

Evetts, J. (2011). Professionalism and management in public sector (Not-for-profit organizations): Challenges and opportunities. In A. Langer & A. Schröer (Eds.), *Professionalisierung in nonprofit management* (pp. 33–44). Wiesbaden: VS Verlag für Sozialwissenschaften.

Gowthorpe, C. (2009). Wider still and wider? A critical discussion of intellectual capital recognition, measurement and control in a boundary theoretical context. *Critical Perspectives on Accounting, 20*(7), 823–834. doi:10.1016/j.cpa.2008.09.005.

Helmig, B., & Boenigk, S. (2012). *Nonprofit mangement*. München: Verlag Franz Vahlen GmbH.

Horak, C., & Speckbacher, G. (2013). Ziele und strategien. In R. Simsa, M. Meyer, & C. Badelt (Eds.), *Handbuch der nonprofit organisation – Strukturen und management* (pp. 159–182). Stuttgart: Schäffer-Poeschel Verlag Stuttgart.

Hustinx, L., & Lammertyn, F. (2003). Collective and reflexive styles of volunteering: A sociological modernization perspective. *Voluntas: International Journal of Voluntary and Nonprofit Organizations, 14*(2), 167–188. doi:10.1023/A:1023948027200.

Johanniter-Unfall-Hilfe e.V. (2005). *Jahresbericht 2005*. Berlin. Accessed August 07, 2014, from http://www.johanniter.de/die-johanniter/johanniter-unfall-hilfe/ueber-uns/bundesgeschaeftsstelle/publikationen/jahresberichte/

Johanniter-Unfall-Hilfe e.V. (2013). *Projektbericht 2013*. Berlin. Accessed August 06, 2014, from http://www.johanniter.de/fileadmin/user_upload/Dokumente/JUH/BG/Publikationen/Jahresbericht/Auslandsarbeitprojektbericht2013.pdf

Keehley, P., & Abercrombie, N. N. (2008). *Benchmarking in the public and nonprofit sectors* (2nd ed.). San Francisco, CA: Wiley.

Kong, E. (2010a). Analyzing BSC and IC's usefulness in nonprofit organizations. *Journal of Intellectual Capital, 11*(3), 284–304. doi:10.1108/14691931011064554.

Kong, E. (2010b). Innovation processes in social enterprises: An IC perspective. *Journal of Intellectual Capital, 11*(2), 158–178. doi:10.1108/14691931011039660.

Kong, E., & Prior, D. (2008). An intellectual capital perspective of competitive advantage in nonprofit organisations. *International Journal of Nonprofit and Voluntary Sector Marketing, 13*, 119–128. doi:10.1002/nvsm.

KPMG. (2012). *Rechnungslegung in der Praxis – Bilanzierungs- und Bewertungsfragen nach deutschem Recht bei Non-Profit-Organisationen*, (Homepage). Accessed January 08, 2014, from http://www.kpmg.com/DE/de/Bibliothek/2012/Seiten/Rechnungslegung-in-der-Praxis.aspx

Lichtsteiner, H., Gmür, M., Giroud, C., & Schauer, R. (2013). *Das Freiburger Management-Modell für Nonprofit Organisationen* (7th ed.). Bern: Haupt Verlag.

Marr, B., & Chatzkel, J. (2004). Intellectual capital at the crossroads: Managing, measuring, and reporting of IC. *Journal of Intellectual Capital, 5*(2), 224–229. doi:10.1108/14691930410533650.

Möller, K., & Gamerschlag, R. (2009). Immaterielle Vermögenswerte in der Unternehmenssteuerung - betriebswirtschaftliche Perspektiven und Herausforderungen. In K. Möller, M. Piwinger, & A. Zerfaß (Eds.), *Immaterielle Vermögenswerte – Bewertung, Berichterstattung und Kommunikation* (pp. 3–21). Stuttgart: Schäffer-Poeschel Verlag Stuttgart.

Mouritsen, J. (2003). Intellectual capital and the capital market: The circulability of intellectual capital. *Accounting, Auditing and Accountability Journal, 16*(1), 18–30. doi:10.1108/09513570310464246.

Nielsen, C., & Madsen, M. T. (2009). Discourses of transparency in the intellectual capital reporting debate: Moving from generic reporting models to management defined information. *Critical Perspectives on Accounting, 20*(7), 847–854. doi:10.1016/j.cpa.2008.09.007.

Oxford Wordpower Dictionary. (2006). In J. Turnbull (Ed.), *Oxford wordpower dictionary* (3rd ed.). Oxford: Oxford University Press.

Petrash, G. (1996). Dow' s journey to a knowledge value management culture. *European Management Journal, 73*(4), 365–373.

Petty, R., & Guthrie, J. (2000). Intellectual capital literature review: Measurement, reporting and management. *Journal of Intellectual Capital, 1*(2), 155–176. doi:10.1108/14691930010348731.

Pfeffer, J., & Salancik, G. R. (2003). *The external control of organizations*. Stanford: Stanford University Press.

Roslender, R. (2004). Accounting for intellectual capital: Rethinking its theoretical underpinnings. *Measuring Business Excellence, 8*(1), 38–45. doi:10.1108/13683040410524720.

Ryan, W. P. (1999). The new landscape for nonprofits. *Harvard Business Review, 77*(1), 127–136.

Salamon, L. M., Geller, S. L., & Newhouse, C. L. (2012). *What do nonprofits stand for? Renewing the nonprofit value commitment*, Baltimore, MD. Accessed December 16, 2012, from http://ccss.jhu.edu/publications-findings?did=389

Schruff, L., & Haaker, A. (2009). Immaterielle Werte in der deutschen und internationalen Rechnungslegung. In K. Möller, M. Piwinger, & A. Zerfaß (Eds.), *Immaterielle Vermögenswerte – Bewertung, Berichterstattung und Kommunikation* (pp. 49–72). Stuttgart: Schäffer-Poeschel Verlag Stuttgart.

Tan, H. P., Plowman, D., & Hancock, P. (2008). The evolving research on intellectual capital. *Journal of Intellectual Capital, 9*(4), 585–608. doi:10.1108/14691930810913177.

TERRA TECH Förderverein e. V. (2006). *Annual report 2006*. Accessed August 07, 2014, from http://www.terratech-ngo.de/de/images/mediathek/jahresberichte/terra-tech-jahresbericht2006.pdf

TERRA TECH Förderverein e. V. (2011). *Rundbrief 2011*. Accessed August 07, 2014, from http://www.terratech-ngo.de/images/mediathek/rundbriefe/terra-tech-rundbrief_2011.pdf

TERRA TECH Förderverein e. V. (2012a). *Rundbrief* 1-12. Accessed August 07, 2014, from http://www.terratech-ngo.de/images/mediathek/rundbriefe/terra-tech-rundbrief_01-2012.pdf

TERRA TECH Förderverein e. V. (2012b). *Annual report 2012*. Accessed August 07, 2014, from http://www.terratech-ngo.de/images/mediathek/jahresberichte/terra-tech-jahresbericht2012.pdf

van Broekhoven, R. A. (2008). *Engaging Donors' Trust*. Accessed February 20, 2014, from http://www.icfo.org/ICFO-Publications

Zambon, S. (2004). Intangibles and intellectual capital: An overview of the reporting issues and some measurement models. In P. Bianchi & S. Labory (Eds.), *The economic importance of intangible assets* (pp. 153–184). Hants: Ashgate.

Zerfaß, A. (2009). Immaterielle Werte und Unternehmenskommunikation – Herausforderungen für das Kommunikationsmanagement. In K. Möller, M. Piwinger, & A. Zerfaß (Eds.), *Immaterielle Vermögenswerte – Bewertung, Berichterstattung und Kommunikation* (pp. 23–48). Stuttgart: Schäffer-Poeschel Verlag Stuttgart.

Chapter 9
Conclusion

A recapitulation and reflection on the main findings brings this dissertation to a close and offers researchers as well as practitioners novel and beneficial insights. Also, six contributions to knowledge, further implications to policy and to practice are presented. Since limitations of the research lead to opportunities for further research, both limitations and opportunities are discussed as well.

9.1 Contributions to Knowledge

The current research makes six contributions to knowledge. First, it addresses disclosure of IC by NPOs, a topic mainly researched from a for-profit perspective so far. It thus adds a new perspective to the literature on IC in NPOs in general and to literature on IC disclosure by NPOs in particular. The few papers that explicitly address IC in NPOs, written by Kong (2003, 2007a, 2007b, 2008, 2010a, 2010b) and Kong and Prior (2008), focused on Australia and are based on literature review, i.e. they include no empirical evidence. However, the third sector in Germany displays unique characteristics based on the principle of subsidiarity and the principle of self-administration. As a result, findings based on research in other countries are not necessarily applicable to German NPOs. Yet the approaches of German NPOs offer insight for NPOs of other countries, for instance, when they accept an assignment from or enter into a partnership with the state and thus lessen the distance between the state and the third sector. Further, the current research is empirical and therefore adds the focus on German NPOs and their particular situation to the third stage of IC research.

A second contribution is that the current research confirmed the existence of a theory-practice gap and highlighted its extent. While in literature IC is regarded as important for NPOs, German donation-soliciting NPOs are not aware of the term intellectual capital and its concept at present. Two consequences for researchers arise from this finding: first, researchers are called to introduce their research to

K. Blankenburg, *Intellectual Capital in German Non-profit Organisations*,
Contributions to Management Science, DOI 10.1007/978-3-319-62655-0_9

practitioners and thus further the discussion about IC of NPOs in research and practice alike; second, while the finding that German donation-soliciting NPOs are not aware of IC and its concept but disclose information on their IC nevertheless is not generalisable; it indicates that practice-focussed research into IC disclosure cannot assume that information on IC was chosen consciously by organisations. As a result, it is not useful to draw inferences from the disclosure of IC on its importance for the respective organisation without ensuring that organisations in question are aware of IC and disclose information on their IC consciously.

The third finding was that longevity, location, and size based on revenue of NPOs did not impact on the way IC was disclosed and are not differentiating factors for German donation-soliciting NPOs. Organisations with different level of internationality, however, face different demands imposed on them by their stakeholders. Also, a connection was detectable between the fundraising performance of NPOs, the size and composition of workforce, and the approach to the disclosure of IC of the respective NPO. These findings provide a valuable insight for further research on the German third sector that is based on segmenting organisations for data collection and analysis.

According to literature, three demands are imposed on the third sector: trust, transparency, and social acceptance (Drucker, 1990; Glassman & Spahn, 2012; Raynard, 1998; van Broekhoven, 2008). The fourth contribution is that the current research established a fourth demand, quality. Crucial resources for German NPOs were established from the empirical data as well. Also, the research offers insight into the dependencies and interdependencies of necessary resources and demands imposed, adding another contribution to knowledge. These original insights contribute to literature on the third sector in general as well as on the third sector in Germany in particular and offer implications for practice, as described in Sect. 9.3.

A literature review by Dumay and Cai (2015) points out various theories that were previously used for research into IC. Four of the theories used most frequently are described in Chap. 5: namely agency theory, stakeholder theory, legitimacy theory, and resource-based-view. Due to the close links of legitimacy theory to institutional theory and resource-based-view to resource dependency theory, these two theories are introduced as well. While every theory is applicable to a certain extent, they cannot entirely explain the motivation of NPOs to disclose information on their IC. However, based on links and similarities, these six theories are combined into a theoretical framework presented in Sect. 5.7. Via this theoretical framework, it is argued that stakeholder theory is at the centre of an explanation for the motivation of IC disclosure of NPOs but resource-dependency theory establishes the initial aim. The aforementioned finding that meeting demands imposed on the organisation and the availability of resources are essential for the survival and success of NPOs, confirm the applicability of resource dependency theory and stakeholder theory to answer the research questions posed. Based on the theoretical framework, the fifth contribution to knowledge is thus that stakeholder theory and resource dependency theory can be used for future research into the motivation of NPOs to disclose information on IC, without researchers having to worrying about ignoring the other four theories.

A sixth contribution is the framework developed based on the findings as well as the question on the necessary extent of external reporting, which offers food-for-thought and is thus a contribution in itself. The framework translates recommendations and calls of several publications into practice: The structure of the framework is inspired by the work of Keehley and Abercrombie (2008), the questions are partly informed by the Wissensbilanz (Alwert, Bornemann, & Will, 2006), the suggestion of Dumay and Rooney (2011) to present narrative reports on the use of IC is adopted, and the calls by Bukh (2003), Arvidsson (2011) and Beattie and Smith (2013) to describe how IC is used for the value creation of an organisation are considered.

Three basic challenges are similar for all NPOs, independent of their country of origin or area of work. They all face limited resources, dependency on stakeholders, and that IC constitutes their competitive advantage. Hence, for research into the motivation of IC disclosure the theoretical framework presented can be applied to NPOs outside of Germany as well. Additionally, the framework developed is neither country nor type of organisation specific. While donation-soliciting organisations depend most on external communication, all other types of organisations are dependent on stakeholders as well. Thus, the framework is of value to any type of NPO and even for-profit businesses that wish to communicate information on their IC can use it as a guideline.

9.2 Policy Implications

The importance of information on IC is accepted within the accounting community (Möller & Gamerschlag, 2009). In 2012 the DRSC took account for this development and introduced a standard regulating group management reports including information on IC. Also, in the last few years, the IIRC developed their <IR> approach including recommendations on the disclosure of information on IC as well. However, as stated in Sect. 3.5, German NPOs are solely obliged to provide a report on income and expenditure and an inventory, but can choose to provide a balance sheet and an income statement instead (Bundesministerium der Justiz und für Verbraucherschutz, 2002). A change in reporting requirements for the latter two would thus only affect few German NPOs directly. Indirectly, most NPOs would be affected by a change in reporting policy due to the demands of their stakeholder who are influenced by the amount and type of information they receive from businesses, which some NPOs therefore use as reference points to begin with. Also, changes in the rules and standards of traditional financial reporting would affect NPOs indirectly through the ongoing professionalisation. Increasingly, volunteers and employees who take on the task of accounting in an NPO have a background in accounting. These members of the workforce would bring new standards and requirements to NPOs and consequently influence their approach to reporting.

At the same time, the heterogeneity of the third sector, the differences in importance of the (intellectual) capitals for NPOs, and the characteristic of IC that it is only of value for an organisation when used for value creation, make a one-size-fits-all approach neither practical nor realizable. Mandatory detailed rules for IC disclosure by German NPOs are thus inadvisable. However, since the interviews showed that some NPOs are unsure as to how they might convey a realistic picture of their organisation (see Sect. 7.2.2), guidance for IC reporting would be helpful. The framework developed and presented in this book is an example of a guideline applicable for every organisation in the German third sector.

Section 8.3.2 includes a paragraph on complexity, which leads to the question whether the scope of information currently demanded from organisations and provided for stakeholders is appropriate (Beattie & Smith, 2013; Gowthorpe, 2009; Nielsen & Madsen, 2009). The principles of orderly accounting according to IFRS (Kuhnle & Banzhaf, 2006) and those of the DRS 20 (Deutsches Rechnungslegungs Standards Commitee e.V., 2012) include the principle of relevance. Both state that only information relevant for a realistic evaluation of the organisation by the target audience should be included (see Table 2.4). Questions not answered by either guideline (IFRS and DRS 20) are: What information is relevant? How detailed should each piece of relevant information be described? In an attempt to answer these questions, the framework presented in this book is based on the notion that one purpose of reports is to provide the legitimisation for the existence of an organisation by highlighting its uniqueness. Thus, information is relevant when it illustrates the uniqueness of an organisation. Since uniqueness of NPOs can mainly be found in its IC, the focus of IC reporting should be on those features differentiating the NPO from other organisations. This issue of complexity versus transparency is at the heart of accounting and should therefore be discussed by practitioners, researchers, and policy makers alike before new standards are introduced or existing ones revised.

In sum, implications for policy regarding the disclosure of information on IC by German NPOs deriving from the current research are threefold. First, mandatory detailed rules for the disclosure of information on IC by German NPOs are inadvisable. Second, guidance for German NPOs that wish to report information on their IC would be helpful. Third, the key question of transparency versus complexity needs to be discussed.

9.3 Implications for Practice

Since the research was practice-oriented, four implications for practice arose. The first implication for practice is the recognition that IC disclosure is important and should receive more attention as it supports securing necessary resources. Practitioners are recommended to support and invest in IC disclosure to ensure the survival and success of their respective organisation in the future. NPOs do not have to disclose information on all the IC available, but, by concentrating on the unique features instead, disclosure becomes less complex and the quantity of information provided in a report decreases while offering all information necessary. This approach helps stakeholders to recognise important information easily, which is essential for their decision making. The framework developed, presented in Sect. 8.4, offers German NPOs a good foundation for reporting information on their IC without having to invest too many resources.

A second implication emerged from the question on the content that should be provided by German NPOs in their publications. Looking at the status quo of current IC disclosure, the literature, and the demands imposed on organisations, German NPOs do not put enough emphasis on representing their human capital in their publications. Human capital is part of the unique features of an organisation which distinguishes it from other organisations. Hence, NPOs should envelop information on human capital to a bigger extent in publicly available documents without a decrease in attention to other intangible capitals. The research also revealed that human resources affect all other demands and resources except one either directly or indirectly. The only demand affected neither directly nor indirectly by any other demand or resource is transparency. Consequently, if German NPOs wish to provide necessary information but keep their disclosure to a minimum, they need to at least address human resources and transparency directly.

Another finding of the current research that leads to the third implication for practice is that fundraising appeals which people can relate to as individuals are more successful. Hence, NPOs should attempt to take this effect into account and break a project down into smaller parts for which funds are raised, if possible. For example, instead of appealing for donations for a building, several individual appeals for the bricks, the windows, a door, a roof, plumbing, etc. could be started. This finding has implications for the fundraising and communication practice of NPOs, which should provide detailed information on the material and projects for which donations are needed in order to more successfully execute fundraising appeals.

Last but not least, the fourth implication arises through the aforementioned theory-practice gap. Currently German NPOs disclose information on their IC based on perceived demands instead of relying on experiences passed on dependably e.g. through recordings, and on reliable research. However, a conscious approach would facilitate a discussion about the importance, the availability, and consequently the management and disclosure of IC for NPOs. Since this theory-practice gap can be approached from the practice side and the research side, practitioners are invited to become involved in closing it.

9.4 Limitations and Opportunities for Further Research

A limitation of the method utilised, i.e. qualitative content analysis, is that data produced is not objective and researchers posing slightly different questions will come to different findings even if they use the same dataset (Krippendorff, 2004;

Steenkamp & Northcott, 2007). Also, researcher choosing to research the same questions and using the same dataset will come to different findings unless they use the exact same methods and methodology. Based on these statements, several measurements were implemented and executed to maximise the credibility and transferability of the findings, as described in Sect. 6.3 in more detail. Thus, while limitation due to bias cannot be excluded with complete certainty, the credibility, transferability, dependability, and confirmability of the current research are high.

Possibilities for further research can be deduced from other limitations. The second limitation is that the focus of the current research is on documents written for external stakeholders. Interesting questions that arise from this focus are for instance: Do internal documents provide information on capitals as well? Does the perspective conveyed in internal documents differ from the one communicated to external stakeholders? As the documents analysed for the current research were prepared by NPOs, they allow insight into the perceptions of the organisations but not into those of stakeholders, which is a third limitation. The perception of stakeholders, however, would provide valuable insight into their actual demands and requirements and would facilitate a validation of the dependencies and interdependencies of demands and resources presented in Sect. 7.4. Consequently, the view of stakeholders on IC, on external documents disclosed, and on demands they impose on NPOs are further topics for future research.

Limitation four and five are that the sample consists of German NPOs and that these organisations are already interested in transparency. An extension of the sample including German NPOs that are not awarded the Spenden-Siegel and thus do not have to follow the requirements set by the DZI would generate further interesting insights into the topic. Also, a comparison to the disclosure of IC by NPOs located in other countries would yield exciting findings. Such a comparison could centre upon various topics: the levels of awareness of IC and its concept in the countries chosen; the effect of different characteristics of the third sectors of the respective countries or of laws and regulations on IC disclosure of NPOs; similarities and differences in the demands imposed upon NPOs; and reasons for the disclosure of IC by NPOs which could lead to a common framework based on the one presented in Sect. 8.4. Also, the applicability of the dependencies and interdependencies of demands NPOs perceive as posed upon them and the resources they view as essential could be verified for NPOs in other countries.

For the development of the framework, the question emerged whether it is adequate and sufficient for NPOs to focus on the disclosure of information on unique characteristics of the link between their IC and their value creation instead of attempting to provide comprehensive information on their IC. A discussion on this question, i.e. the extent of external communication of IC, would add a new perspective and further the discussion on the measurement and reporting of IC. Finally, the usefulness of the framework in practice and its applicability for different types of NPOs or for NPOs of other countries are further opportunities for future research.

9.5 Recapitulation and Reflection

Even though literature on IC in NPOs and on IC disclosure of NPOs exists, the empirical research reported in this book reveals a remarkable theory-practice gap: German NPOs are not aware of the term IC and its concept. At the same time, the research shows that IC is a topic German NPOs have to deal with and they even disclose information on their IC, but without labelling it IC. This implicit way of expressing and reporting IC confirms the choice of qualitative instead of quantitative content analysis as the appropriate approach to find the answers to the research questions posed. The extent of the theory-practice gap uncovered is one of the main findings and only the combination of various methods enabled its discovery. The analysis of the documents alone would have led to the conclusion that German NPOs are aware of IC since they disclose information on it. Yet in combination with the findings from the interviews, a different picture emerged, highlighting that the combination of content analysis of documents and interviews was the right approach.

Some common motivations of NPOs for the disclosure of IC were detectable. One reason is based on the demands imposed on NPOs by stakeholders. According to literature, these demands are social acceptance, transparency, and trust. While these were confirmed by the analysis of the empirical data, quality was established as a fourth demand. These intangible demands, in combination with the deficiency of the traditional financial accounting practice to include IC, are one reason for IC disclosure. Additionally, NPOs need to signal success and competitiveness by describing their mission and aims, the approaches they use to achieve their aims, which resources they need to execute these approaches, and how they secure the availability of these resources. These steps of the value creation process cannot be illustrated by numbers or pictures and are thus a reason for NPOs to choose a narrative form of disclosure, which German NPOs currently prefer. Numbers and pictures support these narratives. Three approaches to narrative disclosure were detectable: objective and factual descriptions, subjective and emotional stories told from the perspective of the NPO, and subjective and emotional stories told by stakeholders. Narrative disclosure additionally facilitates building an emotional link between the organisation and the reader of the publication in question, since it allows the reader to identify with the aim highlighted as well as the beneficiary introduced via his or her conveyed story. An emotional link in turn influences the willingness of people positively to donate time, material, and money and is thus another motivation for IC disclosure. Communication of the mission, aims, and the value creation process of an organisation supports NPOs in recruiting new and retaining existing qualified staff. An awareness of these elements allow employees and volunteers to establish the value of their own work for the organisation, leading to higher job satisfaction and loyalty and resulting in a good work climate. Recruitment and retention of qualified staff is highly important due to an increase in scarcity of qualified staff and an increasing demand for the professionalisation of organisations in the third sector. These challenges, i.e. the pressure to reply to demands from stakeholders, the need to find alternative ways to numerical data to signal success, the challenge to recruit new donors or members, and the scarcity of qualified staff, are common to German donation-soliciting NPOs. An important lesson from the current research is thus that NPOs should not see themselves as isolated. When it comes to finding solutions, organisations do not need to look far to find allies facing the same challenges, independent of their respective areas of work, location, size, and longevity.

Another effect of illustrating the value creation process is to enable stakeholders to evaluate the organisation and the resources it needs realistically. Only if stakeholders are aware of the resources an NPO needs can these resources can be provided. According to the analysis of the empirical data, German NPOs perceive human resources, funding, practices, reputation, and support by external parties as essential resources. Several dependencies and interdependencies of the aforementioned demands and these necessary resources were established. Links confirmed by the analysis of documents and interviews alike were those between reputation and transparency, transparency and trust, human resources and support by external parties, and support by external parties and funding. A further important finding is that while trust does not affect any of the other demands or resources, human resources affects five of the eight resources and demands directly, and two more indirectly. The only demand and resource not affected by any of the other resources and demands is transparency. It is therefore essential for NPOs to be aware of and disclose information on the role of human resources for value creation to obtain positive influences on most of the other demands and resources. The availability of human resources can be supported, for instance, by providing information on the organisational culture, on trainings offered (both structural capital), or on the relationship of the organisation to its staff (relational capital). Transparency is the only demand that needs to be addressed directly, since it is not influenced by human resources or any other resource or demand. On the whole, NPOs disclose information on their IC to satisfy the demands of their stakeholders and to ensure the availability of essential resources for their value creation processes.

The motivations for IC disclosure, the resulting implications for practice, and, due to the confirmation of their applicability, stakeholder theory and resource dependency theory were the basis of the framework developed and presented in Sect. 8.4. A question that emerged during the development of the framework was whether it is necessary to disclose information on all IC available, the whole value chain and every way IC is integrated, or if it is sufficient to focus on the unique features of the IC of an organisation. These unique features are what make an NPO competitive, sustainable, and thus worthy to support compared to other NPOs with a similar aim. Consequently, the framework concentrates on these unique features. The framework is not intended as a substitute to the financial reports required by law but as a supplement. It can be used to inform newly created publications or be integrated in existing publication formats. Since the framework focuses on the unique features of an NPO, it neither supports the disclosure of comprehensive information on the IC of an organisation, nor facilitates comparability with other NPOs. Rather, it does the opposite; it facilitates distinction from other NPOs working in the same field. In short, the framework offers guidance and food-for-thought for German donation-soliciting NPOs that wish to provide information on their unique characteristics and to illustrate of the link between their unique IC and their value creation process in order to increase their competitiveness with minimal investment of resources.

In conclusion, the research presented offers a foundation and several avenues for further research in the fields of IC disclosure, of German NPOs, and of IC disclosure by German NPOs. A main focus of the research in the latter field should be on the theory-practice gap uncovered and, more importantly, ways to minimise it should be determined and executed together with practitioners. The implications for practice identified and the framework developed will support German donation-soliciting NPOs in saving resources while preparing documents for external stakeholders who are essential for facilitating crucial resources. These in turn are necessary for NPOs to survive, to stay competitive, and to achieve their social aim. In other words, the aim for the research project established at its beginning was achieved. Now, the future will show whether the implications and the framework will gain acceptance in practice.

References

Alwert, K., Bornemann, M., & Will, M. (2006). *Wissensbilanz – made in Germany*. Berlin: Bundesministerium für Wirtschaft und Technologie.

Arvidsson, S. (2011). Disclosure of non-financial information in the annual report: A management-team perspective. *Journal of Intellectual Capital, 12*(2), 277–300. doi:10.1108/14691931111123421.

Beattie, V., & Smith, S. J. (2013). Value creation and business models: Refocusing the intellectual capital debate. *The British Accounting Review, 45*(4), 234–254. doi:10.1016/j.bar.2013.06.001.

Bukh, P. N. (2003). The relevance of intellectual capital disclosure: A paradox? *Accounting, Auditing and Accountability Journal, 16*(1), 49–56. doi:10.1108/09513570310464273.

Bundesministerium der Justiz und für Verbraucherschutz. (2002). *Bürgerliches Gesetzbuch* (51st ed.). München: Verlag C.H. Beck oHG im Deutschen Taschenbuch Verlag GmbH & Co KG.

Deutsches Rechnungslegungs Standards Commitee e.V. (2012). *Deutscher Rechnungslegungs Standard Nr. 20 (DRS 20)* (pp. 1–56). Accessed November 23, 2015, from www.drsc.de/docs/press_releases/2012/120928_DRS20_nearfinal.pdf

Drucker, P. F. (1990). *Managing the non-profit organization*. Oxford: Butterworth-Heinemann.

Dumay, J., & Cai, L. (2015). Using content analysis as a research methodology for investigating intellectual capital disclosure: A critique. *Journal of Intellectual Capital, 16*(1), 121–155. doi:10.1108/JIC-04-2014-0043.

Dumay, J., & Rooney, J. (2011). 'Measuring for managing?' An IC practice case study. *Journal of Intellectual Capital, 12*(3), 344–355. doi:10.1108/14691931111154670.

Glassman, D. M., & Spahn, K. (2012). Performance measurement for nonprofits. *Journal of Applied Corporate Finance, 24*(2), 72–77. doi:10.1111/j.1745-6622.2012.00381.x.

Gowthorpe, C. (2009). Wider still and wider? A critical discussion of intellectual capital recognition, measurement and control in a boundary theoretical context. *Critical Perspectives on Accounting, 20*(7), 823–834. doi:10.1016/j.cpa.2008.09.005.

Keehley, P., & Abercrombie, N. N. (2008). *Benchmarking in the public and nonprofit sectors* (2nd ed.). San Francisco, CA: Wiley.

Kong, E. (2003). Using intellectual capital as a strategic tool for non-profit organisations. *The International Journal of Knowledge, Culture and Change Management, 3*(1), 467–474.
Kong, E. (2007a). A review of the strategic management literature: The importance of intellectual capital in the non-profit sector. In *28th McMaster world congress on intellectual capital and innovation* (pp. 1–26). Hamilton, ON: McMaster University. doi:10.1108/14691930710830864.
Kong, E. (2007b). The strategic importance of intellectual capital in the non-profit sector. *Journal of Intellectual Capital, 8*(4), 721–731. doi:10.1108/14691930710830864.
Kong, E. (2008). The development of strategic management in the non-profit context: Intellectual capital in social service non-profit organizations. *International Journal of Management Reviews, 10*(3), 281–299. doi:10.1111/j.1468-2370.2007.00224.x.
Kong, E. (2010a). Analyzing BSC and IC's usefulness in nonprofit organizations. *Journal of Intellectual Capital, 11*(3), 284–304. doi:10.1108/14691931011064554.
Kong, E. (2010b). Intellectual capital and non-profit organizations in the knowledge economy: Editorial and introduction to special issue. *Journal of Intellectual Capital, 11*(2), 97–106. doi:10.1108/14691931011039624.
Kong, E., & Prior, D. (2008). An intellectual capital perspective of competitive advantage in nonprofit organisations. *International Journal of Nonprofit and Voluntary Sector Marketing, 13*, 119–128. doi:10.1002/nvsm.
Krippendorff, K. (2004). *Content analysis – An introduction to its methodology* (2nd ed.). Thousand Oaks, CA: SAGE.
Kuhnle, H., & Banzhaf, J. (2006). *Finanzkommunikation unter IFRS*. München: Verlag Franz Vahlen GmbH.
Möller, K., & Gamerschlag, R. (2009). Immaterielle Vermögenswerte in der Unternehmenssteuerung - betriebswirtschaftliche Perspektiven und Herausforderungen. In K. Möller, M. Piwinger, & A. Zerfaß (Eds.), *Immaterielle Vermögenswerte – Bewertung, Berichterstattung und Kommunikation* (pp. 3–21). Stuttgart: Schäffer-Poeschel Verlag Stuttgart.
Nielsen, C., & Madsen, M. T. (2009). Discourses of transparency in the intellectual capital reporting debate: Moving from generic reporting models to management defined information. *Critical Perspectives on Accounting, 20*(7), 847–854. doi:10.1016/j.cpa.2008.09.007.
Raynard, P. (1998). Coming together. A review of contemporary approaches to social accounting, auditing and reporting in non-profit organisations. *Journal of Business Ethics, 17*, 1471–1479.
Steenkamp, N., & Northcott, D. (2007). Content analysis in accounting research: The practical challenge. *Australian Accounting Review, 17*(43), 12–25. doi:10.1111/j.1835-2561.2007.tb00332.x.
van Broekhoven, R. A. (2008). *Engaging Donors' Trust*. Accessed February 20, 2014, from http://www.icfo.org/ICFO-Publications

Appendix: List of Codes

Codes	Sub-codes	Definition and coding rules	Example
Human capital	Volunteers	Mentioning of volunteers, their value or events, trainings, education etc. for volunteers explicitly mentioned	A huge thank you to our volunteers, who did a fantastic job in preparing this event (D \Annual Report 2011, p. 3)
	Staff	No distinction between employees and volunteers or employees mentioned	Members of staff working in various areas proved their courage by commenting on their individual and personal motives to commit themselves to their tasks (J\Annual Report 2005, p. 3)
	Qualification of staff	Types or forms of qualifications of staff is mentioned such as trainings, workshops, formal education, for both employees and volunteers	We succeeded in recruiting new qualified staff to perform our diverse set of tasks (B \Annual Report 2012b, p. 4)
	Qualities of staff	Characteristics and qualities of individual or groups of volunteers or employees necessary/important for the NPO for instance motivation, commitment	For the reputation of organisations providing social services motivated staff plays an integral part (J\Annual Report 2005, p. 22)
	Professionalism	The words professionalisation or professionalism are used explicitly	Sometimes I ask myself, whether it would make sense to pay someone to facilitate a greater investment of time going into this work and to

(continued)

K. Blankenburg, *Intellectual Capital in German Non-profit Organisations*,
Contributions to Management Science, DOI 10.1007/978-3-319-62655-0

Codes	Sub-codes	Definition and coding rules	Example
			enable us to work a bit more professional, as we do not really work in a professional manner (Mia: 66)
	Recruitment	Strategies and approaches to recruit volunteers, staff, donors, etc.	We hope that our volunteers tell their families and friend about their engagement and maybe arouse their interest to volunteer as well (Raatz, Johanniter-Unfall-Hilfe e.V.: 75)
	Experiences of the interviewee	Reports/stories of experiences of the interviewees themselves	On our way back I said to my wife: this is too big for my taste. She replied: why don't we do it ourselves then? (Elbert.: 29)
Relational capital	Public relations	Descriptions of public relation measures such as events for the public, of publications in the media or of own information material, participation in conferences, public discussions, events for public, publication of brochures and information leaflets	Our online presence is a constant "passive" public relations activity. It offers an interesting platform for to find and to get know our organisation. "Active" public relation activities such as information booth and presentations are not substituted through our internet presence but are enhanced by it (F\Information Booklet_Nr._27, 2008, p. 25)
	Image	Illustration of the way an NPO is perceived by external stakeholders or how it thinks it is perceived as	We represent quality (B \Annual Report 2009, p. 19)
	Relationship to public	Illustration of the nature of the relationship to the public	Since many years we try to pique public interest, combined with the hope that political consequences arise, for those countries in which people suffer from the effects of forgotten disasters (B\Project Report 2013, p. 8)
	Relationship to donors	Description or mentioning of contact with/ to donors, of dependencies, of the nature of the relationship (independent of the type of donor, i.e. individual or company)	Only by providing sufficient information and by staying in contact with donors are we able to help people in need to help themselves (F\Information Booklet_Nr._24, 2005, p. 18)

(continued)

Codes	Sub-codes	Definition and coding rules	Example
	Relationship to press/media	Illustrations or implications of dependencies or of the nature of the relationship to journalists/press/media, e.g. awards by the press or for journalists, articles, papers, etc.	Since the press in this area are tied to us, often I don't have to issue a press release. A phone call to the press is sufficient or a quick invite for the responsible editor to drop by, sit down with us and talk about what might be published next (Schmetz: 11)
	Relationship to partners	Evaluation of co-operations or relationship with/to partners. How is the nature of these relationships? Do any dependencies to partners or parties the NPO cooperates with exist?	Due to technical challenges with the flow of the project we had to find a new local partner (D\Annual Report 2012, p. 7)
	Relationship to beneficiaries	Presentation or evaluation of the relationship to beneficiaries, of dependencies, of the nature of the relationship, i.e. respectful, successful, long-lasting, etc.	Linked offers from a single source and possibly to be found at a single address save beneficiaries unnecessary ways and facilitate aligned assistances (J\Annual Report 2006, p. 16)
	Relationship to politics and officials	Mentioning or valuation of the relationship with politics/officials, of dependencies, of the nature of the relationship to parties, communities, etc. or individual representatives, for instance NPO giving guidance for upcoming decisions to be made, lobbying, transfer of projects by the state, city or community	Due to a change in politics of the Eritrean government the work of NGOs was severely limited and as one of the last remaining active NGOs we had to leave the country (D \Annual Report 2011, p. 5)
	Co-operations	Mentioning of a partner or cooperation, both in general and for a particular project	Within a newly established cooperation with the university medical centre in Vienna [...] (G\Newsletter 2011)

(continued)

Codes	Sub-codes	Definition and coding rules	Example
Structural capital	Structure	Descriptions of responsibilities within the NPO, of allocation of tasks, who reports to whom or is responsible for whom, where the NPO executes its project, presentation of the decision making body or of the departments of the NPO. For example organisation charts or maps illustrating the project countries the NPO is active in	Since the restructuring [...] in 2003, six competence teams started their work (B\Annual Report 2004, p. 25)
	Organisational culture	Description or mentioning of values and views of the NPO, giving every member of the workforce of an organization a common perspective and view on how to handle information, how decisions are made and what values are pursued. Aims of individual projects are not coded with this code	Mr. X, one of the volunteer on duty that day, stated: That's what we are here for—to help other people (C\Yearbook-2014, p. 35)
	Processes	Description of processes/procedures that define the work of the NPO. Not a report of the projects	The membership fee is set by the general assembly (E\Charter: §10)
	Database/IT	Descriptions of the reasons for the use of a database, software or IT in general, for changes of existing/ development of new software. What are the benefits? Why is the particular software/ database/IT relevant? Exception: Links to Web Pages are coded as Public Relations	Further we finally have a new database, which is hopefully going to make our every-day work easier and to help us save time (F\Nr.3_Februar_2008, p. 1)
	Work climate	How are people connected within the NPO? How is their	We live in a community of volunteers and employees who work together trusting each

(continued)

Codes	Sub-codes	Definition and coding rules	Example
		relationship to each other? That is descriptions of the way e.g. volunteers and employees work together, of the perspectives on working together	other (B\Annual Report 2012, p. 2)
	Relationship to staff	Signals as to the relationship of the NPO to the staff, for instance possibilities for staff to get involved in decision making, services for staff, explicitly expresses appreciation of staff	The mission statement of our organisations was developed by our staff in a huge discussion in 1994/1995 [...] (J \Annual Report 2002, p. 3)
	Internal processes	Presentation of internal processes and projects, i.e. those projects beneficiaries and members don't necessarily notice or only feel the effects; further development of processes, for example restructuring of responsibilities, implementation of new software for administrative tasks, further development of services offered	The constant modernisation of our lifeboats progresses and our organisation set the right course for the future (C\Yearbook-2014, p. 68)
	Education/ training	Reporting of possibilities for professionalisation such as training, education, apprenticeships, workshops, etc.	Additionally we offer medical training on a regular basis as well as international and national trainings, using fictitious scenarios to practice how teamwork (B\Project Report 2013, p. 26)
Spiritual capital		Statements that highlight why NPOs and their work is regarded as positive and consequently the support of this work provides a positive emotional return. These statements are not organisation specific and not	In the centre of our work is the human being in its individual and unique dignity (J\Annual Report 2002, p. 3)

(continued)

Codes	Sub-codes	Definition and coding rules	Example
		aimed at any recipient in particular. If statements are organisation specific, they are coded as organisational culture.	
Natural capital		Environmental resources an organisation uses to provide services or manufacture goods, for instance water or air	We regarded the environmental pollution due to the long distance flights and the costs for our participants as too high in the long-run (F \Nr.4_Oktober_2008, p. 2)
Manufactured capital		Description or mentioning of physical objects that organisation can use to produce goods or supply services, for instance cars, buildings, etc.	The library is located in our headquarter and consists of approximately 1200 donated books (E\Report-from-Brasil-2012, p. 23)
Financial capital	Financial statements	Information on financial resources such as expenditures, income, application of funds, independent of the form the information is disclosed in, i.e. numerical or narrative form. Exception: any information on donations or the collection of funds is ascribed to the variable fundraising	The total revenue, consisting of donations, inheritances, return on capital employed, and return on endowment capital, was 39.65 Mio. Euro in 2013(2012: 34.55 Mio. Euro) (C\Yearbook-2014, p. 64)
	Fundraising	All reports on activities to raise funds, description of funds granted by the state or other parties, the way donations are distributed within the NPO as well as other reports on donations collected	With the help of donations we were able to facilitate the urgently necessary repairs. About 65,000 Euro were required (H \Newsletter_0514_Homepage 2014, p. 1)
	Costs of human capital	Report of the cost of staff either expresses in numerical or narrative form	Staff expenses increased compared to the previous year by 4.6% to 265.492 T€ (previous year: 253.900 T€) (J\Annual Report 2013, p. 46)

(continued)

Codes	Sub-codes	Definition and coding rules	Example
Visual Rhetoric	Random picture	Images/pictures without reference to the NPO or its work but that could be used by any organisation, for example pictures of landscape, hands, random people, etc.	*Due to copyright reasons not example is provided*
	Picture of staff	Pictures showing staff/ volunteers/employees are coded "picture of staff" even when the affiliation of the person is only detectable through the caption. Also, the caption of such a picture is not additionally coded as linguistic message	*Due to copyright reasons not example is provided*
	Pictures expressing IC obviously showing the work of the particular NPO	Pictures showing IC with obvious reference to the specific NPO, for instance through a logo on a jacket of a member of staff	*Since these photos cannot be anonymised, no example is provided*
	Picture with caption	Pictures with reference to NPO or its work but only through it caption. If pictures with captions are grouped and described by one caption or part of the same event or work process, the pictures are coded as one unit of coding. However, if pictures with captions are merely located at close proximity but illustrate different aspects of the work of the NPO and have different caption, the pictures are coded individually	*Due to copyright reasons not example is provided*
	Graphs/Tables	Graphs and tables are coded accordingly and a code describing the content is added	*Due to copyright reasons not example is provided*

(continued)

Codes	Sub-codes	Definition and coding rules	Example
	Tacit message	Photos that imply IC but cannot be attributed to a particular organisation, like a nurse talking to an elderly man	*Due to copyright reasons not example is provided*
Facts	Data on NPO	Data of NPOs such as contact details, locations, project countries	*To ensure anonymity, no example is provided*
	Data on output	Reports on number of beneficiaries reached, services offered, countries the NPO is active in, activities executed and all other numerical data describing the output of a NPO. If a sum is mentioned as well as the numbers of the individual components, only the sum is coded	Currently around 2000 families are supplied with food, medication and water (D \Newsletter 2-2013, 2013, p. 2)
	Data on staff	Numerical data on staff independent of the type of work, i.e. volunteers, employees, youth group, part-time, fulltime	180 employees and around 800 volunteers work for C (C \Technical brochure 2012, p. 4)
	Data on interviews	Factual data of the interview such as the date, type, lengths, language of the interview, the place it was conducted	*(code was not used)*
	Data on interviewee	Factual data on the interviewee. What information is available on the interviewee? Name, position/tasks within the NPO, etc.	I work for this organisation since 1.5 years by now. Initially I started my career in corporate communication for a commercial business (Raatz, Johanniter-Unfall-Hilfe e.V.: 13)
	History of NPO	Information on the history of the organisation	And in eastern Germany we started in 1990, that is as soon as it was possible, and then such an association was founded in nearly every Bundesland (Representative of Albert-Schweitzer-Kinderdorf in Sachsen e.V.: 9)

(continued)

Codes	Sub-codes	Definition and coding rules	Example
Stories and citations of individuals		Reports on the work, value or impact of an NPO using stories, citations of individuals or by describing particular events	Together with the university medical centre in Vienna we managed to provide a 10-year old girl from Rumania with a specially tailored prostheticarm. Mid July 2011 the girl and her parents came to Vienna. [. . .] (G\Newsletter 2011, p. 1)
Type of donors and target groups		Descriptions of existing donors and target groups of services or mailings, for instance	Our average supporting member is 80+ years old.(Raatz, Johanniter-Unfall-Hilfe e.V.: 80)
Style of address		Information on internal guidelines/rules for external communication, for example How fundraising appeals are phrased	And I think that's how it should be, we don't have the demands of a specialist journal or a scientific paper, but we want to convey live stories and experiences of our beneficiaries (Representative of Albert-Schweitzer-Kinderdorf in Sachsen e.V.: 59)
Medium used for external communication		Mentioning of media or channels used or explicitly not used for external communication	We stopped printing brochures as those are out of date rather quickly and we had to throw them away after only one year (Elbert: 6)
Form of external communication		Discussions on the form of external communications, the advantages and disadvantages of or experiences with certain forms of communication	We noticed that it is important to inform readers immediately how they can donate, that is to provide the information on the account for donation (Schmetz: 35)
Perspective on IC	IC as liability	Statements implying that IC is a liability for the organisation	Difficult balancing act in the collective bargaining policy: On the one hand J needs to remain attractive as an employer and stay true to our own demands on faire remuneration. On the other hand, in the light of insufficient refinancing, payroll costs need to be limited (J\Annual Report 2010, p. 10)
	IC expresses explicitly	Mentioning of IC or any of the capitals	The immaterial assets are mainly software that was

(continued)

Codes	Sub-codes	Definition and coding rules	Example
		explicitly, including immaterial assets (which was the only term explicitly used!)	purchased, licenses for data-base- applications for cost accounting, operational accounting, and customer relationship management (B \Annual Report 2008, p. 22)
Demands	Trust	Mentioning of trust and the value of trust	We are grateful for the interest in our work, the trust you granted us and your support as our work would not be able without it (F\Nr.9_Newsletter 2012, p. 1)
	Transparency	Mentioning transparency as a strategic aim or an important value, also report on transparency certification	Transparency is a very important foundation for trust which affects the amount of donations we collect (Elbert: 19)
	Social acceptance	Signals for social acceptance of projects, services in general and the processes in particular, such as awards, official certification, orders from the state to provide a particular service	Crucial was the high quality of the services provided on the one hand and the resulting high appreciation by the public (J\Annual Report 2004, p. 17)
	Quality	Mentioning of quality standards, description of quality management, certifications verifying the quality of an organisation	Crucial was the high quality of the services provided on the one hand and the resulting high appreciation by the public (J\Annual Report 2004, p. 17)
Necessary Resources	Human resources	Claims that human resources are essential for the work/survival of the respective organisation	To realise the concept presented, we need employees who support, carry and live this idea and who implement it to the satisfaction of the beneficiaries as well as their own (A\Concept_January_2011, p. 15)
	Funding	Statements that funding is crucial for the work/survival of the respective organisation	The continuation of the projects is thus dependent on donations (B\Annual Report 2003, p. 15)
	Practices	Essential for the work/survival of the respective organisation	In order to meet the constantly increasing demands adequately, an effective risk management is of vital importance (J\Annual Report 2005, p. 26)

(continued)

Codes	Sub-codes	Definition and coding rules	Example
	Reputation	Mentioning that reputation/image is essential for the work/ survival of the respective organisation	Essential for successful fundraising is a positive image in the public eye (J\Annual Report 2006, p. 30)
	Support by external parties	Claims that support by external parties is essential for the work/ survival of the respective organisation	The project failed due to unexpected administrative difficulties. The conditions for the building projects imposed by the government would have lead to an enormous increase in costs (D\Annual Report 2006, p. 5)
DZI		Mentioning of the DZI, the relationship to the DZI, its influence, etc.	Due to the Spendensiegel we are limited to a certain level of administrative expenses. We cannot be generous with the donations we receive since we are only allowed to use a certain percentage for administration and advertisements etc. (Representative A of ProBrasil e.V.: 200)
Comparison to other NPOs		Comparison of the organisation the interviewee represents with another organisation or other organisations	Maybe that is due to us being rather small and not as visible as bigger organisations that come to your mind easily in that situation, I can imagine (Representative B of Steinschleuder e.V.: 163)

Reference

Representative of Christophorushilfe e.V. (2014, August 05). Telephone conversation with "Representative of Christophorushilfe e.V."

K. Blankenburg, *Intellectual Capital in German Non-profit Organisations*, Contributions to Management Science, DOI 10.1007/978-3-319-62655-0

MIX
Papier aus verantwortungsvollen Quellen
Paper from responsible sources
FSC® C105338

If you have any concerns about our products,
you can contact us on
ProductSafety@springernature.com

In case Publisher is established outside the EU,
the EU authorized representative is:
Springer Nature Customer Service Center GmbH
Europaplatz 3, 69115 Heidelberg, Germany

Printed by Libri Plureos GmbH
in Hamburg, Germany